Fchs7Ed
228

THE
TRAINING
OF THE URBAN
WORKING
CLASS

THE
TRAINING
OF THE URBAN
WORKING
CLASS
A History of
TWENTIETH CENTURY
AMERICAN Education

paul c. violas

University of Illinois at Champaign, Urbana

Rand McNally College Publishing Company / Chicago

Rand McNally Education Series
B. Othanel Smith, Advisory Editor

78 79 80 10 9 8 7 6 5 4 3 2 1

Library of Congress Catalog Card Number 77-77707

To my Father and Mother
who understood the
distinction between
education and
training

Contents

Preface

This essay is the result of my desire to understand the relationship between what American intellectuals said about education and what children experienced as they were initiated into American society, especially those experiences that occurred within the public schools. My curiosity about this question was stimulated by a penetrating question posed by David Tyack during our many discussions on educational history and historiography. He questioned the amount of influence that the ideas of intellectuals or, as he called them, mandarins, actually exercised on the programmatic aspects of public schooling. The possibility that American intellectuals had not actually influenced American schooling ran counter to my general assumption that there existed an intimate relationship between social and intellectual history. Tyack also suggested that much of the recent work in educational history centered around a rather amorphous concept of social control and failed to specify the purposes or the beneficiaries of this control. These discussions convinced me that my own research program, which began with *Roots of Crisis*, should be expanded to include an examination of public schooling at the programmatic level.

It seemed that the most direct way to assess the impact of intellectuals on schooling and to clarify the notion of social control would be to revisit the early twentieth-century schools as they were undergoing the sweeping changes that shaped the nature of public education. This, of course, cannot literally be done. The past can only be revisited through the historical imagination, and this imaginative reconstruction can approximate historical reality only if it is based upon sufficient evidence bequeathed to the historian by those who lived the era under study.

Thus, I attempted to assemble as much primary material as possible in order to re-create as accurate a picture of this transformation as I could. The general plan of attack involved three strategies: first, to examine the statements of educational leaders regarding the overall purposes of schooling; second, to look at what practicing schoolmen, including administrators and classroom teachers, said about the changes transpiring in their schools; and third, to study other descriptions of actual school programs such as school surveys, course outlines, and journalistic accounts of particular schools. Throughout the study I made a concerted effort to correlate these three strategies.

The overwhelming amount of data available on the subject dictated the first restriction on the study. Since my main interest and my training are in urban history, I decided to confine the study to urban schooling. Moreover, I believe that Arthur M. Schlesinger was correct when he noted that by the twentieth century the city had become "the center of national equilibrium." Although I maintain that the study of urban schooling is critical to any understanding of American society in this century, the claim should not be taken as a deprecation of the importance of rural educational developments.

The first phase of the research was basically exploratory, in which I attempted to determine what educational changes were most important in the transformation of the schools. It began with a survey of the major educational journals published during the last decade of the nineteenth century and the first four decades of the twentieth century and continued with examination of the annual proceedings of the National Education Association. I then turned to the school surveys, which by 1940 had been conducted for nearly every urban school system. This was followed by a study of the annual superintendents' reports from New York City, Chicago, and Cincinnati. My investigation uncovered seven significant educational innovations that defined the character of twentieth-century urban schooling in America. They included compulsory school attendance, Americanization, the play movement, student extracurricular activities, vocational training, vocational guidance, and the emergence of the professional school administrator. At this point I decided to limit the study to an examination of these seven innovations, even though several interesting but less important aspects of urban schooling, such as the character education movement, would not be included. Plans for discussing the last topic in this essay were also dropped when, in preparing the first draft, I read David Tyack's book, *The One Best System*, and discovered that his work, together with Joseph Cronin's *The Control of Urban Schools*, had more than adequately covered the area.

As the first phase of my research drew to a close, it became appar-ent that many of these innovations began outside the public school and had continuous support from individuals and groups not formally asso-ciated with the schools. Most of these allies of public education were drawn from three areas: social reformers from the settlement houses and the playground movement; officials from various branches of the state and federal governments; and businessmen and industrialists. Thus, in the second phase of the research it became necessary to examine sev-eral sources not commonly found in educational bibliographies. These consisted of books, pamphlets, journal articles, and speeches by people in these areas, as well as a variety of governmental reports and publica-tions. The two most valuable journals for this phase were *Charities and The Commons* and *The Playground.*

The last phase of the research consisted of studying works pertinent to the topics that had been isolated for analysis—the annual reports of the U.S. commissioners of education, numerous bulletins issued by the U.S. Bureau of Education, reports of associations such as the Society for the Promotion of Industrial Education, and books by individuals such as Paul Hanus, Ebert Fratwell, Edith Abbott, Ellwood Cubberley, and Meyer Bloomfield, who had been involved in one or another of these innovations. In this phase, as in each of the preceding phases, an effort was made to examine a variety of sources that might reveal what was actually occurring in the schools and how the ideas of the so-called mandarins related to the actual programmatic changes in the schools.

This research disclosed a plethora of evidence demonstrating a strong relationship between the ideas of intellectuals and social policy decisions affecting public schooling. The innovations had been deliber-ately planned with definite ends in view, and the mandarins had been instrumental not only in the construction of the ends, but also in the development of the means for achieving those ends. Moreover, the co-cept of social control was clarified through identification of the purposes and the beneficiaries of that control. Underlying all of the educational innovations analyzed were considerations related to the changing nature of work resulting from the predominance of corporate industry in the American economy. Railroads, steel, coal, oil and other industrial trusts and mammoth companies had developed procedures that sub-divided the labor process and relegated the average factory worker to a tedious round of dehumanizing actions requiring neither human skill nor intelligence. Corporate managers were faced with the problem of inducing the worker to accept such conditions and thus avoid the bitter labor strife that plagued American capitalism in the late nineteenth and early twentieth centuries. Most intellectuals and educational leaders believed that the development of corporate industry and its organization of the workplace was natural and inevitable. They felt, too, that because most men would have to labor under such conditions those men should learn to accept them. The devices of social control that were built into each educational innovation were designed to acclimate the worker to these conditions with as little pain and alienation as possible. If such adaptation could be accomplished, the mandarins believed, the nation would prosper and the worker would ultimately benefit. This essay is largely a study of the socialization of urban working-class children by the American public school as that institution attempted to adjust those children to their inevitable industrial futures.

In the field of historical inquiry, it is easier to accumulate than discharge intellectual debts. Some specific items can be readily acknowledged with footnote citations. Others, however, cannot be easily reduced, nor should they be relegated to the bottom of a page. These debts are to scholars whose works helped delineate the questions or suggested research paths which determined the ultimate configuration of the present effort. The intellectual heritage of this essay can be traced to Merle Curti's demonstration of the nexus between social ideals and educational practice. Lawrence Cremin and Bernard Bailyn persuasively argued that one cannot analyze the historical development of education while ignoring the learning that takes place in the larger social order and the relationship between that order and schools. Although this essay analyzes the relationship differently than Cremin or Bailyn, their admonitions were learned. The influence of Edward Krug's carefully researched analysis of the role of social efficiency in the evolution of the American high school is evident. The highly informative, pioneering work of Joel Spring in the areas of extracurricular activities, playgrounds, and vocational guidance has been influential. Spring has developed insights which are relevant to most of the critical historiography in this decade. In similar vein, the work of Marvin Lazerson on vocationalism in Massachusetts, Sol Cohen's interpretation of industrial training, David Tyack's study of school administration, and Michael Katz's analysis of nineteenth century school reformers were important. I have valued most the influence and support of Clarence Karier. During the past fourteen years, as teacher, colleague, and friend he has been part of a continuous and stimulating dialogue. While none of these scholars should be held responsible for any of the ways I may have distorted their ideas, I gratefully acknowledge my debt to each.

In researching and preparing this essay I have received generous assistance from my colleagues, my students, and the University of Illinois. James Anderson, Joe Burnett, Walter Feinberg, David Hogan, Clarence Karier, and Russell Marks have each read and offered critical commentaries on parts of the manuscript. A special debt is owed to Frederic Jaher for his careful editing and helpful substantive suggestions. Extended discussions with Mobin Shorish on the manpower model of education and with David Hogan on the organization of the industrial workplace have clarified my understanding of those crucial topics. A seven-year dialogue with John Erickson of the University of Iowa Journalism Department has been central in the development of many of the ideas included in the following chapters. Moreover, during the past years my academic unit, Educational Policy Studies, has had a large number of first-rate graduate students who have helped to establish an intellectual atmosphere that has stimulated a vigorous exchange of ideas. The University of Illinois Research Board provided funds for research assistance during two years and the diligent work of Jon Fennell, Timothy O'Hanlon, and Spiro Rasis hastened the completion of the manuscript. I am most thankful for the truly superb collection of resources on educational history available at the University of Illinois library and the helpful attitude of all the library's personnel. I would also like to thank my friend Richard Ognibene and his colleagues at Siena College for inviting me to share my conclusions with them in February of 1974, when those conclusions were still in an embryonic stage. Their comments were most helpful. The careful, patient, and compassionate attention that Barbara Franklin and Linda Roberts devoted to typing the several drafts of the manuscript is likewise appreciated. While I am indebted to all of these people, none of them bears responsibility for any shortcomings that may remain in the essay. My largest debt remains to be acknowledged. It is to my family: my wife, who edited the many revisions and provided useful comments as well as continuous ego support, and my four children, who understood, or at least managed to mask their disappointment, when their dad was unavailable to participate in many of the everyday activities which constitute an important part of growing up.

Chapter 1

The Crisis of Transition

The closing quarter of the nineteenth century witnessed a rapid disintegration of the rural orientation of American society.[1] Any attempt to understand the development of American urban education in the twentieth century must first recognize the sense of urgency and crisis created by this disintegration. Intellectuals and educators were most anxious to find an alternative organizing social principle that would replace apparent disorder with harmony. A common reflex was to abandon voluntaristic efforts in favor of compulsory, institutional, governmental, and bureaucratic solutions to social and individual problems. This response appeared in such areas as charity, social work, insurance, and medicine, but was nowhere more apparent nor more important than in schooling.

The fundamental and rapid transformation of the social and economic basis of American life that occurred in the 40 years following the Civil War led historian Samuel Hays to assert that "Seldom, if ever, in American history has so much been altered within the lifetime of a single man."[2] As industrialism displaced agriculture, the nation lost its decidedly rural village orientation and assumed an urban character. Familiar channels of business, such as the individual entrepreneur and the partnership were rudely and often violently cast aside in favor of corporate capitalism and monopolistic arrangements. Even the intellectual underpinnings of the older social order were

---

1. Robert H. Wiebe, *The Search for Order* (New York: Hill and Wang, 1967).

2. Samuel P. Hays, *The Response to Industrialism, 1885*–1914 (Chicago: University of Chicago Press, 1957), p. 1.

1

severely buffeted by successive waves of new and seemingly revolutionary ideas, beginning with the Darwinian challenge and extending through the pragmatic theology of the social gospel. Moreover, the very composition of the American people was drastically reshaped as massive waves of immigrants threatened the widely held belief in the virtue of a homogeneous national character. These important forces of transformation did not escape the scrutiny of intellectuals and school officials as they urged a national reformation of the public schools to restore order and rationality to American society.

THE RISE OF THE CITY

The centrality of urbanism in this era of social change is underscored not only by the fact that other developments occurred primarily in the city, but by the fact that urban growth rapidly outdistanced population increases in the countryside. The federal census of 1790 disclosed that only 5.1 percent of the total population lived in cities.[3] There were only eight cities over 8,000, the two largest being Philadelphia with 43,000 and New York with 33,131. In contrast, the 1900 census showed that the urban population had climbed to 39.75 percent of the total. The most significant increases occurred in the last half of the nineteenth century when urban growth accelerated nearly three times as fast as rural growth.[4] Even more spectacular were the growth patterns of certain individual cities. During the 1880s, for example, Chicago doubled its population, while Omaha mushroomed from 30,500 to 140,000 and Kansas City spurted from 60,000 to 132,000.[5] The disquieting decline of rural dominance in a society that for over 200 years had considered itself a land of yeoman farmers accentuated the traditional American suspicion that the city was the breeding ground of evil.[6]

The association of urban life with vice and disorder seemed confirmed by the discovery that the mercurial rise of the city was accom-

---

3. A city is defined as a place with over 2,500 persons.

4. Samuel Eliot Morrison and Henry Steele Commager, *The Growth of the American Republic,* 2 vols. (New York: Oxford University Press, 1956), 2: 911.

5. Arthur M. Schlesinger, *The Rise of the City, 1878–1898* (New York: Macmillan, 1933), p. 64; and Bernard A. Weisberger, *The New Industrial Society* (New York: Wiley, 1969), p. 32.

6. See for example Morton and Lucia White, *The Intellectual vs. the City* (New York: Mentor, 1962).

panied by numerous and serious social problems. Statistics reported at the turn of the century by the *Chicago Tribune* showed a 500 percent increase in homicides between 1881 and 1898.[7] Thomas Nast and Lincoln Steffens disclosed widespread municipal corruption. Jacob Riis discovered urban slums and introduced the top half of American society to the other half. Robert Hunter and other settlement workers vividly portrayed the poverty that blighted many lives in the city. Such revelations convinced many Americans that action was necessary to save the soul of America. The effort to curb municipal corruption often relied upon political innovations designed to reduce immigrant and working-class political participation and influence. Some reformers turned to settlement houses to ameliorate economic and social problems while others considered city parks and playgrounds as a source of uplift. Most of the early reform efforts began as voluntary individual or group actions, but the enormity of the tasks encouraged reformers to seek institutional or governmental support. In nearly every instance the reforms were intimately related to education and the public schools.

INDUSTRIALIZATION

The city was the locus of several activities that changed the structure of American life in the last third of the nineteenth century and the most important of those activities was industrialization.[8] During this period, many farm hands became factory hands.

Among the various factors that facilitated industrialization, the advent of the corporation was most responsible for fundamental alterations in the nature of factories. One of the major advantages of the corporation was the relative ease of amassing capital through the public sale of shares of ownership in the enterprise. While the corporate-owned enterprise expanded in size and continued to utilize increasingly complex and expensive machinery, the single entrepreneur or partnership arrangement often found it difficult to obtain sufficient capital to purchase the expensive new machinery that would

---

7. Schlesinger, *Rise*, p. 114.

8. See Morrison and Commager, *Growth of the Republic*, p. 915: David Brody, ed., *Industrial America in the Twentieth Century* (New York: Crowell, 1967), p. 1; Weisberger, *Industrial Society* p. 13; and Howard Mumford Jones, *The Age of Energy* (New York: Viking, 1970).

enable them to transform their shops into factories. The influence of the corporation on American industry is illustrated by the fact that by 1904 almost 70 percent of the manufacturing work force was employed in corporate-owned factories.[9]

It was not surprising that the expanding complexity and size of corporate industry provided a receptive setting for the gospel of efficiency spread by Frederic Taylor and his disciples, a gospel that accelerated the decline of craftsmanship in American industry.[10] A major aim of the efficiency movement was to organize the factory in order to facilitate the greatest productivity with the least expenditure of manpower and other resources. One means to this end was to subdivide each operation into its simplest component, devise the one best way for the worker to do that operation, and offer incentives to induce him to complete it at top speed. The highly skilled artisan who had spent years of apprenticeship to develop his abilities was an anachronism in an age when most tasks had been so subdivided and simplified that by 1923 Henry Ford could report that over 85 percent of the jobs in his factory could be learned in less than one month and almost half required less than one day's training.

Around the turn of the twentieth century, the factory workplace in corporate industry became highly specialized and standardized. Because most of the work slots required little skill, initiative, or intelligence, those occupying these positions were machine tenders who, as many contemporary observers noted, became mere extensions of their machines. Requirements for these jobs were spelled out not in terms of skills but in terms of personality structures, patterns of habits, and conditioned reflexes. In contemporary terminology, this level of the hierarchy was the "rank and file of the industrial army." Machines, however, needed more than tending; they also had to be repaired. Maintenance men required some skills—the ability to apply at least limited practical scientific knowledge and to exercise a degree of independent initiative. Moreover, the machine tenders also needed tending, a task requiring foremen with a range of abilities somewhat similar to those of the maintenance corps. Employees at this level were often referred to as the "noncommissioned officers of the industrial army." At the top of the hierarchy were the "commissioned officers," ranging from engineers

---

9. Weisberger, *Industrial Society*, p. 18.

10. Samuel Haber, *Efficiency and Uplift* (Chicago: University of Chicago Press, 1964).

and plant managers to corporation presidents. Although some requirements such as system loyalty and cooperativeness were common to all levels of the labor force hierarchy, most contemporary observers believed that each level required specialized individuals and hence specialized schooling. A similarity of tasks and requirements within each level allowed an employee to move horizontally from one job to another, but it became increasingly difficult for one to move vertically. By the end of the first decade of the twentieth century, those who understood the specialization characteristic to the structure of corporate industry recognized that a Horatio Alger would become increasingly uncommon.

This specialization of the workplace meant that the rank and file required substantially less skill in the industrial arena than the artisan or farmer had displayed in the workshop or on the farm. Skill dilution was a striking feature of modern corporate industrialism. Accompanying this decline in skill requirements was an equally significant transformation in what one might call the culture of work. Order, regularity, punctuality, strict adherence to work schedules and blueprints, and the ability to cooperate with co-workers were but some of the attributes necessary in the new work culture. As Herbert G. Gutman has noted, these requirements produced an intense cultural conflict between the industrialists and a large segment of the working class whose cultural commitments were preindustrial or traditional in nature.[11] This problem was compounded by the fact that by the turn of the century much of the American industrial working class was made up of immigrants who possessed not only preindustrial but also non-Anglo-Saxon cultural values. This placed the immigrants in a particularly vulnerable position as targets for those who wished to preserve the cultural homogeneity of the nation and for corporate industrialists who demanded a working class with cultural values compatible with the requirements of the modern factory workplace. As Americanization programs developed to process immigrants into Americans, industrialists moved swiftly to insure that these programs produced citizens who would also be acceptable industrial workers. It seemed necessary either to restructure industrial work or to acculturate the industrial working class. Acculturation meant changing the attitudes, habits, and consciousness, or world view, of the working

---

11. Herbert G. Gutman, "Work, Culture, and Society in Industrializing America, 1815–1919," *American Historical Review 78* (June 1973),: 531–88.

class. Considering the distribution of wealth and power in American society at this time, it should come as no surprise that the latter alternative was adopted. Early in the twentieth century, this effort was institutionalized within the public schools.

Although the corporate form of business organization contributed to the development of an new kind of industrial workplace, the imposition of organization regularity upon a single factory or firm was but part of the changing nature of industrial enterprise. By the late 1890s, when many corporations had merged, trusts controlled two-fifths of all manufacturing capital and two-thirds of all railroad trackage.[12] The resulting concentrations of wealth and power seemed to document the conservative Social Darwinist position that the most capable enterprises would survive the struggle of the marketplace. This concentration of power, however, often occasioned fear of monopolistic abuse. Concrete problems arose as some of these large combines, such as Standard Oil, displayed selfish concerns for profits, using their monopolistic power to raise rather than lower prices. While contemporary critics recognized the inevitability of big business, many felt that the captains of industry would have to be restrained. They usually suggested that increased size brought increased efficiency which if the few selfish moguls of industry could be restrained, ultimately would be passed on to the rest of society in the form of lower prices and a higher standard of living.

The major economic reforms of the Progressive Era were advertised as attempts to protect the public through governmental regulation of certain aspects of the marketplace. This seemed to suggest a dichotomy, with reformers attempting to protect the public against the evil machinations of the selfish titans of business. This dichotomy, accepted by many contemporary reformers, has also shaped our present understanding of the Progressive Era. Indeed, much of the subsequent historical analysis of this era is dependent on a paradigm that projects big business as the antagonist of liberal reform.[13] This perspective presents a "devil theory," with the businessman cast as the initiator of most of the evil that abounds in American society. Conversely, within this paradigm any effort at reform must be viewed as an alternative to the evil machinations of business interests. Because

---

12. Brody, *Industrial America*, p. 2.

13. See Arthur M. Schlesinger, Jr., *The Age of Jackson* (New York: New American Library, 1955), p. 173.

many liberal reforms have thus escaped critical analysis, our understanding of the evolution of public schooling has suffered.[14]

Several historians have recently challenged this rather simplistic dichotomy. Robert Wiebe, for example, has shown that businessmen were not a cohesive group, for they supported diverse and often conflicting economic programs. The works of Gabriel Kolko and James Weinstein indicate that corporate industrialists and businessmen, as opposed to noncorporate or entrepreneural types, generally found it in their own interests to support the liberal social and economic reforms of the Progressive Era.[15]

If these historians are substantially correct, then the older analysis of big business as the bastion of rugged individualism, unqualified opposition to government regulation, single-minded devotion to maximum profits, and general opposition to social reform, must be modified. It seems more accurate to recognize that the leaders of corporate business were sometimes willing to forego large profits in order to gain predictable returns in a rational market. Many of them understood that social reform was necessary to obtain the conditions for a rational market; so, rather than oppose the liberal reformers, they often cooperated with them to correct social maladjustments and obtain stability and harmony.

NEW PHILOSOPHIES

While chaotic conditions in the marketplace seemed to drive men to support reforms designed to restore economic order, equally disquieting developments in the intellectual world spurred efforts for stability in that sphere. The certitudes of Scottish Realism, the unifying force of transcendentalism, and the sometimes lofty moral absolutes of

---

14. See, for example, Raymond Callahan, *Education and the Cult of Efficiency* (Chicago: University of Chicago Press, 1962). Callahan finds school administrators helpless because of their vulnerablity to the demands of powerful business interests. He suggests that the administrators were forced to accept the tenets of efficiency. A less dichotomous view of the relation between big business and educators, however, might suggest otherwise. As will be shown in later chapters, they usually shared the basic beliefs and attitudes of the corporate industrialists and were in agreement with programs designed to fulfill the requirements of corporate industry.

15. Robert Wiebe, "Business Disunity and the Progressive Movement," *The Mississippi Valley Historical Review 44* (March 1958): 665; Gabriel Kolko, *The Triumph of Conservatism* (Chicago: Quadrangle, 1963); and James Weinstein, *The Corporate Ideal in the Liberal State, 1900–1908* (Boston: Beacon, 1969).

Evangelical Protestantism all seemed incapable of explaining or guiding the turbulent events of the late nineteenth and early twentieth centuries. When these systems began to lose their credibility as organizing or explanatory guides, new rationales were sought. Protestant theology changed radically as the social gospel was advanced by men like Washington Gladden and Walter Rauschenbusch. Philosophy experienced a similar upheaval as William James, Chauncy Wright, Charles S. Pierce, and John Dewey developed varying brands of pragmatism. Even the tradition-bound discipline of law felt the influence of Louis Brandeis's, Roscoe Pound's, and Oliver Wendell Holmes's sociological jurisprudence. Significantly, these theories all sought to ground reality in the social present. All agreed that in their respective fields truth and standards of conduct were not to be discerned by appeals to tradition or to an absolute moral code, but by an examination of the interaction of present social forces. Ultimately, this stance lent intellectual credence to the forces that were strengthening the nexus between the individual and society.

THE STRANGERS IN THE LAND

Compounding the trauma triggered by these intellectual, demographic, and economic transformations was the spectre of immigration. Because of the sheer volume of immigration, many contemporary social critics considered it the major issue of the age. Statistics for the last half of the nineteenth and the early years of the twentieth century disclose an increasing flow of immigrants into the U.S. The 1860s found a total of 2.3 million immigrants seeking new homes in America. This total increased dramatically to 5.2 million during the 1880s and reached its zenith of 8.8 million in the first decade of the twentieth century. By 1900, of the total U.S. population of 76 million, over 10 million were foreign born and 26 million had foreign-born parents. In other words, foreigners composed almost half of the U.S. population and an even greater percentage in some urban areas and in certain important categories. According to the 1890 census, almost four out of five children of school age in New York and Chicago had foreign-born parents. For a nation so recently aware of urban problems, these figures were bound to be ominous.

By the mid-1880s, the immigrant question began to receive the anxious attention of many Americans. Perhaps most reflective of this concern was Josiah Strong's *Our Country*, first published in 1886. As Jergen Herbst has noted, the book "mirrors the thoughts and aspirations of this dominant segment of American society towards the close of the nineteenth century."[16] Strong observed that since the Civil War immigration had increased steadily, and he accurately predicted that the increase would accelerate. He feared that it would become increasingly difficult to assimilate larger numbers of immigrants to American Anglo-Saxon standards. While there was little doubt in Strong's mind that the newcomer was inferior and contributed to many of the nation's social problems, he nevertheless remained somewhat optimistic that reasonable numbers of immigrants could be successfully assimilated. He saw the public school as an important engine for this assimilation: "In the United States the common school has a function which is peculiar, viz., to Americanize the children of the immigrants. The public school is the principal digestive organ of the body politic."[17]

Although Strong's qualified optimism would continue as one strain in the American response to immigration, a more pessimistic view soon emerged. This negative response developed mainly in reaction to the changing immigration patterns. During the 1860s, almost 88 percent of the immigrants were from northwestern Europe, while less than 2 percent were from southeastern Europe. As the century drew to a close, however, the percentage of southeastern Europeans dramatically increased, the upsurge began in the mid-1880s and reached a high of over 70 percent of the total in the first decade of the twentieth century. Even before this vast increase of immigrants from southeastern Europe, the "old immigration" pattern dominated by immigrants from northwestern Europe evoked reactions typified by Josiah Strong, namely, that too great an increase might hinder assimilation. Critics argued that these new immigrants were so inferior that they could only deteriorate the racial stock of the nation. Borrowing concepts from the new sciences of genetics, anthropology, sociology, and psychology, they argued the innate inferiority of the new immi-

---

16. Josiah Strong, *Our Country* (Cambridge, Mass.: Harvard University Press, 1963), p. xix.

17. Strong, *Our Country*, pp. 52, 53, 55, 89, 200–218.

grants. This reaction, widespread among the general population, was formulated by many of the best minds in the nation.[18]

Many of these arguments were summarized in David Starr Jordan's article, " Closed Doors on the Melting Pot." Professor Jordan, a renowned zoologist and president of Leland Stanford University, argued that national survival depended on the preservation of the original racial characteristics—self-control and a love of freedom—that had sustained the emerging democracy. The new immigrants, according to Jordan, brought different and inferior racial traits that were incompatible with democracy. He thus proposed legislation to ban those immigrants who endangered the purity of the Nordic races that had previously dominated the nation.[19] Such sentiments were often expressed by those seeking to close the gates to further "undesirable" immigrants.

The millions of new immigrants and their children who already lived in the country were viewed as an educational problem. Most of those who addressed this problem adopted a stance that comprehended both the optimism of Josiah Strong and the pessimism of David Starr Jordan. They tended to agree with Jordan's assessment that the new immigrants were of a lesser breed than the old immigrants, while retaining Strong's confidence that, given the correct educational environment, America could change anyone for the better. In their view the immigrants possessed some cultural qualities that, properly blended with American culture, would enhance both the newcomers and the nation if new educational methods and new institutions facilitated the Americanization process.

PUBLIC SCHOOLS AND URBANIZATION

Public schools were thus expected to relieve the anxieties aroused by immigration and by new economic and intellectual trends. The rapid disintegration of rural hegemony and the corresponding ascendancy of

---

18. See John R. Commons, *Races and Immigrants in America* (New York: Macmillan. 1907); Edward A. Ross, *The Old World in the New* (New York: Century, 1914); Jack London, *The Valley of the Moon* (London: Mills and Boon, 1914); Francis A. Walker,"Restriction of Immigration," *The Atlantic Monthly*, June 1896, p. 828; Booker T. Washington, "Atlanta Exposition Speech," in *Up from Slavery* (New York: Doubleday, Page, 1901); and Woodrow Wilson, *History of the American People* (New York: Harper and Brothers, 1901), pp. 212–14.

19. David Starr Jordan, "Closed Doors on the Melting Pot," *The American Hebrew*, September 26, 1924, pp. 538 and 592.

urbanization meant that many of the older village-oriented devices for social control had become anachronisms. The educative experiences of the family farm affected an increasingly smaller portion of the population, and large-scale industrialism diminished the opportunities for children to gain vocational competence through apprenticeships. The minimal skill demands of industry further reduced the skill levels of much of the work force. Industrial requirements were now cast in terms of behavior rather than skill. Modern industry demanded stability, rationality, and cooperativeness of its employees, and corporate leaders cooperated with school reformers in designing new educational programs to meet these demands. Increasingly, psychological theory indicated that behavior could be most reliably controlled through emotional and attitudinal training. Educational experiences that emphasized the concrete and allowed students to learn by doing rather than by precept would, it was thought, develop in them dispositions to react in predictable ways in given situations. In short, those concerned with the failure of the older intellectual and religious underpinnings of social order looked to the school to develop a new type of student with the social and moral habits necessary for the modern age.

The various reforms designed to produce a better citizen, a well-trained and adaptable worker, and an intelligent consumer coalesced in the campaign to Americanize immigrants. The general reaction to the new immigrants emphasized their differences and hence underlined the demand for a differentiated curriculum designed to meet the needs of the learner. Not surprisingly, those needs were made to coincide with the requirements for the new industrial worker. The doctrine of individual differences and its curricular manifestations threatened the ideology of "democratic education." Ellwood Cubberley, one of the most influential educators of the era, accurately plotted this course as he predicted: "Our city schools will soon be forced to give up the exceedingly democratic idea that all are equal, and that our society is devoid of classes, as a few cities have already in large part done, and to begin a specialization of educational effort along many new lines in an attempt better to adapt the school to the needs of these many classes in the city life."[20]

This new outlook necessitated a massive transformation of existing techniques. The American public school had traditionally been an institution where children learned the rudiments of literacy and the basic elements of citizenship. Attendance had been voluntary and often irreg-

---

20. Ellwood P. Cubberley, *Changing Conceptions of Education* (Boston: Houghton Mifflin, 1909), p. 57.

ular. The pedagogy of the little red school house had been based upon the premise that to educate a man one must train his mental faculties. In theory, at least, the basic mission of the school had been intellectual training for contemporary psychology held that if the child's mind was adequately trained his correct behavior as an adult could be assured. Most children attended school only long enough to gain rudimentary literacy. A few, usually children of the more privileged classes, remained in school beyond the early elementary years. Their education was designed to prepare them for the positions of community leadership that they were to hold as adults by developing their capacity for independent decision making. The classical curriculum, designed to produce leaders, emphasized cultural education and rigorous intellectual exercises. This traditional educational ideal was not considered appropriate for the growing number of working-class pupils who swelled school attendance at the end of the nineteenth century. It survives, nevertheless, in a somewhat modified form, in those schools and curriculum tracks most heavily populated with children from the upper social and economic classes.

The large urban schools, with their factory-like appearance, which emerged at the end of the nineteenth century, were radically different from the traditional American school. Attendance was no longer voluntary, and as increased numbers of working class children were compelled to attend school for extended terms, intellectual training fell into disrepute. Educators despaired over intellectual training for children whose intellects they suspected were inadequate for the content of the traditional curriculum. Moreover, psychologists were beginning to suggest that the intellect was not, after all, the most effective level for control of behavior; they suggested instead that the nonintellectual wellsprings of human behavior were far more significant than the mind. These could be controlled most effectively by instilling appropriate habits and dispositions to react in prescribed ways to specific kinds of situations. The technique for this training involved having the student practice the desired response in a controlled situation. The modern child would "learn by doing rather than by precept"; activity became more prominent than books.[21] The new schools were total institutions

---

21. Some educators used the phrase "learn by doing" to describe processes different from those discussed in this study. For example, in the physical sciences the laboratory method, in which the student actually conducted the experiment, could be called a "learn by doing" exercise because the student would engage in an activity in order to understand a certain principle. As the term was applied to the working-class student, however, it meant that the child would engage in an activity to develop a habitual response that would not require the understanding of a principle. Thus the statement: "learn by doing *rather than* by precept."

that attempted to influence all aspects of the children's lives and particularly all aspects of their development into adults compatible with the new industrial requirements. The public schools were now engaged in more than literacy development. Like the Protestant churches of the preceding decades, they were engaged in the total development of the child.

SYNOPSIS

The following chapters will examine some of the more significant aspects of the massive transformation that American education and public schooling underwent during the first few decades of the twentieth century. One important change resulted from the passage of compulsory school attendance laws in all of the states by 1919. Legislative proponents of this measure were usually looked upon as altruists, interested in raising literacy standards and in diffusing knowledge among the populace. Chapter two will show that fear rather than beneficence provided the impetus for compulsory schooling. Educators and political leaders were afraid that immigrant and working-class children untrained in the public schools would become a disruptive force in the emerging urban-industrial society. The public schools were perceived as the state agency most strategically located to restructure the nation's children and produce the desired new industrial working class. To compel attendance in the public schools, it was widely argued, was simply a strategy to protect the state.

The immigrants, with their odd costumes, strange languages, non-Protestant religions, and other unusual customs, were the focus of many attempts by American reformers to restructure aberrant lifestyles. Some of the earliest reforms began outside the schools in settlement houses and other philanthropic agencies. By the turn of the century, the thrust of these efforts was captured by the Americanization campaigns that surfaced in the schools. Chapter three examines the development of this Americanization movement.

In order to change lifestyles, engender acceptable reality structures, and implant the habits and responses appropriate for future industrial laborers, education had to control many aspects of the child's life. Chapter four, accordingly, traces the history of the play movement. Prior to 1885 there were no organized public playgrounds in America, but by 1910 nearly every city in the country had officially organized and supervised playgrounds. Those that were not part of the public school system generally had close alliances with the schools. Analysis of this movement reveals that it was much more than an effort to give urban children a place to exercise their desires for play. The play forms fostered on American public playgrounds were rooted in a sophisticated set of psychological theories which held that the kinds of attitudes, values, and habits exercised during a child's play would be reproduced in his adult behavior. By providing carefully selected play activities, the playground movement implanted in the child behavior patterns appropriate for an industrial worker. These lessons were not taught through the intellect, but were transmitted by training the child's emotions in a controlled environment. The child who played in the urban playground learned by doing.

The application of progressive education's slogan, "learn by doing," is similarly part of the story told in chapter five, an overview of the widespread use of extracurricular activities in the public schools. Activities such as student self-government, clubs, and music organizations were designed to give children practice in acting out appropriate responses to selected social situations. It was generally assumed that because these activities would influence children to derive satisfaction from group and system loyalty they would enable the children to adapt more easily to the assembly lines and production teams in the modern factory. Extracurricular activities had the added advantage of giving school authorities access to the student's out-of-class life, thus increasing the school's probable effect on him.

The most important twentieth-century innovation in the public school curriculum was undoubtedly the introduction of the differentiated curriculum. The changing character of the student body suggested that since various types of children faced differing life possibilities, they required a school curriculum based upon their projected life future. It is difficult to obtain accurate statistics regarding the number of students who were directly affected by the introduction of vocational education.[22] Although some estimates place the number at about 10 percent,[23]

---

22. In part, the problem occurs because of the general unreliability of school statistics during the early twentieth century. Different parts of a superintendent's annual report often contained conflicting figures, and the U.S. Bureau of Education's statistics were usually based upon incomplete returns of questionnaires. In the case of vocational education the problem is even more complex because of the shifting definition of many of the categories of vocational studies. For example, it is often difficult to discern whether a report is referring to the number of students who had studied a single vocational course, such as typing, or to the number of students who were pursuing a vocational curriculum, such as commercial education.

23. David B. Tyack, *The One Best System* (Cambridge, Mass.: Harvard University Press, 1974), p. 190.

this figure seems rather low for urban public schools. Based upon incomplete reportings from the entire nation, for example, it appears that as early as 1906 about 20 percent of the total public high school student body was following a vocational curriculum, that is, either technical, manual, industrial or commercial courses of study.[24] The share of the high school student population who pursued vocational curricula in urban systems was significantly higher. Vocational students constituted approximately 25 percent of the total high school population in New York City during 1909, about 57 percent in Cincinnati during 1911, 33 percent in Chicago during 1913, and 56 percent in Elyria, Ohio during 1918.[25] These figures represent the early stages of the vocational movement and reflect only the high school populations. "Prevocational" programs were later introduced in the junior high schools to extend the vocational movement into the lower grades. It seems reasonable to conclude that the proponents of vocational training were at least moderately successful in their announced effort to extend vocationalism to a significant percentage of urban school students.

Chapters six and seven examine the evolution of the differentiated curriculum and its motivating idea, vocational education. Industrial education was strategically important not only because it was designed to produce a future industrial proletariat from working-class children, but also because it embodied most of the pedagogical techniques used in the educational movements discussed earlier. More than any of the other innovations, it exemplified popular educational slogans of its age: "learn by doing" and "education for life." Moreover, industrial education was an extremely complex innovation seeking to train a working class that would match the hierarchy of skills within the corporate work force. Its primary aim was not to develop skills among the vast majority of the students, for corporate industry required but a small number of workers who possessed skills. Technical high schools and manual training programs prepared this small cadre to become the elite corps of the industrial army—the foremen, engineers, and repairmen.

---

24. Calculated from figures in *Report of the Commissioner of Education for the Year 1906* (Washington, D.C.: U.S. Government Printing Office), 2: 697, 1053, and 1095.

25. *Annual Report of the New York City Superintendent of Schools* [hereafter cited as *New York Annual Report*], *for the Year Ending July 31, 1909*, p. 104. This figure reached almost 50 percent by 1914, as disclosed in *New York Annual Report*, 1914, p. 106. *Annual Report of the Public Schools of Cincinnati* [hereafter cited as *Cincinnati Annual Report*] *for the Year Ending August 31, 1911; Annual Report of the Chicago Board of Education* [hereafter cited as *Chicago Annual Report*] *for the Year Ending 1913*, p. 255; and "Educational Survey of Elyria, Ohio," *Bulletin of the U.S. Bureau of Education, 1918*, no. 15, p. 77.

The diversity of corporate industry's work force prompted the formation of the vocational guidance movement discussed in chapter eight. Various levels of the hierarchy required different types of workers, differing personality structures, and, in some cases, intelligence, initiative, and skill. Clearly, some mechanism was needed to sort the children into the appropriate categories in order to train each for his projected life. Vocational guidance provided this tool.

Chapter 2

Compulsory Schooling

As they stood at the door of the twentieth century, American intellectuals and educators cast an anxious and often longing glance at the rapidly receding decades of their youth. Although clouded by nostalgia, their view of the American past, which probably resembled historical reality only partially, shaped their programs for the new century. Two somewhat conflicting visions of the American past emerged in educational literature. The first was based on the folklore of rugged frontier individualism,[1] while the second recalled the neighborly cooperativeness of the nineteenth-century American rural village.[2] Both interpretations are woven into the fabric of American folklore, and both contain a measure of truth. Most educators sensitive to the nation's pressing social problems were especially troubled by the apparent disintegration of the village-oriented, rural *gemeinschaft*.[3] They hoped to recapture the lost opportunities for informal education and social control intrinsic in ante-bellum village life. Educators who believed that the village was losing its impact on future citizens offered the public school as an alternative. "The work of public education is with us," said Ellwood Cubberley, "to a large

---

1. See, for example, John Dewey and Evelyn Dewey, *Schools of Tomorrow* (New York: E.P. Dutton, 1962), pp. 122–23. In addition to railing against the rugged individualism of pioneers, Dewey often hailed the community spirit of New England villagers.

2. See Ellwood P. Cubberley, *Changing Conceptions of Education* (Boston: Houghton Mifflin, 1909), p. 16.

3. For an unsympathetic view of the nineteenth-century village and its disintegration see Sherwood Anderson, *Winesburg, Ohio* (New York: Viking Compass Editions, 1958), pp. 70–71.

degree, a piece of religious work. To engage in it is to enlist in the nation's service."[4] The dean of Stanford's School of Education was not the only American educator to conceive the work of the public school as religious in nature, nor was he the last to suggest that the nation was an appropriate object of religious devotion.

Although the anarchic frontier and the village community were conflicting visions of the American past, the public education policy recommendations that flowed from each myth were fundamentally the same: the school was to develop cooperative and socially concerned individuals equipped to contribute to the welfare of the nation. The perceived importance of this task for the future of the society dictated that no child escape the regenerative influence of the public school. This reflex was a major factor in the turn-of-the-century crusade for compulsory school attendance.

This chapter focuses on the evolution of compulsory attendance in urban schools. It begins with a brief outline of the relevant legislation and then examines the relation between these laws and child labor laws. The effect of the new student population on schools and schoolmen is discussed next, followed by an analysis of compulsory education's fundamental purpose: to protect the state by socializing children for acceptable citizenship. The chapter closes with a survey of various enforcement agencies—truant officers, school censuses, visiting teachers, and truant schools.

COMPULSORY ATTENDANCE LEGISLATION

The ideal of public responsibility for school facilities has a long tradition in the United States. The assertion that the state has the right and obligation to compel children to attend the schools, however, is of much more recent vintage. The first state compulsory attendance law was the Massachusetts code enacted in 1852. Massachusetts during the 1840s was already undergoing many of the stresses of urbanization, immigration, and industrialism that other sections of the nation

---

4. Cubberley, *Changing Conceptions of Education*, p. 68.

would face later in the century,[5] so it was also the leader in developing ideas and institutions to deal with the problems spawned by these social forces. By 1870, only one other state and the District of Columbia had followed Massachusetts' lead. During the succeeding thirty years, however, the rush to compulsion swept thirty-two states. The 1907 legislative year found the children in only nine Southern states outside the pale of compulsory attendance laws. These same states had resisted the seemingly irrepressible tide of modernity in the nineteenth century and had capitulated to the demands of urban industrialism only at the point of drawn sabers and blasting cannons. They recognized the value of public schools as a replacement for the discarded plantation system of schooling primarily through the prodding of Northern industrialists, especially those associated with philanthropic foundations.[6] By 1918, when the last bastion finally surrendered, all of the states had adopted compulsory attendance laws.

The several states and territories differed in the time of enactment of compulsory attendance laws and in the age limits for required attendance. Of the 34 states and territories that had compulsory attendance laws in 1902, the beginning compulsory age was 7 years in 15 states and 8 years in the rest. The terminal compulsory age was 12 years in one state, 14 years in 20 states, 15 in 6 states, and 16 years in the remaining 7 states and territories. The trend by 1918 was clearly to confine a child in school for increasingly longer periods of his life. 21 states had lowered the starting age to 7, while 26 retained the eighth year as the compulsory entry age. Only 9 states allowed children to leave school at age 14; 7 others insisted on attendance until age 15, and 31 required attendance until age 16. By 1954, all states required children to attend school until their sixteenth birthday.

5. For a description of these problems and the rhetoric supporting compulsory schooling in Massachusetts see Michael B. Katz, *Irony of Early School Reform* (Boston: Beacon, 1970).

6. See James D. Anderson, "Education for Servitude" (Ph.D. diss., University of Illinois, Urbana , 1973). This is not meant to imply that there was little interest in education in the post–Civil War South prior to the active campaigns for schooling conducted by Northern philanthropists. The Reconstruction governments in most of the Southern states attempted to develop public schools, and the freedmen had made extensive provisions for black schools. The purpose is to note the influence of Northern industrialists in spurring the realization that compulsory public schooling could be used to socialize children in much the same manner that the plantation system had.

CHILD LABOR AND SCHOOL ATTENDANCE

The crusade for compulsory school attendance laws was intimately related to the gradual elimination of child labor in industry and mines. The early child labor laws were inspired by humanitarian reformers who wanted to stop the brutal oppression of children, which they believed inhibited the child's normal development, rendered him useless to society during his adult years, and thus undermined the strength of the nation.[7] Child labor laws in Illinois, for example, began with the 1872 act forbidding the employment of youths under 14 in mines. An act in 1877 extended the state's protection by prohibiting the employment of children younger than 14 in occupations designated morally or physically dangerous. By 1897 the state had outlawed the employment of any child under 14, barred those under 16 from engaging in hazardous employment, and limited the work hours for children under 16 to ten hours per day and sixty hours per week. In addition, all establishments that employed children under sixteen were required to post a list of their names.[8]

These child labor laws, laxly administered and easily avoided, were not the basic cause of the gradual disappearance of children from the ranks of the employed. Some employers found the legal restrictions too cumbersome, but others simply found it unprofitable to employ children, who were often unreliable and irresponsible. Of greater importance were the southern and eastern European immigrants, who provided industry with an alternative supply of cheap labor, and the more sophisticated industrial machines, which took over many of the jobs children had formerly performed. In any case, the traditional American reliance on work as a moral instructor for its young was gradually and generally abandoned.

For humanitarian reformers, getting children out of the mines and factories was only one side of the crusade to save the nation. Edith Abbott, a Chicago social reformer, indicated the double nature of the effort when she said:

A well-enforced compulsory education law must proceed or accompany a child labor law if child labor is really to be prohibited or even regulated. A good compulsory education law, well enforced, may in fact prevent child labor, whereas a child labor law unaccompanied by

7. See Clarence Karier, Paul Violas, and Joel Spring, *Roots of Crisis* (Chicago: Rand McNally, 1973), p. 79.

8. Edith Abbott and Sophonisba P. Breckenridge, *Truancy and Nonattendance in Chicago Schools* (New York: Aron Press, 1970), Appendix V, pp. 440–46.

a compulsory education law takes children out of the factories and workshops only to throw them into the streets.[9]

A child on the city streets or even in many city homes was not considered in the best interests of the nation. Most reformers believed that compulsory attendance in the public schools would be the antidote for social degeneration. Children evicted from the work bench were to be placed at the school desk.

THE EFFECT OF THE NEW CLIENTELE

One significant problem associated with the enforcement of compulsory schooling was the effect these pupils would have on the school. Soon after the 1889 compulsory education law in Illinois went into effect, the Committee on Compulsory Education of the Chicago school board advised that:

> this class of unfortunates, who, either from improper training and unwholesome surroundings at home, or from unnatural perversity of disposition evade their school duties, and who, when brought to school by the attendance agent, cause sufficient disturbance to have absence heartily desired by the teacher and principal, should be placed in a separate room or building and under a different system of discipline.[10]

Teachers in other cities also found it difficult to deal with these unwashed students from the unfortunate classes. School Superintendent Maxwell reported in 1902 that "the freezing out of disagreeable children by principals and teachers" was one of the four chief causes of truancy in New York City.[11]

Immigrant and working-class children dominated this "class of unfortunates" or "disagreeable children" now herded into the schools for regular, extended attendance. Their permanent presence led school officials to initiate programs to separate the most disagreeable of them from the other students. These problem children were usually offered significantly different kinds of training in the course of their regeneration. Four years after Maxwell had expressed his disapproval

---

9. Abbott and Breckenridge, *Truancy and Nonattendance*, p. 74.

10. Quoted in Abbott and Breckenridge, *Truancy and Nonattendance*, p. 61.

11. *New York Annual Report*, 1902, p. 91.

of the tendency of teachers and principals to freeze such pupils out of school, E. E. Meleney, the associate superintendent in charge of compulsory education for New York City had "become convinced that children of evil tendencies should be eliminated from the regular classes of the public schools." He recommended that they be placed in special schools to "be trained by specialists competent to deal with serious problems."[12] Similarly, the Cincinnati superintendent recommended segregation into special ungraded schools for those students who could not adjust to school discipline. In the same discussion of "school deportment" he pointed to the overriding purpose of schooling: "Not less, but more important than book lessons learned are the habits of behavior acquired, the cultivation of right dispositions and temper, the easy and habitual respect for the teacher's authority and confidence in her good will."[13] Although it was deemed necessary to get lower-class and immigrant children off the streets, their presence in schools that had been modeled on middle-class, Anglo-Saxon, Protestant values was troublesome. One early response was to incarcerate the more intractable of the underprivileged in truant schools and parental homes while they learned the appropriate values and modes of behavior. This policy, the schoolmen believed, benefited both the nation and the children.

THE INTERESTS OF THE STATE

National interests, however, were uppermost in the minds of the champions of compulsory schooling. Buffalo's superintendent of schools, Henry P. Emerson, emphasized the priority of the claims for safe citizenship in his 1902 address to the National Education Association. "Our compulsory education laws are based on the theory that a community, for its own protection, as well as the good of the child, must make it impossible for any boy or girl to grow up in ignorance, a stranger to the ennobling influences which every good school exerts."[14] A similar objective for compulsory attendance was

---

12. *New York Annual Report*, 1906, p. 257.

13. *Cincinnati Annual Report*, 1900, p. 35; similar response can be seen in the Chicago schools. See *Chicago Annual Report*, 1911, p. 133.

14. Henry P. Emerson, "Influences that Make for Good Citizenship." in *National Education Association Addresses and Proceedings* [hereafter cited as NEA Addresses and Proceedings], (Washington, D.C.: National Education Association, 1902), p. 192.

expressed by Graham H. Harris, president of the Chicago Board of Education in 1900.[15] Fourteen years later, a committee of teachers and administrators conducting a self-survey of the Chicago schools demonstrated the continuity of the belief when it argued that the educational care of certain classes of students should be considered as a measure for civic self-protection.[16] The sentiment was most succinctly and candidly stated, however, in a 1914 bulletin of the U.S. Bureau of Education:

> Since all classes of our heterogeneous society are active factors therein, the State maintains schools to render its citizenship homogeneous in spirit and purpose. The public schools exist primarily for the benefit of the State rather than for the benefit of the individual. The State seeks to make every citizen intelligent and serviceable.[17]

Compulsory school attendance was viewed by many of its proponents as a preventive measure against the civic decay that impaired the functioning of the state. The schools were expected to make each child serviceable and safe for citizenship.

The civic purposes of compulsory school attendance laws surfaced in the subsequent judicial interpretation of the legislation. In a summary of the legal interpretation of such legislation, Newton Edwards said in 1940: "In requiring attendance upon state schools, or others substantially equivalent, the legislature does not confer a benefit upon the parent, nor primarily upon the child; it is only doing that which the well being and safety of the state itself requires."[18] Most supporters of enforced attendance agreed that such statutes were justifiable because the safety of the state required that all children, and especially lower-class children, submit to the socialization processes of the schools, which they believed would propagate safe citizenship. Clearly, the intent of the compulsory attendance laws was not wholly child-centered.

This rationale for mandatory schooling placed the individual in a precarious relationship to the state. It justified many invasions of privacy and liberty. One of the more interesting statements of national

---

15. *Chicago Annual Report*, 1900, p. 14.

16. *Chicago Annual Report*, 1914, p. 376.

17. William H. Hand, "Compulsory School Attendance, Part II: Need of Compulsory Education in the South," *Bulletin of the U.S. Bureau of Education*, 1914, no. 2, p. 105.

18. Newton Edwards, *The Courts and the Public Schools* (Chicago: University of Chicago Press, 1940), p. 480.

interests was made by James B. Aswell, superintendent of public education for Louisiana, in a 1907 address to the National Education Association. With rhetoric that became increasingly familiar in the twentieth century, Aswell argued that all members of a society are so interconnected that the actions of each affect all. The state, as the protector of all, has the right to control each child's education because "the child is a ward of the state." The child's right, he claimed, is "to demand such opportunity as will enable him to render, in his own way, the most efficient service and thus become a valuable asset to the state, worthy of citizenship."[19] Following similar logic, Ada Van Stone Harris, an assistant superintendent in the Rochester, New York schools, told the 1907 meeting of the National Education Association that the safety of the state was sufficient justification for any educationally centered intrusion into the home. She believed that in many instances the state rather than the home should determine the kind of training a child received.[20]

Two years earlier, Julia Richman, a district superintendent of schools in New York City, had phrased the problem more concretely, warning the NEA of the need to compel immigrant children to attend school. She argued that in a nation of immigrants, where foreign-born children would become voters and perhaps political leaders, the school should play a vital role in determining the quality of citizenship. The "civic problem" created by the presence of immigrant masses could be met only through regular school attendance and adequate Americanization programs in the public schools. Richman recommended a national cooperative effort between the federal immigration authorities and local schools to locate, tabulate, and guarantee the school attendance of all alien children in the nation. These children could not be left under the influences of either the street or their parents. Only the public school could regenerate alien children and thus save the nation. Like many other twentieth-century educators, Richman believed that as the schools conducted the "holy service" of "the making of a true American citizen out of the immigrant child," they played a role in society similar to that played earlier by

---

19. James B. Aswell, "Is the Child a Ward of the State," *NEA Addresses and Proceedings*, 1907, p. 152.

20. Ada Van Stone Harris, "What Should the Public Do for the Care and Training of Children Before They Are Admitted to the Public School?" *NEA Addresses and Proceedings*, 1907, p. 157.

the churches.[21] As will be seen, this "holy service" replaced and replicated the older work of the churches as the schools increasingly engaged in the process of reality structuring and moral training.

Some educators, viewing as essential the school's mission of shaping good citizens, began to argue that the school should have unlimited access to the formative years of childhood and, in special cases, even beyond. By 1911, the NEA included in its "Declaration of Principles" a provision that would have kept some children in permanent custody. Instead of an arbitrary age limit on compulsory schooling, the NEA opted for the development of physical and mental maturity standards for all students. Those "failing to meet such maturity tests at school-age limit should remain under public supervision and control, either until they reach maturity, or permanently."[22] Charles A. Ellwood, a professor of sociology at the University of Missouri, echoed this sentiment when he characterized the compulsory education laws as "failures" because "instead of securing the proper training for citizenship which must be the foundation of successful free institutions, they let every year vast numbers through their net." Children were allowed to escape from the beneficent influence of the school after they had served a definite term of years, even if they had not responded to the school's influence and become competent citizens. As an alternative Ellwood suggested that educators devise definite educational standards and requirements and "then let every child in the state be 'sentenced,' as it were, by a rational compulsory education law, to complete this requirement of education in our public schools before they are permitted to go forth and take their place in the world of work." Such legislation would, he thought, "have a eugenic value for the race," for those who could not satisfy the requirements for citizenship would be "turned over to proper institutions for their care and training."[23] Presumably, these institutions would prevent such undesirables from procreating. These proposals would give the state power to confine indefinitely those who did not satisfy an official norm for citizenship. Although Ellwood's proposal was not enacted into law, it illustrates the potential threat to personal liberty posed by the state benefit theory. His proposals, moreover, were not atypical.

---

21. Julia Richman, "The Immigrant Child," *NEA Addresses and Proceedings*, 1905, pp. 113 and 121.

22. "Declaration of Principles," *NEA Addresses and Proceedings*, 1911, p. 32.

23. Charles A. Ellwood, "Our Compulsory Education Laws," *Education* 34 (May 1914): 572, 575, and 576.

RESPONSE TO TRUANCY

The home environment and other social conditions deemed perni-
cious to good citizenship could not be allowed to influence the
future citizen without the intervention of the school. Although the
immigrant home was viewed as deleterious, it was not the only perceived threat. All environmental circumstances that did not conform
to the middle-class morality and the social ideals of school officials
became objects of reformation. Particularly illustrative of this view are
the discussions and programs surrounding truancy and nonattendance.[24] Poverty, indifferent or inadequate parents, vicious neighborhood conditions, and immigrant values were the usually cited causes
for the truant or nonattending child. Reformers and educators blurred
the distinction between these categories, so reference to one usually
implied inclusion of all. They linked various economic, social, and
ethnic factors to truancy and poor citizenship with little or no supporting evidence; in fact, hard data frequently contradicted these
correlations.

The fiftieth annual report of the Chicago Board of Education contained such unsubstantiated conclusions. The president of the board,
Alfred R. Uron, after citing the large number of children of foreign
parentage in Chicago, concluded, "It is evident that Chicago, as a
cosmopolitan city, must maintain compulsory education to safeguard
the educational interests of its future citizenship."[25] He apparently
found the number of foreigners a sufficient indication of their threat.
The same report contained an analysis of the truancy problem in Chicago by William Bodine, the superintendent of compulsory education.
His study of 4,230 cases of truancy for the year showed that only
1,234 truants came from "poor" homes while 1,061 were from
"good" homes and 2,035 were from "fair" homes. Although his own
figures stated that almost three-fourths of the truants came from good
or fair homes, he concluded that, "While a good boy may come
from a bad home and a bad boy may come from a good home, the
fact remains that the environment of the insanitary and improvident
home is now, and always has been the dominant breeder of the
backward, truant, delinquent or subnormal child."[26] While Mr.

---

24. Especially valuable is Anthony M. Platt, *The Child Savers: The Invention of Delin-*
quency (Chicago: University of Chicago Press, 1969).

25. *Chicago Annual Report*, 1911, p. 31.

26. *Chicago Annual Report*, 1911, p. 136.

Bodine's allegation may seem a bit curious in light of his statistics, it does underscore the threats perceived by reformers. It also reveals the intent of the compulsory attendance movement. This intent was further clarified in a statement by Edith Abbott and Sophonisba Breckenridge, two of the leading Chicago reformers: "In the well-to-do sections of the city, the problem of attendance, while it may be a school problem, is not a social problem of importance as it is in the poor and congested neighborhoods."[27]

The discussion of the "habitual truant" by Abbott and Breckenridge is also instructive. They noted with approval that "the persistent truant or extremely incorrigible boy who comes from a good home, and who has parents able to devote time and effort to getting him to school, is likely to be returned to his home, while another boy whose offense has been much less grave may be sent to the Parental School if home conditions are less favorable." In their analysis of the economic backgrounds of the inmates of the Chicago Parental School, the two reformers discovered that 80 percent were from poor or very poor homes. From this they concluded not only that poverty is an important cause of truancy, but also that "the families that furnish the truant candidates for the Parental School are not only poor but foreign."[28]

A similar pattern developed in New York City. Attendance statistics for 1900–1901 reveal, for example, that the truant officers investigated a total of 76,073 cases. The breakdown by borough was 34, 180 for Manhattan and the Bronx, 25,931 for Brooklyn, 14,180 for Queens, and 1,782 for Richmond. The first two boroughs had much larger populations than the others and contained most of the immigrant and poor districts. Most significantly, all of the 621 children committed to truant schools were from these immigrant and poor boroughs.[29] Six years later, in his report on the causes of truancy, Superintendent Maxwell emphasized the large number of foreigners in the city.[30]

In reference to juvenile justice practices implemented at the turn of the century, Anthony Platt has said, "The child savers set such high standards of family propriety that almost any parent could be accused of not fulfilling his proper function. In effect, only lower-

27. Abbott and Breckenridge, *Truancy and Nonattendance*, p. 94.

28. Abbott and Breckenridge, *Truancy and Nonattendance*, pp. 157, 158.

29. *New York Annual Report*, 1901, p. 61.

30. *New York Annual Report*, 1907, p. 335.

class families were evaluated as to their competency, whereas the propriety of middle-class families was exempt from examination and recrimination."[31] Schoolmen exhibited this bias in their evaluation of truancy as well. In large measure, the compulsory attendance effort was directed at immigrant and working-class children, whose regeneration was seen as particularly vital for the security of the state.

The attendance or truant officer became an important agent for enforcing compulsory schooling. The experience of Chicago reflects developments in other urban areas. The Chicago Compulsory Education Department was organized in 1888 with three officers. The corps was increased to 12 the following year[32] and to 40 by 1908.[33] Over the next six years the force expanded to 53.[34] The early efforts of these officers aimed at voluntary compliance. The Committee on Compulsory Education reported in 1890 that "no interference with parental authority, no arrests had been made, not a single case of prosecution or persecution, the strength of moral persuasiveness had been used."[35] The use of moral persuasion placed this effort directly in the tradition of nineteenth-century voluntarism, a tradition that would soon seem outdated in urban-industrial America. The late 1890s saw the demise of voluntarism in Chicago. In 1898, the superintendent of compulsory education would report that the first prosecution had been successful. He justified the change in policy by arguing that:

> We should rightfully have the power to arrest all these little beggers, loafers and vagabonds that infest our city, take them off the streets and place them in schools where they are compelled to receive education and learn moral principles. . . . we certainly should not permit a reckless and indifferent part of our population to rear their children in ignorance to become a criminal and lawless class within our city.[36]

31. Platt, The Child Savers, p. 135.
32. Mary J. Herrick, The Chicago Schools (Beverly Hills: Sage Publications, 1971), p. 63.
33. Chicago Annual Report, 1908, p. 17.
34. Chicago Annual Report, 1914, p. 405.
35. Quoted in Abbott and Breckenridge, Truancy and Nonattendance, p. 63.
36. Chicago Annual Report, 1898, p. 170.

SCHOOL CENSUS

Truant officers soon discovered that the Promethean task of chasing reluctant students through the street of major cities was as inefficient as it was difficult. A more effective technique was the school census. The idea of enumerating school-age children was not conceived in the twentieth century. School censuses had been previously conducted in many states to determine the distribution of state financial support to the local districts rather than to enforce attendance. These censuses were usually carelessly taken, so their findings only approximated the real numbers. Leonard Ayres estimated that "the errors in some cases were as high as 25 percent."[37] By the turn of the twentieth century, educators proposed to develop accurate school census procedures in order to use the information to enforce school attendance laws. The census would inform school officials of the number and location of potential students. It was a means of "getting the name of the child on the books of the school so that he is not thereafter lost sight of by the educational authorities until, by age or schooling, he is no longer within their jurisdiction."[38] The development of a permanent census board in New York illustrates the effort to enumerate school-age children in American cities during the early years of this century.[39]

Superintendent William Maxwell recommended in his 1905 annual report a law that would utilize the municipal police to locate potential truants. He suggested that parents be required to report their children to the local precinct station. The police would then inform them when it was time for the child to enroll in school, and in this way "keep every child in the city under inspection."[40] Three years later, the state of New York passed a school census law requiring the larger cities in the state to maintain a permanent census board under the control of the mayor, the superintendent of schools, and the police commissioner.[41] This law paralleled Maxwell's earlier recommendations and included a penalty of

---

37. Leonard Ayres, *Laggards in Our Schools: A Study in Retardation and Elimination in City School Systems* (New York: Charities Publication Committee, 1909), p. 191.

38. John Dearling Haney, *Registration of City School Children* (New York: Teachers' College, Columbia University, 1910), p. 16.

39. For information regarding comparable developments in other cities see Haney, *Registration of Children*, pp. 60–101; Abbott and Breckenridge, *Truancy and Nonattendance*, pp. 211–26; and W. S. Deffenbaugh, "Compulsory School Attendance Laws in the United States, Part I," *Bulletin of the U.S. Bureau of Education*, 1914, no. 2, pp. 12–15.

40. *New York Annual Report*, 1905, p. 97.

41. *New York Annual Report*, 1908, p. 170.

$20 for parental failure to comply. In addition, house-to-house enumeration by police officers was mandated. Maxwell was clear about the intent of the statute: "The end first sought by the accumulation of this information is a stricter and better enforcement of the compulsory education and child labor laws."[42] The state commissioner of education claimed that as a result of the census law 23,241 children were found to be unlawfully out of school in New York City.[43] By 1918, all but three states had passed legislation either requiring or permitting a school census.[44]

WORK CERTIFICATES

The census effort was essentially an accounting problem: to find and keep track of school age children. The task was complicated by the fact that most states had attendance laws that allowed employed children between 14 and 16 years of age to escape the protective custody of the school. These children received work certificates and often refused to attend school even if they lost their job and were unable to obtain other employment.

The response of educators to what they called the "14 to 16 problem" enlightens those seeking to understand the aim of compulsory attendance laws. Chicago's William Bodine urged the schools to make "better provision for the correction and care of children between 14 and 16 years of age who are beyond parental control and who prefer idleness to school attendance or employment." He recommended the establishment of a central juvenile employment bureau "to expedite the employment of boys and girls as soon as possible after they secure their age and school certificates." Maxwell argued similarly that the employment certificates were unfortunately often seen as licenses to remain away from school and to roam the streets until the child produced evidence from an employer that he would be given regular employment.[45] In the same vein, a specialist from the U.S. Bureau of Education proposed that the certificate be given not to the child, but to the employer,

---

42. *New York Annual Report*, 1905, pp. 170–71.

43. Quoted in Deffenbaugh, "Compulsory School Attendance," p. 13.

44. Frederick Earle Emmons, *City School Attendance Service* (New York: Teachers' College, Columbia University, 1926), p. 25.

45. *Chicago Annual Report*, 1911, p. 138; *New York Annual Report*, 1912, p. 241.

who would return it to the school authorities upon termination of employment.[46] In this way, the school would be able to compel the child to return to the classroom. These arguments and recommendations all contained the demand that the child be in school or at work, because, at least after age 14, either, would fit him for citizenship. Idleness, or "roaming the streets," was commonly regarded as a distinct threat.

As child labor became less important to urban employers, the cry for reform took a somewhat different tack. Abbott and Breckenridge noted that because of increasing reluctance of employers to hire workers under 16, the jobs open to child laborers were mostly "uneducative, undisciplinary, 'blind-alley' occupations that are likely to lead to nothing but a 'dead-end' and unemployment in the future."[47] Although they conceded that in many homes poverty was great, they insisted that "the 'necessity' of the work must be estimated not by the poverty in the home, but in terms of its educative value *from the point of view of their later industrial life and their fitness for citizenship.*"[48] They proposed a system of mandatory but part-time continuation schools and a system of employment counseling to supervise and guide the child who had left school.

THE VISITING TEACHER

If many jobs were considered dysfunctional in the education of the future citizen, many homes were similarly viewed. The visiting teacher was a new school program, a predominantly urban one, intended to neutralize the effects of undesirable homes and to promote more regular school attendance for children whose homes were deficient.[49] Like most educational reforms in the early twentieth century, the "visiting teacher" was an experiment first conducted by organizations outside the schools and later shifted to the regular school structure. Many of the early efforts were directed by settlement workers who cooperated with school officials in giving "personal attention to children whose whole-

---

46. Deffenbaugh, "Compulsory School Attendance," p. 15.

47. Abbott and Breckenridge, *Truancy and Nonattendance*, p. 328.

48. Abbott and Breckenridge, *Truancy and Nonattendance*, p. 330 (emphasis added).

49. Sophia C. Glein, "The Visiting Teacher," *Bulletin of the U.S. Bureau of Education*, 1921, no. 2, pp. 5–7 and 18.

some development was being endangered by the ignorance, neglect, or destitution of their parents or guardians."[50] The visiting teacher thus extended the influence of the school into homes unwilling or unable to provide acceptable standards of family life. Her mission included providing better study areas and medical attention for the children and employment counselling for the parents. The visiting teacher also was charged with interpreting the purpose of the school to ignorant parents, a task that sometimes involved justifying inequities within the system. In Indianapolis, for example, many black parents were opposed to racially segrated schools. The chief truant officer reported in 1909 that the visiting teacher had successfully transformed that hostility into "a growing consciousness that the school is working with the home for the best interests of the child."[51]

TRUANT SCHOOLS

While the visiting teacher tried to adjust a child's home environment, conditions in some homes were irremediable; in these cases the social and moral development of the child demanded his removal from degrading environmental influences. The parental or truant school was established as a custodial institution where the potential delinquent could be sent for varying terms and kept under constant supervision in order to assure his proper development. Many of the fears and expectations of school reformers at the turn of the century are reflected in the programs and rationale for the truant schools. The intent of these schools was to transform truants and classroom incorrigibles into receptive public school students. Superintendent Maxwell expressed these objectives in behavioral terms. "The truant school is a place for the development of habits of punctuality, order, cleanliness, obedience, application to study, and right conduct. In terms that the boys understand it is an opportunity to learn that 'school is a good thing' and 'a square deal.'"[52] It was hoped that the socializing effect of the truant school would allow the boys to return to regular schools or, at the very

---

50. Glein, "Visiting Teacher," p. 5.

51. Quoted in Deffenbaugh, "Compulsory School Attendance," p. 22.

52. *New York Annual Report*, 1906, p. 254; see also *New York Annual Report*, 1909, p. 166; and *Chicago Annual Report*, 1912, p. 75.

least, prepare the most recalcitrant of them for safe and productive citizenship.

Maxwell echoed popular sentiment when he said, "A term in a truant school should not be regarded as a form of punishment but as a means of reformation."[53] Many students in these schools had committed no crime for which they should be punished; rather, their circumstances and patterns of behavior suggested a probability that they would become a menace to society if not afforded an opportunity for wholesome development. James S. Hiatt summarized the rational when he advised, "It is wiser and more economical for the state to step in and form the character of these boys before they become criminals than to spend millions for reform purposes when it is almost impossible for them to retrace their steps to manhood."[54] Sentence to the truant school was perhaps a classic example of the modern liberal concept of fitting the punishment to the offender rather than to the offense, for in many cases there had been no offense. While school authorities might not look upon confinement as punishment, it was undoubtedly so considered by school inmates. In most states, children could, theoretically, be confined until the authorities were convinced that they had been reformed, but in practice most were released or paroled within one year. In any event, they could not be detained beyond the compulsory school age.[55]

Truant schools reflect the assumptions of their founders in both housing and geographic setting. Living units in the schools were usually organized into cottages meant to approximate wholesome family conditions. Truant schools served primarily an urban population, but because they were designed to give the children farming experience most of the schools were located in rural areas.[56] The Chicago Parental School, for example, was located at Bowmanville on a 70-acre farm. This placement typified the residual American fear of the city and its faith in the rejuvenative power of agrarian life.[57]

The educational programs in the truant schools also reflect the traditional assumptions of educators, for most placed a heavy emphasis on

53. *New York Annual Report*, 1906, p. 254.

54. James S. Hiatt, "The Truant Problem and the Parental School," *Bulletin of the U.S. Bureau of Education*, 1915, no. 29, p. 18.

55. Hiatt, "The Truant Problem", pp. 26–27.

56. See, for example, Hiatt, "The Truant Problem."

57. For an interesting discussion of this faith at the turn of the century see Peter J. Schmitt, *Back to Nature: The Arcadian Myth in Urban America* (New York: Oxford University Press, 1969).

work. Maxwell described the New York program as providing "school-rooms, work-shops and abundant opportunities for gardening and farming and dwellings in which the conditions of a well-ordered home are as far as possible imitated."[58] Thomas MacQueary, superintendent of the new Chicago Parental School, proposed in 1900 to include in the curriculum physical training (with emphasis on military drill), manual training, a modified version of academic preparation, as well as moral and religious training. Those familiar with truant reformation would agree, he said, that the truant "should be given more manual training in the shop and outdoors and less book work." While it was important to spend some effort on the academic subjects, MacQueary was convinced that unless these subjects were modified and closely correlated to the shop work, they would continue to be of little interest to the truant boys. With his assertion that "it is important, no doubt, to 'teach the children to think,' but it is even more important to teach truants to feel and act," MacQueary justified the emphasis on shop work in his program.[59] A 1915 study of parental schools in 13 cities revealed that in 4 cities one-half of the curriculum was devoted to industrial work and only 3 devoted all their curriculum to academic work.[60] This emphasis on work and industrial training represented an effort to prepare these children for the labor requirements of corporate industry, but it also reflected an older reliance on work as a moral trainer for children. Educators were convinced that appropriately supervised labor would train children to become better citizens. This belief accorded with their view that children between ages 14 and 16 should be either in school or employed.

   In their assessment of the results of the truant school experience Abbott and Breckenridge offer helpful insights into goals of truant school. They were most pleased that the students had acquired "superior manners," and their report contained numerous comments, from mothers of former truant-school inmates: "He always gets a chair for me to sit down and never used to"; "He always hangs up his clothes now"; and he "cleaned the house nicely" when asked.[61] They were, however, concerned at the large percent of student inmates who had violated parole. Their report ignored the academic progress of the boys and dealt exclusively with the effects of the truant school on moral and

---

58. *New York Annual Report*, 1909, p. 166.
59. *Chicago Annual Report*, 1900, pp. 15–25.
60. Hiatt, "The Truant Problem," p. 27.
61. Abbott and Breckenridge, *Truancy and Nonattendance*, pp. 171–72.

social behavior. Success was judged by the approximation of the students' behavior to middle-class moral and social standards.

The truant school epitomized the sentiment behind the turn-of-the-century crusade for compulsory schooling. It reflected the fear of family disintegration in the urban setting and the necessity for state intervention in the lives of unfortunates. By insuring that potentially wayward youths would become good citizens, this institution protected the nation against their demoralizing effects. The rejuvenation was to be accomplished by the state, which, through its beneficent interference, assured the institutionalization of appropriate urban-industrial values. Such intervention was not considered punishment, but protection.

COMPULSORY ATTENDANCE AND LITERACY

The history of the drive for compulsory school attendance, with its auxiliary components such as the visiting teacher, school census, truant officers, and truant schools, suggests important clues about the nature of American schooling in the twentieth century. The movement demonstrated that the public schools were valuable agencies of the state as educators fought to extend its authority into the lives of individuals in order to create behavior patterns acceptable in the emerging industrial society. In their debates and literature, the proponents of compulsory attendance showed little concern for standards of literacy, perhaps because minimum literacy, the ability to read and write, was not really a problem by the final decades of the nineteenth century. The census of 1890, for example, shows that only 13 percent of persons over ten years of age were illiterate. The figures for the major urban and industrial states reveal even lower rates, with the illiteracy rate for Massachusetts at 6.22 percent, New York at 5.53 percent, Illinois at 5.25 percent, and California at 7.67 percent. Figures for the largest cities show a similar configuration.[62] With the decline of illiteracy, leaders of the compulsory attendance movement turned their attentions to the behavior patterns of children of immigrant and working-class parents. Reformers believed that without the salutary influences of public schooling these children would remain unacceptable for citizenship. Like the Protestant churches of the past, the public schools of the twentieth century were to define

---

62. U.S. Census Office, *Eleventh Census, 1890* (Washington, D.C.: U.S. Government Printing Office, 1895), vol. 1, part 2, pp. xxxiii, lvi.

social reality for their initiates and channel their adult behavior along routes established during the formative years. The older, rural-oriented devices of social control had broken down with the erosion of rural hegemony at the end of the nineteenth century, so new shackles to restrain unacceptable behavior were to be forged in the crucible of the public school; henceforth, voluntarism would be too expensive a luxury.

Chapter 3

Americanization

Mass migration from southeastern Europe compounded the sense of undesirable change felt by many native Americans. Immigrants, with their peasant dress, unusual customs, strange religions and alien languages, symbolized the triumph of the atomized and corrupt city over the cohesive and healthy rural village or farm. It is not surprising, then that they became the subject of much debate and the object of many reform programs. Revised public school programs, settlement house activities, and laws to exclude southeastern European newcomers from the United States were part of the effort to solve the immigrant problem. Underlying these attempts to purify the national community by excluding, Americanizing, and improving the social lot of immigrants was the belief that those living in America must be a part of it. Often, the tone of these efforts resembled that of earlier religious revivals. Like the revivals, most of the efforts to deal with the immigrant included commitment to dogmatic regularity, profound concern for the salvation of the individual unregenerate, and fear for the welfare of the community. In a somewhat different although not conflicting sense, the immigrant question can be seen as part of the search for order that characterized this era. The immigrant was perceived as an abrasive and disruptive factor in American society, and thus it was thought necessary to encourage or compel him to conform to the national social and economic system. The effort to fit him into the emerging economic order of corporate industrialism was a most significant aspect of the Americanization programs, which also included large doses of social and cultural uplift.

Since most of the reformers accepted new technology and business organization as central components of modern American capitalism, they agreed that Americanization programs should prepare immigrants to take their place in corporate industry. This theoretical consensus, however, did not yield a uniform programmatic response to the immigrant question. For analytic purposes, those who addressed the question can be grouped into three broad categories: exclusionists, assimilationists, and cultural pluralists. Exclusionists sought to prohibit the immigration of "undesirable" peoples to the United States. Assimilationists, more complex in their prescriptions, called for changing the character of immigrants to fit them into the American social order. The techniques for implementing this transformation, however, provoked continuous debate among proponents of different methods. The least popular of the Americanizers were the cultural pluralists. They suggested a new conception of the national community, one that allowed diverse groups to exist and function within a broad, but comprehensive federation of ethnic enclaves.

EXCLUSIONISTS

One proposed solution to the immigrant problem demanded federal legislation to ban immigration from southeastern Europe. This argument rested on the premise that peoples substantially different from the Anglo-Saxon type diminished the country's vitality. Many exclusionists believed that southeastern Europeans were innately inferior peoples, unfit for American citizenship. Such explicit racism was not limited to the right-wing sectors of American society; it also appeared in some of the period's leading intellectuals and professionals.[1]

The Immigrant Restriction League illustrates the role played by intellectuals and professionals in the drive to bar the gates of Ellis Island to the tired, the hungry, and the oppressed of southeastern Europe. The league was formed in 1894 in Boston under the aegis of Samuel B. Capen, president of the Boston School Committee; Joseph Lee, president of the Massachusetts Civic League and later a central figure in the playground movement; Robert T. Paine, vice-president of the Boston Municipal League; Robert DeCourcy, a Harvard professor of climatology; and Prescott Hall, a lawyer.[2] By 1921, the league's

---

1. See, for example, Thomas F. Gossett, *Race, The History of An Idea in America* (New York: Schocken Books, 1965), pp. 287–339.

2. John Higham, *Strangers in the Land* (New York: Atheneum, 1969), p. 102.

national committee included such well-known academics as John R. Commons and E. A. Ross; the nationally renowned head resident of Andover Settlement House, Robert Woods; the presidents of Harvard and Stanford Universities; and presidents of four lesser-known institutions of higher learning.[3] Years of unstinting labor by this group and others finally resulted in successful passage of the 1924 immigration law that significantly and selectively reduced southeastern European immigration. The influence of the league and the findings of psychologists Robert M. Yerkes, Carl C. Brigham, and H. H. Laughlin were of critical importance in the congressional deliberations.[4]

Two prominent committee members, E. A. Ross and Robert Woods, were also deeply committed to assimilation. In many of his sociological works Ross analyzed the processes of socialization and assimilation.[5] He even noted the power of socialization forces on the southeastern European immigrant as he marveled at "the change a few years of our electrifying ozone works in the dull, fat-witted immigrant."[6] In a more direct and sympathetic manner, Robert A. Woods spent his entire adult life in settlement work. Nevertheless, both men concluded that the country could not assimilate a continued flood of immigrants from southeastern Europe.

---

3. Complete membership of the committee was A. Lawrence Lowell, president, Harvard University; David Starr Jordan, chancellor, Stanford University; R. E. Blackwell, president, Randolph-Macon College; Leon C. Marshall, dean, University of Chicago; K. G. Matheson, president, Georgia School of Technology; E. D. Warfield, president, Wilson College; Charles F. Thwing, president, Western Reserve University; E. A. Ross, professor, University of Wisconsin; John R. Commons, professor, University of Wisconsin; Edwin B. Craighead, professor, State University of North Dakota; William M. Irvine, master, Mercersburg Academy; Madison Grant, George Shirased, Owen Wister, attorneys; James T. Young, professor, Wharton School of Finance; James Ailshie, chief justice, Supreme Court; Thornton Cooke and James Dinkins, bankers; Henry Holt, publisher; Lucien Howe, physician; William Kent, member of the U.S. Tariff Commission; Franklin MacVeagh, former U.S. secretary of treasury; Robert A. Woods and Henry Fairchild, social workers. Letterhead on letter from Prescott, secretary of league's executive committee, to E. A. Ross, February 12, 1921, in Ross collection, Wisconsin Historical Society, Madison, Wisconsin.

4. See Russell Marks, "Testers, Trackers and Trustees" (Ph.D. diss., University of Illinois, 1972), pp. 108–20; for a discussion of the congressional debates see Higham, *Strangers in the Land*, ch. 11; Joseph Henry Taylor, "The Restriction of European Immigration 1890–1924" (Ph.D. diss., University of California, Berkeley, 1936); and Oscar Handlin, *Race and Nationality* (Boston: Little, Brown, 1957), ch. 5.

5. See Clarence J. Karier, Paul Violas, and Joel Spring, *Roots of Crisis* (Chicago: Rand McNally, 1972), pp. 40–65.

6. E. A. Ross, *Foundations of Sociology* (New York: Macmillan, 1905), p. 391.

The similarities in the exclusionist and the assimilationist positions suggest that both were part of a larger campaign to purify the American community. Their congruence is evident in a 1902 article by A. A. Bradley, written to explain a resolution advanced by the Associated Charities of Boston in support of a bill to limit and regulate immigration. The members of the association, working to assimilate and uplift immigrant charity recipients, saw unrestricted immigration as an obstacle to their educational and charitable efforts. Bradley concluded that God had given Americans a special trust, and further adulteration of the American community with unassimilable immigrants would most assuredly violate that stewardship.[7]

The seemingly contradictory aims of assimilation and exclusion converge again in Charles A. Brooks' *Christian Americanization*. Americanization according to Brooks was "a spiritual process" that enlightened the immigrant to Anglo-Saxon ideals and values in order that he might share in the benefits of American society. He demanded that all immigrants be given the opportunity to become truly American, for he believed that those who made the effort could attain the lofty spiritual peaks of complete Americanization. For those who would not, Brooks demanded a course of action which put his assimilation ideals squarely in the philosophical camp of the exclusionists: "If they are incorrigible, they should seek another home where they can enjoy their kind of culture unmolested by Americanism."[8] Many of these alleged incorrigibles were encouraged to do just that by Mitchell Palmer, U.S. attorney general during the "red scare" deportations at the end of World War I.

ERASE AND COLOR

The assimilationists clashed over methodology and the meaning of Americanization. The earliest and most simplistic approach might be termed "erase and color." Through this process, which had to be directed by Americans, the immigrants' background would be blotted out and replaced with an American way of life. The immigrant was

---

7. A. A. Bradley, "To What Extent Does Unrestricted Immigration Counteract the Influence of our Educational and Charitable Work?" *Charities*; April 5, 1902, p. 330.

8. Charles A. Brooks, *Christian Americanization* (Council of Women for the Home Missions, 1919), pp. 13–16, 64.

simply the sheet on which American standards would be painted. These assimilationists differed from the exclusionists in assuming that the immigrant was capable of reaching the Anglo-Saxon American standard while the exclusionists felt that the immigrant was too defective for such uplift. For both groups, however, the goal was a purified and thus unified community.

Marion Brown, principal of the New Orleans City Normal School, outlined this position as she alerted the 1900 NEA convention to the pressing social and political problems caused by the growing proportion of children with foreign-born parents. Brown's solution was to educate the children up to the American standard, defined as the "Anglo-Saxon ideal." This effort had to be undertaken by school teachers on behalf of the immigrant child because "their parents are no longer to be depended upon for safe guidance."[9] William Maxwell assumed a similar stance in arguing for a Department of Hygiene under the jurisdiction of the school system. He asserted that such a department would force immigrant parents to upgrade their homes to "the American standard of living."[10] Because schoolmen felt it was all too likely that the parents would infect their children with ideals other than those which Principal Brown or Superintendent Maxwell believed were essential to Americanism, the school's goal was to erase the last vestiges of those other ideals and color the child with the more acceptable American principles.

IMMIGRANT GIFTS

Many assimilationists disagreed that all vestiges of the immigrants' former cultural traits should be obliterated. The "immigrant gifts" approach stressed the valuable traits of the various ethnic minorities and searched for ways in which these useful traits could be molded into the American culture. The most successful settlements operated on the assumption that because the foreigner possessed qualities that

9. Marion Brown, "Is There a Nationality Problem in Our Schools?" *NEA Addresses and Proceedings*, 1900, pp. 585–90; a somewhat similar view was expressed by Rabbi Charles Fleischer, who argued that the schools should develop a "national religion" to facilitate the transformation of immigrant children into "state devoted children and citizens." See Charles Fleischer, "Education and Democracy," *Arena* 27 (May 1902): 488.

10. *New York Annual Report*, 1907, pp. 138–39.

America could not afford to forfeit, the settlement house should accommodate America and the immigrant to each other. The Anglo-Saxon mold would be modified by the mixture of immigrant traits, and the resulting amalgam would be a richer yet more unified society.

Subtle but significant shifts in the immigrant gifts or melting pot idea transformed it into the most sophisticated theory of assimilation. Part of the problem with the melting pot was that some immigrants were difficult to melt. The idea of "democratic participation" emerged in response to both sociological theory and practical experience in assimilation among immigrant neighborhoods. Because the immigrant had gifts to offer to Anglo-Saxon culture, he was to be more than a passive vessel into which the new ideals were poured. Participating in his own Americanization would give him a stake in the enterprise and thus help insure its success. This philosophy shaped much of the work of Jane Addams, who believed that immigrant organizations and social groups could be vehicles for absorption into the host country.[11]

Urban sociologists, Robert E. Park and Herbert A. Miller, summarized the democratic participation approach in their *Old World Traits Transplanted*: "We must make the immigrants a working part in our system of life, ideal and political, as well as economic." The intelligent means to this end was to "seize on everything in his old life which will serve either to interpret the new or to hold him steady while he is getting adjusted."[12] This meant that Americans should accept immigrant societies and institutions such as the foreign language press as potential Americanizing forces rather than oppose them as sources of exclusiveness among the immigrant peoples. Park and Miller did not believe that all immigrant institutions or values were useful to the Americanization process, but they contended that Americans often failed to sense the harmony between immigrant and indigenous values. One example they offered was that of the Russian Jew, whose preoccupation with artistic and religious interests frequently led to "maladjustment in America." Because these activities reflected the Jewish devotion to learning, Park argued that this commitment, if it could be deflected from Old World religious concerns

---

11. See Karier, Violas, and Spring, *Roots of Crisis*, pp. 66–83.

12. Robert E. Park and Herbert A. Miller, *Old World Traits Transplanted* (New York: Harper and Brothers, 1921), pp. 204, 295.

into more productive scholarly channels, would enable the Jew to occupy a useful intellectual status in America.[13]

That Park and Miller were not simply engaged in academic speculation is evident from widespread efforts to use the immigrant or foreign language press for Americanization. One of the primary figures in this effort was Frances A. Kellor, who presented her program to the twenty-fourth annual convention of the National Association of Manufacturers in 1919.[14] Kellor discussed the serious problems that employers faced with their immigrant employees, notably the problem that John Dewey had mentioned in his study on the Poles: that it would become increasingly difficult for employers to obtain competent foreign laborers as many of the most intelligent arrivals would leave this country either to return to their native lands or to go to other labor-hungry countries such as Canada or Latin America.[15] She also predicted increased labor strife as foreign laborers were organized by ethnic leaders and influenced by radical foreign ideologies. Kellor characterized Americanization as "a good business proposition," for the most effective way to insure that these immigrants would remain loyal American factory workers was to make them part of the society for which they toiled.[16]

A significant source of resistance was the widespread retention of old country habits, especially in consumption patterns. The recently arrived used foreign-made foods and other products. Demonstrating an insight that social scientists discovered only years later, Kellor argued that consumerism was a major force for binding an individual to his industrial environment. Here, she asserted, was the basis for cooperation between the American businessman and the 1,739 foreign language newspapers with a circulation exceeding 10 million. The vehicle for this cooperation was to be the Association of Foreign Language Newspapers. A group that Kellor represented had recently purchased this agency, which funneled nationwide advertising into the local foreign language newspapers. She proposed that by diverting a portion of their advertising expenditures to the association businessmen would initiate the foreign worker to American consumer prod-

13. Park and Miller, *Old World Traits*, p. 265.

14. Frances A. Kellor, "Industrial Americanism," in *Proceedings of the Twenty-Fourth Annual Convention of the National Association of Manufacturers of the U.S.A.* (New York: Issued from the Secretary's Office, 1919), pp. 361–68.

15. John Dewey, "Conditions Among the Poles in the United States," *Confidential Report* (Washington D.C.: U.S. Government Printing Office, 1918).

16. Kellor, "Industrial Americanism," pp. 361–62.

ucts and thus promote Americanization. Kellor maintained that this effort would ultimately result in "pro-American control" of these important institutions in the ethnic communities, especially since the editors of the immigrant press were influential men in their respective communities. Acculturation through propaganda would reinforce acculturation through consumerism. Her proposal intimated that the editors, influenced by this remunerative source of advertising, would inject a pro-American bias in their editorals and news coverage. She predicted, "If we can make seven-tenths of the advertising in the foreign language press American instead of foreign, we will begin to get, without any suggestion on our part, pro-American editorials and pro-American news."[17] This proposal and the experience of the Creel Committee with the immigrant press during World War I indicate that Park and Miller were indeed insightful in arguing that effective Americanization programs should exploit existing immigrant societies and institutions.

CULTURAL PLURALISM

A relatively rare reaction to both the exclusionists and the assimilationists was voiced first by Horace Kallen and later by Randolph Bourne, both of whom attacked the schools and settlements for trying to force immigrants into an Anglo-Saxon American mold.[18] They claimed that Americanization crusades were motivated by fear of ethnic difference and that conformity to the dominant culture was undesirable and impossible. Kallen believed that a person's ethnic heritage could not change

17. Kellor, "Industrial Americanism, p. 368. For other elaborations of this plan to control the immigrant press see T. Coleman DuPont, "The Inter-Racial Council: What It Is and Hopes to Do," *Advertising and Selling*, July 5, 1919, pp. 1–2; a two-page advertisement paid for by the American Association of Foreign Language Newspapers, Inc., "Good Americanism is Good Business," *Advertising and Selling*, July 5, 1919, pp. 32–33; Frances A. Kellor, "The Plan and Purpose of American Association of Foreign Language Newspapers," *Advertising and Selling*, July 5, 1919, p. 506; and Frances A. Kellor, "Industrial Americanization and National Defense," *North American Review*, May 1917, pp. 724–33.

18. Horace M. Kallen, "Democracy Versus the Melting Pot," *Nation*, February 18, 1915, pp, 190–94, and February 25, 1915, pp. 100, 217–20; and Randolph S. Bourne, "Trans-National America," *The Atlantic Monthly*, July 1916, pp. 86–97. For a more extended analysis of Kallen's theories of cultural pluralism see Jay Harvey Wissot, "A Critical Evaluation of the Origins, Meaning, and Implications for Education of Horace M. Kallen's Cultural Pluralism" (Ph.D. diss., University of Illinois, Urbana, 1974).

without serious consequences to the individual. Bourne agreed, adding that the potential strength of the American nationality lay in a confederation of nationalities with each contributing its own unique creative power to the whole. These cultural pluralists were convinced that their alternative would result in an orderly, cooperative, and harmonious society.

In a sense the different responses to the immigrant problem were simply variations on one theme: how to create order in a chaotic society. All agreed that the individual could not be left to his own devices as he searched for identity and meaning in the urban-industrial world of twentieth-century America, but the cultural pluralists differed from the others in their insistence that diverse groups could live together in harmony. This belief, flying in the face of established American social and religious practices, was too revolutionary to be given a serious hearing. The other Americanizers, both exclusionists and assimilationists, called for a homogeneous community. The underlying assumption shared by the exclusionists and the assimilationists was that American society should not become a polyglot collection of different peoples with potentially conflicting traits or value systems. Although conflict raged over the methodology, the various Americanization efforts all sought to produce an organized, integrated, and harmonious social system with a central core of values to which all Americans, old and new, would subscribe. It should be noted that this classification of responses to the immigrant problem, although useful for analytic purposes, is somewhat artificial and simplistic. Few participants in the Americanization crusade operated entirely within one of these categories; most were pragmatic in approach, adopting the tactic which seemed most appropriate to the immediate problem they faced. An examination of the settlement programs designed to produce a unified national community demonstrates the instrumental character of the Americanization effort.

SOCIAL SETTLEMENTS

The social settlement movement was an early and continuous force in the Americanization crusade. The first American settlement, the Neighborhood Guild, was organized in 1886 by Stanton Coit at 146 Forsyth Street in New York City. It was soon followed by the New York College Settlement, by Hull House in Chicago, and by the East Side House in

New York City.[19] During the next three decades, settlements were established in nearly every city in the United States. Although the various settlements devised many different programs, all were founded on a common sentiment, as expressed by Vida D. Scudder on behalf of the standing committee of the Association of College Settlements in 1899. She noted that the settlements were trying to become organized centers of cohesive community life in the disorganized urban slums. "To this attempt," Scudder believed, "Christianity and patriotism alike call us. Placed at the point where the problems of our civilization gather most thickly, settlements may become efficient though modest agents in that spiritualizing of our great material democracy."[20] Some 23 years later, Robert A. Woods, one of the leading figures of the settlement movement, said, in a national assessment of the movement compiled for the Russell Sage Foundation, "The settlement proposed that the best equipped youth in a high spirit of devotion should undertake a mission toward building up the state at the precise point of its greatest disintegration." He also felt that "the peculiar American cause of disintegration in neighborly relations. . .is immigration." By 1922, over 90 percent of the settlements were located in immigrant districts.[21]

The settlement movement reflects many of the ambiguities and paradoxes of American social thought and action. One cannot fail to be impressed by the profound concern for human suffering and the genuine altruistic impulses that moved settlement residents like Lillian Wald or Jane Addams. The fact that they preferred to call themselves "residents" indicates a deep sympathy for their immigrant clientele. Nevertheless, there was another side to their work that conflicted with their benevolent attitude toward the slum dwellers. Although they claimed that the cause of suffering stemmed from an unfair distribution of wealth, they began with attempts to reform the victim. Unable to overcome the traditional American belief that virtue brings worldly rewards, residents worked to uplift the immigrant so that he might be more virtuous and thus more successful. This endeavor to change the immigrant was an expression of the typical American rationalization of blaming the victim of social injustice for his plight. Settlement workers did not hesitate to challenge the worst aspects of the industrial system, but their most

---

19. Robert A. Woods and Albert J. Kennedy, *The Settlement Horizon* (New York: Russell Sage, 1922), pp. 33–40.

20. Vida D. Scudder, "College Settlements Association: 1890–1900," *Tenth Annual Report of the College Settlement Association (Boston: A. T. Bliss, 1899), p. 10.*

21. Woods and Kennedy, *Settlement Horizon*, pp. 39, 67, 326.

intensive efforts were directed at enabling the immigrant to fit that system. Restructuring the immigrant was, for them, a critical aspect of system reform. They seemed unable to imagine that an individual might have some legitimate conflict with even a good social system. They were captives of the contemporary social theory that the individual must not simply be a part of his social milieu, but must so thoroughly embody its characteristic values, attitudes, and behavior patterns that he becomes an expression of that milieu in his everyday life.

A second paradoxical aspect of the settlement movement arises from the residents' rejection of the depersonalization inherent in contemporary institutional charity. Their initial reaction was to confront social problems on a personal or face-to-face basis with their clients. One of the earliest discussions of the settlement movement defended this approach: "The settlement movement strikes at the root of the tree. Not contrivances, but persons, must save society. And wheresoever society at all needs saving, there people must go in ample number and so the best trained ability. The resources of society are largely in persons. The needs of society are in persons."[22] Once they became involved in the regeneration of immigrants, however, residents found the process exceedingly complex and difficult. They quickly looked for allies and found them in the public schools, in business, and in governmental agencies. Residents began to think of the settlement as a laboratory where social experiments could be conducted and, when successful, transferred to other agencies.[23] Ultimately, this attitude resulted in institutionalization and depersonalization of the welfare system. Looking back over the years from the vantage of 1934, Lillian Wald observed that the settlement programs had prepared the way for many of the social welfare reforms of the New Deal era.[24] Thus, an effort that rooted and never entirely surrendered the ideal of face-to-face social reform became a catalyst for the development of the bureaucratic

---

22. Robert A. Woods, "University Settlements," *The Andover Review* 17 (October 1892): 337.

23. See Arthur C. Holden , *The Settlement Idea: A Vision of Social Justice* (New York: Macmillan, 1922), p. 77; Woods and Kennedy, *Settlement Horizon*, pp. 319, 324, 381, 393. Morris I. Berger has demonstrated the influence of the New York settlements on the establishment of kindergartens in the public schools. See "The Settlements, the Immigrant, and the Public School" (Ph.D. diss., Columbia Teachers' College, 1956); also see Lillian Wald, *The House on Henry Street* (New York: Henry Holt, 1915), pp. 117–20, regarding settlement involvement in the institution of classes for defective children in the public schools.

24. Lillian D. Wald, *Windows on Henry Street* (Boston: Little, Brown, 1934), pp. 319–21.

response to public welfare and social regeneration that has characterized twentieth-century America.

The ideal of personal contact required the residents to maintain a
special relationship with the neighborhood, namely, that of a neighbor.
Also embedded in the settlement ideal was the notion of expertise. The
residents were not simply neighbors, but special neighbors. They
believed it was essential to combine the knowledge of the evolving
science of sociology with the culture of a university-trained youth and
the warm humanitarianism of a philanthropist if they were to understand
the needs and potentialities of their neighborhood. In this way, they
could aid and direct the regenerative processes that would bring the
immigrant up to American standards. The demand for special skills
resulted in functional specialization both within and among the various
settlements; it eventually led to the professionalization of social work, a
phenomenon that precluded the kind of personal contact that the ideal
envisioned.[25]

SETTLEMENT CLUBS

Settlements conducted a variety of programs for immigrants, none more
significant than their club activities. As one commentator on the settlement movement observed, "The policy of the average settlement is so
bound up with the administration of its club system that it is well to
inquire further into the latter before attempting to study the deeper
social significance of the movement as a whole."[26] The settlement clubs
began in an almost accidental fashion because of the demands of time
and space. Residents pressed for time to meet and interact with individual children, arranged to meet with groups at specified times. Lillian
Wald recalled that the first clubs at Henry Street began as such an expedient. "It soon became evident that definite hours must be set aside for
meeting different groups if our time was not to be dissipated in fragmen-
tary visits."[27] The physical fact that most early settlements were in resi-

---

25. For an interesting account of this professionalization of social work and its results,
see Roy Lubov, *The Professional Altruists* (Cambridge, Mass.: Harvard University Press,
1965).

26. Holden, *The Settlement Idea*, p. 64.

27. Wald, *House on Henry Street*, p. 180.

dential dwellings meant that the groups had to be limited in size. The residents were actually experimenting in what has since been called small group dynamics, although they failed to develop the conceptual analysis employed by later social psychologists. The practical application of these dynamics furthered the settlement objectives of social integration, uplift, and control.

The first settlement club came into being in 1886, when Stanton Coit brought a street gang called the Lilly Pleasure Club under the protection of his Neighborhood Guild and persuaded the members to rename it the O.I.F. (Order, Improvement, Friendship) Club.[28] It was both richly symbolic and aptly prophetic that the first settlement club was formed from a street gang and that its name was changed from one implying an unrestricted pursuit of youthful impulses to one suggesting the sublimation of those impulses into socially approved channels.

The most insightful residents recognized that little difference existed between the dynamics of a gang and those of a well-organized club. Wald commented that the Henry Street Settlement "defined a gang as a club gone wrong."[29] The task was to redirect the gang's energies into activities that would yield desirable social results. The club, according to Wald, "almost always consciously . . . functioned as a means of education, and as a source of mental and spiritual enrichment as well as of 'good times.' "[30] The initiative for this enrichment was the club leader, who made it "his business to see that the club gets the benefit of the advantages which the settlement is able to offer."[31] The leader was to set the tone of the group and serve as an example for its members. It was a settlement axiom that "a group seldom rises above the stature of the leader."[32] The leader's task was to instill correct social and moral behavior in the members through participation in the rich variety of club activities. Miss Wald argued that the qualities of the leader were more important than the program of the club.[33] Club programs and activities were simply means to more significant settlement ends.

---

28. Woods and Kennedy, Settlement Horizon, p. 42.
29. Wald, *House on Henry Street*, p. 78.
30. Wald, *Windows on Henry Street*, p. 156.
31. Holden, *The Settlement Idea*, p. 65.
32. Wald, *Windows on Henry Street*, p. 157.
33. Wald, *House on Henry Street*, p. 181.

Basic to the settlement club project was a pedagogical principle also fundamental in progressive educational theory: effective teaching must utilize the individuality of each student, and the successful teacher must understand the individual student. This precept was implemented partly through the dynamics of small group interactions within the club. "The intimate relations fostered by such recreations led boys to boast of their adventures," noted Robert Wood, "to discuss the rules which governed their dealings with one another, and thus to reveal the ways their minds were made up. Deep-seated hopes and aspirations were laid bare in the plans they outlined." The leader was to explore the home and neighborhood environment of each club member in order to relate club objectives to real life. Sometimes an undesirable environment had to be changed to uplift the child. The desire for a community modeled after the rural village is implicit in this statement of Andover House's head resident: "No mere public care for children can take the place of that conspiracy between family, teacher, and friends through which well-conditioned households safeguard the delicacy of a child's perceptions and her relationship with others."[34] Only when the club leader understood the innermost secrets and ambitions as well as the social background of each member could he control the proper development of that member's attitudes and social outlooks.

Henry Street resident Rita Wallach Morganthau, writing in the twentieth-anniversary report of that organization, outlined the objectives of club activity:

> The aim of the club work is the development of the child's character and personality and the club leader's function is to give the child all the cultural material at her command, so as to produce the desired development of the child, "a development which will include the expression of his own powers, the creation of control over them, and the direction of them to the necessary, to the useful and to helpful social activities."[35]

The headworker of the college settlement in New York explained that club work expanded to include girls over 16 in order to keep them with the settlement "from their baby days to their maturity." She noted happily that even with limited club activities the residents exerted con-

---

34. Woods and Kennedy, *Settlement Horizon,* pp. 74, 95.

35. Rita Wallach Morgenthau, "Work for Girls and Young Women," *Report of the Henry Street Settlement, 1893*–1913 (New York: Henry Street Settlement, 1913), p. 31.

siderable control over the members.[36] Through their influence, settlement workers sought to inculcate attitudes that would facilitate the members' inclusion into industrial society. The social ideal advocated by the settlement clubs was comprised of self-restraint, discipline, cooperation, and service. Woods and Kennedy, discussing settlement dedication to the moral idiom behind the bureaucratic thrust of modern America, stated, "Once the moral principle that the whole is more important than the sum of its parts is definitely grasped, club members jointly and severally have a practical motive for cooperation, the intrinsic force of which is never thereafter lost."[37]

This ideal was implemented by more than rhetoric. As Elizabeth Williams, head resident of the New York College Settlement, suggested, "The central idea in all the clubs is self-government, but the continued insistence on order and the respect due for the rights of others, certainly helps to make a boy better fitted for contact with his fellow men."[38] The very structure of the club meetings, which stressed constitutions, decorum, and rules for procedure, was an object lesson deliberately conceived by the residents. Club leaders soon learned to use the power of peer pressure in a small group setting to achieve settlement objectives. Williams indicated that the leader should apply this pressure to shape the norms for group behavior: "With a group of younger boys it is not difficult to give it the right spirit so that they hold their members to a high standard of conduct both within and without the club. The task is not so simple when they have passed the impressionable age, though not hopeless, but the kindergarten is the best place in which to lay the foundations of civic virtue."[39] The power of example exerted by well-trained leaders sympathetic to individual members made the settlements effective agents for Americanizing immigrant slum children. It deemphasized conceptual or intellectual training and correspondingly intensified nonintellectual training through learning by doing. The principle of learning by doing placed the settlement movement directly within the mainstream of twentieth-century pedagogy, making it an eddy flowing into what later became known as progressive education.

---

36. Fean Gurney Fine, "Report of the New York Settlement," *Second Annual Report of the College Settlements Association* (New York: Brown and Wilson, 1892), p. 12.

37. Woods and Kennedy Settlement *Horizon*, p. 76.

38. Elizabeth S. Williams, "The Settlement in Recreation," *Eleventh Annual Report of the College Settlements Association* (Boston: A. T. Bliss, 1900), p. 10.

39. Elizabeth Williams, "Report of the Head Worker," *Fourteenth Annual Report of the College Settlements Association* (Philadelphia: Innes and Sons, 1903), p. 29.

FROM CULTURE TO VOCATIONALISM

Americanization required an intimate, organic relationship between the immigrant and American society. Settlement workers initially believed that this relationship could be nurtured if the immigrants were brought into contact with the host culture. The early college-bred settlement resident, who had already drawn deep draughts from the cup of higher learning, passed it on to the immigrant—often in the form of clubs that replicated the resident's college experiences. The executive committee of the Dennison House emphasized "the necessity and privilege of bringing the joy and freedom of the higher learning to those who will receive it."[40] Over two decades later, Robert Woods praised higher learning as the supreme liberating and acculturating avenue available to man. He noted that the most highly privileged were "those who have the possession—above all price—of their full potential selves. This is what the higher education brings."[41] In the interval between these declarations, however, residents became much less sanguine about the possibility of integrating immigrant masses through higher learning and culture.

Similar disenchantment appears in Jane Addams' realization that many of the college instructors brought to Hull House had failed to ignite a flame of curiosity among the neighbors.[42] This concern was reflected in her more general attack on traditional schooling: "We are impatient with the schools which lay all stress on reading and writing, suspecting them to rest upon the assumption that the ordinary experience of life is worth little, and that all knowledge and interest must be brought to the children through the medium of books."[43] Addams pessimism was confirmed by resident Anna Davies, who said, "If culture is the acquaintance with the best that has been written and thought by the greatest of the world of intellect, its growth among the masses seems hopeless." She maintained that culture "leaves untouched the masses of genuine working people who have frankly accepted their occupation, or

40. Executive Committee, "Boston Settlement: Report of the Head Worker," *Fourth Annual Report of the College Settlements Association* (Philadelphia: Avil Printing, 1894), p. 44.

41. Robert A. Woods, "Academic Community Service," *Intercollegiate Community Service Quarterly* 3 (January 1918): 6.

42. See Jane Addams, *Twenty Years at Hull House* (New York: New American Library, 1960), pp. 294–300.

43. Jane Addams, *Democracy and Social Ethics* (Cambridge, Mass.: Harvard University Press, 1960), pp. 180–81.

its like, as a life long task for themselves and probably for their children, and have no hint of brillancy in themselves and their future."[44]

The problem was to find a substitute for higher learning that would absorb the immigrant masses into the urban-industrial social order. Jane Addams summarized the dilemma as she reported, "The residents of Hull House feel increasingly that the educational efforts of a settlement not be directed primarily to reproduce the college type of culture, but to work out a method and an ideal adapted to the immediate situation."[45] The immediate situation, she believed, was that many were "doomed to the unskilled work which the permanent specialization of the division of labor demands." The solution was not to be found, according to Addams, in technical education because polytechnics of a high order "do not even pretend to admit the working man with his meager intellectual equipment. They graduate machine builders, but not educate machine tenders."[46] Guided by their belief in the inevitability of the machine economy and by their low estimate of the mental capacity of the working classes, most settlement workers became champions of educational programs designed to train machine tenders for willing acceptance of their functional calling. This transition from cultural education to vocational training is even less surprising when one recalls the long tradition in American social and religious thought that glorified work as a "calling" with divine sanctions and uplifting qualities. This aspect of settlement work foreshadowed similar curricular reform in the public schools.

It would probably be a mistake to suggest that this rationale for vocational training emerged in full bloom from the social philosophy of the settlement movement. Vocational education actually evolved from a series of experiments conducted in the settlements. Again, Addams pointed the way when she noted that domestic training and trade instruction both emerged from the Hull House club program and eventually demonstrated their worth.[47] The annual reports for the College Settlements Association during the 1890s document a hesitant but increasingly important growth of club work in the area of trade training and household arts. The Philadelphia settlement, whose door "never opened without a horde of curly-headed Jews or little picaninnies pour-

---

44. Anna Freeman Davies, "The Settlement in Education," *Eleventh Annual Report of the College Settlements Association* (Boston: A. T. Bliss, 1900), pp. 15, 16.

45. Addams, *Twenty Years*, p. 300.

46. Addams, *Democracy*, pp. 202, 203.

47. Addams, *Twenty Years*, pp. 301–2.

ing into the hall," began a carpentry class for "colored boys" as early as October, 1893.[48] In 1895, the Dennison House of Boston reported that its club work was teaching "housewifely arts" to girls and manual skills to boys.[49] By the turn of the century, all three of the settlements in the College Settlements Association had conducted successful experiments with trade training and household arts. The direct relevance of domestic education to Americanization was spelled out by Emma Beard in her report on the cooking school in the New York Settlement. She noted that the classes intended to teach "the true American home ideal." The method of instruction was in keeping with current pedagogical theories, for residents hoped that the classes would "unconsciously teach the value of light, cleanliness, order, and the general fitness of things." This school taught not only cooking, but a way of living.[50]

A survey of immigrant sections of Boston conducted by the residents of the South End Settlement House in 1903 contained similar conclusions regarding the educational needs of immigrant children. The residents claimed that "poverty and lack of interest" caused many immigrant children to leave school before earning the elementary diploma. The problem of poverty, they believed, lacked an immediate solution, but the question of interest engaged the residents. Immigrant children lost interest in school because "the necessary routine of language, geography and arithmetic is a heavy burden for children who cannot in any way connect these studies with their home lives." The survey recommended industrial training as an alternative that was acceptable to parents and their children. The residents indicated their belief that most immigrant children would follow the occupational paths of their parents as they stated, "The special importance of industrial training on the immigrant districts is emphasized by a glance at the list of parents' employments." All the parents were engaged in manual labor. A list of parents' employments included in the survey disclosed that industrial training was especially appropriate to immigrant districts, where parents were universally engaged in manual or semiskilled labor. In their justification for domestic training for girls, residents again sug-

---

48. Helena S. Dudley, "Report of the Headworker," *Fourth Annual Report of the College Settlements Association* (Philadelphia: Avil Printing, 1894), p. 22; and Katherine Bement Davis, "Report of the Headworker," *Fifth Annual Report of College Settlements Association* (Philadelphia: Dunlap, 1894), p. 27.

49. Helena S. Dudley, "Report of the Headworker," *Sixth Annual Report of the College Settlements Association* (Philadelphia: Dunlap, 1895), p. 36.

50. Emma Burlen Beard, "The Cooking School," *Thirteenth Annual Report of the College Settlements Association* (Philadelphia: Innes and Sons, 1902), p. 37.

gested that they could predict the destiny of immigrant children. These girls would become wives shortly after leaving school. Since the object of education is "to fit for life," the residents concluded that "it is not the acquisition of facts but cultivation that the foreign girls need for their future happiness and usefulness, correct ideas of life, and freedom from superstition, rather than definite knowledge about trade winds and syntax."[51] Residents felt that they could provide the best "education for life" by training the children for the activities that they supposedly would perform in later adult life. Immigrant and working-class children would "learn by doing" rather than through inculcation of concepts or culture.

Once settlement residents accepted the varying capacities of their neighbors and the inevitability of the machine economy, the development of vocational guidance and placement became a logical and humanitarian next step. Residents believed that a child was usually doomed to frustration and failure if he embarked upon an education that was beyond his capacity or irrelevant to his work life. Settlements expended much energy to save the immigrant child from the pain of failure in school and, most importantly, in later life. The Henry Street Settlement in New York, for example, got involved in vocational guidance through its scholarship fund. The fund gave financial aid to deserving youths between the ages of 14 and 16 so that they might stay in school to receive vocational training.[52] This effort led the residents to cooperate with the public schools in establishing a Vocational Guidance Bureau in Public School 147.[53] Indeed, many of the leaders in the early guidance movement, notably Meyer Bloomfield and Frank Parsons, began their work in the settlements.

The settlements inaugurated many pragmatic experiments to relieve the most immediately painful conditions in the immigrant slums. These activities yielded a variety of programs that were subsequently offered to public agencies such as schools. In addition to vocational training and guidance, the programs included kindergartens, penny lunches for school children, school savings banks, visiting teachers, and special classes for deficient or defective children. They were designed to bring the immigrant into the mainstream of American society by giving him a

---

51. Robert A. Woods, ed., *Americans in Process: A Settlement Study* (Boston: Houghton Mifflin, 1903), pp. 298, 299, 303.

52. Wald, *House on Henry Street*, pp. 137–44; Margaret Brown, "Vocational Scholarships," *Report of the Henry Street Settlement*, pp. 45–46.

53. Lilian Wald. *Windows*, p. 144.

role in it and a stake in its success. While these practical and particularistic endeavors apparently were not preconceived to implement any overall settlement social policy they were, nevertheless, generally in accord with the settlement leaders' vision of a good society, a vision shared by the leaders of corporate industry. This fact helps to explain the close cooperation and support offered to individual settlements by men such as Seth Lowe, a leader of the National Civic Federation.

THE NEW INDUSTRIAL MAN

This congruence of ideals does not imply that the settlements conspired to further the interests of corporate industry. It simply means that corporate leaders and settlement house residents agreed on the basic social structure necessary to fulfill the promise of American life. They also agreed that a new type of man was required for this new society. Americanization of the immigrant and socialization of the native were part of the effort to produce that new man.[54]

Many settlement residents envisioned an ideal society that would combine enlightenment, humanitarianism, and the American Protestant belief in the brotherhood of man.[55] In the emerging society, brotherhood would replace class conflict, cooperation would supplant competition, harmony would triumph over discord, and pain and the possibility of individual failure would be significantly reduced, if not eliminated. Most important, individuals would be included in the social system as functionally interdependent parts. There was a dual purpose in developing a cooperative man who would identify with the larger social order. In the first place, this kind of worker was needed in the modern factory with its highly specialized labor force. Secondly, and perhaps more importantly, the emergence of such a worker would counter what many capitalists desperately feared—the development of a proletarian class consciousness that would demand a redistribution of wealth, power, and status.

---

54. Interestingly, once the conception of Americanization was programmatically implemented, many of the Americanizers began to discuss the need to Americanize all children, regardless of the nativity of their parents.

55. For a similar analysis of this vision in the writings of Jane Addams, see Karier, Violas, and Spring, *Roots of Crisis*, pp. 66–84.

Robert A. Woods forcefully articulated this ideal in noting that "the success of cooperation awaits the appearance of 'the cooperative man.' Settlements half unconsciously and yet fixed with purpose during three decades have been developing this creature. Three simple lines of effort have been carved out." This effort, Woods said, consisted of finding "worthy industrial careers" for boys and girls; developing industrial training programs "that would make those subject to such discipline more desirable candidates for certain broad classes of positions"; and "training children in the practice of association, that they might be capable of effective and responsible action as members of highly organized producing corps." Such activities were necessary because, as Woods observed, "even simple handicrafts demand accuracy, neatness, order, perseverance, and initiative." He reasoned that since the public schools "were sending out thousands of children with no specific training for the work they were to undertake," industrial training programs would have to develop the child's vocational interests and provide "a kind of discipline which prepares the mind for wage-earning." Woods attributed the eventual inclusion of industrial training in the public school curriculum to the pioneering examples of the settlements and to direct agitation by settlement residents. He encouraged settlements to guide working-class children into appropriate career choices because "working-class parents lacked the breadth of view, connections, and experience through which more favored classes direct the careers of their children."[56]

Woods acknowledged that his ideal was compatible with the interests of the new corporate industrialists. "Residents sympathized greatly with those who, in the administration of industries and mercantile establishments, are striving first to regularize employment and, secondly, to organize group loyalty and initiative among employer personnel." The important lesson of the years of struggle "to rear a generation better equipped both technically and morally for a highly integrated industrial system" was that the "typical tenement background stunts rather than fosters productive capacities." Cohesion required a "homegeneous population" according to Woods, who also felt that national progress was slowed because "we are engaged in a vast problem of political cooperation involving the welding of many nationalities into one."[57]

---

56. Woods and Kennedy, *Settlement Horizon*, pp. 140, 212, 213, 214, 217.
57. Woods and Kennedy, *Settlement Horizon*, pp. 220, 221.

AMERICANIZATION AND PUBLIC SCHOOLS

Settlement residents had always considered the public schools their natural ally in the effort to direct the immigrant masses into the mainstream of American society. The schools quickly accepted the challenge offered by the increasing numbers of unassimilated newcomers. Their efforts proceeded along two distinct lines: adult education for those beyond the reach of compulsory schooling laws, and school programs for the children of immigrants. In both, mastery of the English language was considered crucial for Americanization. "To be great, a nation need not be of one class; it must be of one mind,"declared Professor John R. Commons. "If we think together, we can act together, and the organ of common thought and action is common language."[58] This sentiment was reiterated in 1916 by Frederic Farrington of the U.S. Bureau of Education and by Franklin K. Lane, U.S. secretary of the interior.[59] The belief that a common language would unify the American people was indeed insightful. Americanizers, and most other educational reformers, worked to create a reality with which Americans could personally identify. Reality structuring required the use of symbols, images, and metaphors, the emotional content of which everyone would feel in a similar fashion. Translating them into different languages would subtly but surely change their content in ways that might undermine a unified sense of social reality in the citizenry. A common language was rightly deemed essential for a common social reality.

Urban schools have been providing English language instruction for adult immigrants since the early years of the twentieth century. New York City's enrollment in evening English classes for foreigners spiraled from 18,938 in 1901, to over 40,000 in 1907. By 1907, almost 10,000 of the 17,295 students attending evening schools in Chicago were enrolled in English classes for foreigners.[60] The Cincinnati superintendent reported in 1903 that English for foreigners was one of several evening school subjects offered in the public schools;[61] by 1909 he

---

58. John R. Commons, *Races and Immigrants in America* (New York: Macmillan, 1907), p. 20.

59. Frederic Ernest Farrington, "Public Facilities for Educating the Alien," *Bulletin of the U.S. Bureau of Education*, 1916, no. 18, p. 9; quoted in Fred Clayton Butler, "Community Americanization: A Handbook for Workers," *Bulletin of the U.S. Bureau of Education*, 1919, no. 17, p. 30.

60. *New York Annual Report*, 1901, p. 50; *New York Annual Report*, 1907, p. 544; and *Chicago Annual Report*, 1907, p. 144.

61. *Cincinnati Annual Report*, 1903, p. 101.

referred to Americanization as "one of the important functions of these schools."[62] Farrington reported in 1916 that six of the ten states with over half a million foreign-born whites provided support for evening English classes for immigrants. Of the 429 school systems that responded to his questionnaire, 376 provided evening facilities for foreigners to learn English.[63]

Although many cities engaged in the campaign to Americanize the adult alien through English language classes, success was limited. In New York the average attendance in 1901 was only 27 percent of the enrollment, and in Cleveland less than one-half of one percent of the alien men were enrolled. Part of the problem was that after working all day men were too tired to attend evening classes. Americanization classes were also plagued with inappropriate methodological approaches. Sociologist Herbert Miller recalled his visits to several Cleveland Americanization classes. In one class, "hulking laboring men" were copying, "I am a yellow bird. I can sing. I can fly. I can sing to you." While in another they were reading a third grade book "about a robin that said 'God loves the flowers and birds too much to send the cold to freeze them.' "[64] Although such materials probably did not increase the adult alien's motivation for evening school, the limited success of the program may also have been due to his resistance to such efforts to obscure his ethnicity.

Community leaders in many cities with large immigrant populations initiated campaigns to increase attendance at evening Americanization classes. By 1915, foreign language posters advertising the classes were commonly found in locations frequented by foreigners. Several cities used public school children as messengers to deliver notices of such classes to their alien parents. Over 400,000 such notices were distributed by student messengers in Chicago between 1914 and 1915. Other cities sought the cooperation of churches, motion picture houses, and committees of foreigners in publicizing their classes.[65] A common aspect of these drives was the close cooperation between big business,

---

62. *Cincinnati Annual Report,* 1908, p. 8.

63. Farrington, "Public Facilities," pp. 15, 20, 21.

64. *New York Annual Report,* 1901, p. 50; Herbert Adolphus Miller, *The School and the Immigrant* (Cleveland: Survey Committee of the Cleveland Foundation, 1916), pp. 20, 92–93.

65. Farrington, "Public Facilities," pp. 30, 81.

the public schools, and ameliorative agencies such as the YMCA and the settlements.[66]

In contrast to the many ineffective adult alien education programs, the effort at Rochester, New York was deemed a success.[67] In an article entitled "An Americanization Factory," George Mason lauded the program and attributed its success to the new approach developed by its director of immigrant education, Charles E. Finch. Whereas other programs had treated the adult alien like a child by using primary readers and discussing simplistic topics, Finch's approach was to "treat an adult like an adult." By using adult learning materials such as newspapers, Finch's program proposed to give aliens practical knowledge about their surroundings and their everyday problems. The immigrants were taught English words and moral lessons that would help them as workers, consumers, and voters. The effect of this program, Mason implied, was to make the alien more compatible with American industrial life, for it provided "an opportunity for the clever teacher to make very real to his pupils the 'one for all and all for one' ideal in American government." Mason concluded his article with an allusion to the Lawrence and Paterson strikes, which he thought might have been avoided by better preparation of the alien workers.[68] Despite its success, the Rochester experiment was not replicated in many other cities. Until World War I, the Americanization movement had no central authority to coordinate local efforts and avoid duplication of unsuccessful experiments.

The increasing American commitment to participation in World War I heightened the sense of urgency in the Americanization crusade. This movement, like so many other aspects of national life, experienced the organizing influence of a greatly expanded federal government. The central agency in the Americanization crusade was the Department of Labor's commissioner of naturalization. In 1906, Congress provided for "a uniform rule for the naturalization of aliens throughout the United States, and, to accomplish this uniformity, created a federal administra-

---

66. See Gerd Korman, *Industrialization, Immigrants and Americanizers* (Madison: State Historical Society of Wisconsin, 1967), esp. ch. 6; and Peter Andre Sola, "Plutocrats, Pedagogies and Plebes" (Ph.D. diss., University of Illinois, Urbana, 1972), esp. pp. 155–61, and pp. 226–32.

67. The Rochester program was cited as "worthy of special mention" in "The Public Schools of San Francisco," *Bulletin of the U.S. Bureau of Education*, 1917, no. 46, p. 354.

68. George Mason, "An Americanization Factory," *The Outlook*, February 23, 1961, pp. 439–48.

tive bureau charged with the administration of this law."[69] Before this regulation, local cooperation between federal judges and the public schools was sporadic and uncoordinated. By 1915, though, the Bureau of Naturalization was furnishing to the local school systems the names and addresses of all the declarants for citizenship and petitioners for naturalization. The 1915 regulations of the Department of Labor stated that the purpose of this policy was to bring

> these prospective citizens into contact, at the earliest moment, with the Americanizing influences of the public school system and thereby contribut[e] to the elevation of citizenship standards. By insuring comprehension of the true spirit of our institutions on the part of the aliens admitted to citizenship, the bureau may hope to make their acquisition serve as a strengthening influence upon the moral, social, political, and industrial qualities of those institutions.

The regulations also made the bureau a "clearing house of information on civic instruction." This body displayed the common tendency to mix the exclusionist and assimilationist impulses by stating that "without relaxing its efforts at excluding unfit aliens from citizenship, it is endeavoring to stimulate preparation. Its ideal in this respect is to promote the attainment by aliens of such qualities for the citizenship they seek as will better fit them for its duties."[70]

This goal was pursued along several lines, the most visible being the institution of an Americanization Day. The first such ceremony was held in Philadelphia on May 10, 1915. Attention to this event was insured by the fact that President Wilson addressed the new citizenship recipients. The event inspired many other cities to follow the example, and July Fourth was designated Americanization Day in numerous states. It also prompted one correspondent to write that "America does not consist of groups. A man who thinks of himself as belonging to a particular national group in America has not yet become an American."[71] The bureau prompted these Americanization Days to publicize and gain support for its effort to fit aliens for their responsiblities as citizens.

---

69. *Annual Report of the Commissioner of Naturalization to the Secretary of Labor* [hereafter cited as *Annual Report of the Commissioner of Naturalization*] for the Year Ending 1916 (Washington, D.C.: U.S. Government Printing Office), p. 33.

70. Quoted in *Annual Report of the Commissioner of Naturalization*, 1916, p. 33.

71. Quoted in *Annual Report of the Commissioner of Naturalization*, 1916, p. 37.

The bureau sent personal letters to 207,584 candidates for citizenship in 1916. These letters announced the citizenship classes and advised the aliens that they would be able to learn the English language, make a better living, and become better citizens if they accepted the opportunity thus offered.[72] Three years later, the bureau obtained the cooperation of the Boy Scouts of America in delivering the letters. This was believed to be a more effective form of communication, for aliens would have visible evidence of the nation's concern for their assimilation in the person of the young scout at their doors.

The bureau traced its difficulty in securing regular attendance in the classes to the lack of a standard course of instruction. As a remedy, the bureau developed a plan of instruction that included a text and teacher's guide in citizenship, an outline of the naturalization law, and a card system to classify each student and report his progress. These materials were distributed to the army and navy for use in their schools for enlisted men, many of whom were foreign born, as well as to thousands of public school systems throughout the country for use in both the adult alien and the regular school civics classes.[73]

An interesting twist to the bureau's efforts was added in 1920 when it promoted the study of national government through "pilgrimages to the nation's capital." The first such pilgrimage was conducted by an adult citizenship class from Bayonne, New Jersey. The class visited the houses of Congress and various governmental agencies, where they viewed the originals of the "sacred documents of the Nation."[74] The deliberate use of religious terminology like "pilgrimages" and "sacred documents" reflects the tone of religious revivalism that permeated the Americanization movement. Like religious pilgrimages, these trips used experiential devices to evoke appropriate emotional responses.

Enthusiasm for the bureau's programs spread quickly. In July of 1915, the bureau contacted all cities with a population of over 2,500; within one month, 38 had responded positively, and within one year over 600 had agreed to cooperate with the bureau's program. By the close of the 1919 school year, 2,240 of the 2,400 cities with a population of over 2,500 participated in the federal government's Americanization program. During 1921, over 117,000 adult aliens were enrolled in

---

72. *Annual Report of the Commissioner of Naturalization*, 1916, pp. 38, 70.

73. *Annual Report of the Commissioner of Naturalization*, 1916, pp. 39–42.

74. *Annual Report of the Commissioner of Naturalization*, 1920, p. 39.

such classes, and in 1923 the bureau distributed over 126,000 copies of its citizenship textbook.[75]

Government centralization and control became more pronounced during America's military involvement in World War I. By April of 1918, every state had created a state council of defense. In many states, these councils included community councils in school districts and precincts. At the request of the U.S. Bureau of Education, the National Council of Defense asked each state council to appoint an Americanization committee to assist the Bureau of Education in its national program and to develop state programs. In addition to coordinating the Americanization work of all voluntary agencies, such as settlements and the YMCA, the councils disseminated war information prepared by the Creel Committee. As described by a member of the National Council of Defense, "The State Council of Defense will thus become, not only the correlating agency for the work of Americanization societies, but will center in itself work representing the three departments of the Federal Government most concerned with Americanization—the Department of the Interior Bureau of Education, the Committee on Public Information, and the Department of Labor Bureau of Naturalization."[76]

This effort and its results were described in part by George Creel in 1920:

> The loyalty of "our aliens," however, splendid as it was, had in it nothing of the spontaneous or the accidental. Results were obtained only by hard, driving work. The bitterness bred by years of neglect and injustice were not to be dissipated by any mere war-call, but had to be burned away by a continuous educational campaign. The *real* America had to be revealed to these foreign-language groups—its drama of hope and struggle, success and blunders—and their minds had to be filled with the tremendous truth that the fight against Germany was a fight for all that life has taught decent human beings to hold dear.
>
> This campaign succeeded because the Committee avoided the professional "Americanizers," and steered clear of the accepted forms of "Americanization." We worked from the *inside*, not from the outside, aiding each group to develop its own loyalty league, and utilizing the natural and existing leaders, institutions, and machinery. We offered co-operation

---

75. *Annual Report of the Commissioner of Naturalization*, 1916, p. 48; *Annual Report of the Commissioner of Naturalization*, 1919, p. 34; *Annual Report of the Commissioner of Naturalization*, 1921, p. 16; and *Annual Report of the Commissioner of Naturalization*, 1923, p. 17.

76. Elliott D. Smith, address in "Americanization as a War Measure," *Bulletin of the U.S. Bureau of Education*, 1918, no. 18, pp. 21, 22.

and supervision, and we gave counsel, not commands. As a consequence, each group had its own task, its own responsibility, and as soon as these facts were clearly understood the response was immediate. [77]

The approach adopted by the Committee on Public Information closely resembled the Americanization proposals of Robert Parks. In particular, it seemed to follow his notion of working from within the structure of the immigrant community, using immigrant leadership and institutions to implement the government's objectives. This was evident in specific practical recommendations, as well as at the more general theoretical level. At the practical level, for example, the committee foreshadowed Park's suggestion that the immigrant press could be a powerful force in the Americanization process. The foreign language press became an important conduit for the government's war propaganda. Creel noted that "96 percent of the papers availed themselves to the material. Very many of the papers used all but a few releases, and it was a frequent occurrence to have foreign-language papers come in carrying on their front page two or three columns of the Bureau's material." [78]

Although war concerns accelerated the move to centralize Americanization programs, it would be wrong to attribute the efforts of the Naturalization Bureau and the National Council of Defense to wartime hysteria, particularly since the Naturalization Bureau's effort predated the outbreak of hostilities. The logic from which the programs developed was simply an extension of the premises underlying older reactions to the immigrant question.

The Americanization of immigrant children posed problems similar to those faced by the adult Americanization programs. The schools sought to integrate the immigrant children into the mainstream of American society by making them a functional part of it. The first requisite for success was compulsory attendance laws. Once school officials were able to force the children to attend school they soon discovered that they were dealing with variegated raw material requiring differential methods and programs. As early as 1899, Dr. W. S. Christopher, a member of the Chicago Board of Education, noted, "If the schools are to do the best for these immigrant children, and do their share in blending these nationalities into a common American type, the national peculiarities of these children must be known, and they can only be known by

---

77. George Creel, *How We Advertised America* (New York: Harper and Brothers, 1920), p. 184. I am indebted to Stephen Yulish for bringing this source to my attention.

78. Creel, *How We Advertised America*, p. 192.

systematic, scientific study."[79] The child study movement had always contended that if certain results were desired, then the teacher should understand the individual child in whom the change was to be wrought. With the influx of immigrant children into the schools, this theory was reinforced for educators now discerned not only individual peculiarities in each child, but also racial pecularities in each ethnic group. It was generally agreed that the schools would have to deal with these traits if they hoped to blend the immigrants into American society.

These efforts resulted in school programs with two broad complementary objectives. The first was met by programs designed to fit the children with functional specialties that would contribute to their usefulness and thus to their integration into American society. Such areas as vocational guidance, industrial education, and domestic education had special relevance for the immigrant child's passage to American adulthood.[80] The second objective was to give the immigrant child a sense of identity with American ideals and American standards of citizenship. Only when this was accomplished, many schoolmen believed, could a homogeneous community emerge with a sufficient sense of national unity to fulfill the promise of American life. This second purpose was addressed in regular curricular offerings, extracurricular activities, and many other aspects of school life.[81]

Regardless of whether they were attempting to develop functional specialization or a unified sense of community within which those specialities could be applied, the schools wrestled with the problem of language. The intricacy of the English language presented serious difficulties for newly arrived, foreign-born children, and educators realized the inefficiency of allowing these children to founder in the regular classes until they had gained an adequate command of English. The experiment of the Educational Alliance in New York City showed a way to eradicate the problem. The Educational Alliance was born in 1891, in response to the influx of Jewish immigrants from Russia. Supported and run by New York Jews, one of its important purposes was to prepare foreign-born, non-English-speaking, Jewish children for attendance in the public schools. These children would often spend several months in the Alliance program, where they were taught English and patriotism. One observer of the Alliance program said, "When the children have learned the language and have become Americanized in their dress and

79. *Chicago Annual Report*, 1899, p. 74.
80. These curricular innovations will be examined in detail in subsequent chapters.
81. These will be examined in subsequent chapters.

habits they are transferred to the public schools."[82] During the first decade of the twentieth century, many urban public schools followed the principle of the Alliance program by setting up separate classes for non-English-speaking immigrant children. Cleveland had what they referred to as "streamer classes" by 1901. Similar provisions were instituted as early as 1904 in New York.[83] In all cases, the objective was first to teach the child English and then to move him into the appropriate grade level within the regular program. These special classes were designed to integrate the immigrant child into normal school life as rapidly and smoothly as possible.

The Americanization of immigrant children in the public school and its adult alien education counterpart in the settlement ultimately had the same objective. Both attempted to integrate the newcomer into society by making him a functional part of urban-industrial America. Before he could become a part of this social order, it was believed that the immigrant would have to adopt appropriate values, attitudes, and behavioral patterns. The Americanization crusade was but one of several movements within the larger effort to defuse the potential explosiveness of an unassimilated and discontented alien proletariat. The Americanization crusade, however, was not an isolated effort. There were several similar attempts to restructure urban children, especially those from the lower social and economic classes so that they might better meet the labor requirements of corporate industry. The play movement was one such effort.

---

82. David Blaustein, "From Oppression to Freedom," *Charities* 10 (April 4, 1903): 338.

83. Miller, *School and the Immigrant*, p. 72; *New York Annual Report*, 1904, p. 160; and *New York Annual Report*, 1905, p. 64.

Chapter 4

The Play Movement

As American society became increasingly aware of the problems raised by immigration, urbanization, and industrialization, many intellectuals began to examine the potential of play and recreation as a means to mitigate these difficulties. No previous generation had evidenced so great a concern for the play activities of its youth. Intellectuals developed theories to explain the psychological, physiological, and sociological bases of play. Municipal playgrounds were constructed in every city. A new vocation, the play leader, emerged, and a national organization, the Playground and Recreation Association of America, appeared in 1904 to organize, standardize, and promote recreation. Public school programs and architecture were modified to accommodate the new interest in the educational use of child's play. A common theme in the recreation movement was the faith that play encouraged socially productive attitudes, values, and habits.

THEORIES ABOUT PLAY

A number of theories were advanced in support of the play movement. One of the earliest was Herbert Spencer's conception of play as the expenditure of surplus energy in more or less aimless activity. Spencer explained that children in modern society, relieved of most of the burdens of making a living, could devote large reserves of energy to play.[1] Although this formulation implied that play was an

---

1. Herbert Spencer, *Principles of Psychology* (New York: D. Appleton, 1896), vol. 2. ch. 9.

essential aspect of childhood, it did not suggest how or why play could be a training device. Most play movement enthusiasts considered Karl Groos's work an improvement on Spencer's theory. After extensive study of animal play, the German psychologist analysed human play and concluded that Spencer had erroneously characterized play as an aimless activity. Groos noted the frequency with which play manifested activities later useful in the adult life of both man and animals. It functioned essentially as a preparatory exercise for developing responses and muscles necessary in adult life.[2] While the Groos theory explained the educational dimension of play, it still left unanswered questions about those play activities seemingly unconnected to future adult functions.

It was at this juncture that American theoreticians became most creative and productive. Walter B. Hill, the chancellor of the University of Georgia, projected the direction of American theories of play in his 1902 address to the National Education Association.[3] He cautioned that while fun was an expression of natural impulses, in civilized communities it must be bounded by ethics. This could be accomplished if man's natural wit was deliberately trained and cultivated, channeling spontaneous fun into acceptable outlets. Americans were most concerned with the use of play as a control mechanism, and so the idea that fun should have a moral purpose was an important beginning in the construction of a more complete conceptual framework for the play movement.

A second component of the framework was provided by G. Stanley Hall's speculations regarding the development of impulses for fun and play in children as a part of their natural growth pattern. Hall, a prominent psychologist and the founder of the child study movement, contended that children relive or "recapitulate" the total experience of the human race. Instincts appropriate to that distant past, Hall believed, found expression is play. If many of these activities were not directly useful for the child's future functions, they were, nevertheless, essential for his successful voyage through the evolutionary development of the race.[4]

---

2. Karl Groos, *Play of Man*, trans. Elizabeth L. Baldwin (New York: D. Appleton, 1901).

3. Walter B. Hill, "Psychology and Ethics of Fun," *NEA Addresses and Proceedings*, 1902, pp. 286–97.

4. G. Stanley Hall, *Adolescence* (New York: D. Appleton, 1908), vol. 1, ch. 3, vol. 2, chs. 7 and 8.

Utilizing Hall's basic conceptual framework, Joseph Lee and G. T. W. Patrick extended the recapitulation theory of play. Patrick, a psychologist, argued that the burden of civilization repressed natural instincts while cultivating will, concentration, and abstraction. Children, passing through an earlier evolutionary stage, were unable to sustain such efforts and even most adults could sustain them for only limited periods. Patrick interpreted the play of children and the recreation of adults as cathartic reversions that offered a respite from higher mental efforts. Because some forms of play were more desirable than others, he recommended development of healthy recreational opportunities.[5] The understanding that play and recreation could be structured to yield specific behavioral outcomes in other spheres of life had significant application to the problem of developing a working class with personality types and behavioral patterns required by corporate industry.

Theoretical work along this line was extended by social worker Joseph Lee, "the father of the American play movement." One of his earliest works noted the importance of lessons learned in play and enunciated the bellwether slogan of the play movement: "The boy without a playground is father to the man without a job; and the boy with a bad playground is apt to be father to a man with a job that had better have been left undone."[6] Lee analyzed play as a facet of the recapitulation theory. Recalling the growth stages developed by G. Stanley Hall, Lee organized human growth into babyhood-childhood, the dramatic age, the big injun age, and the age of loyalty. Each was dominated by different instincts that found expression in a variety of play impulses. While the impulse for play could not be denied, Lee maintained that it was possible and desirable to channel the impulses into activities that instilled socially acceptable habits.[7]

John Dewey was also concerned with the social outcomes of play. In a brief article for Monroe's *Cyclopedia of Education*, he outlined the educational implications of play. Expressing the priorities of pragmatism, the philosopher claimed that the important considera-

---

5. G. T. W. Patrick, "The Psychology of Play," *The Pedagogical Seminary* 21 (September 1914): 469–84.

6. Joseph Lee, *Constructive and Preventive Philanthropy* (New York: Macmillan, 1902), p. 123.

7. Joseph Lee, *Play and Playgrounds*, pamphlet, American Civic Association, 1908; and Joseph Lee, *Play in Education* (New York: Macmillan, 1921).

tions were not why play impulses occurred but rather under what conditions. Dewey differentiated play, work, labor, drudgery, amusement, and recreation. Play, he asserted, was an intrinsically enjoyable activity performed "without reference to ulterior purpose."[8] Work, on the other hand, was directed toward an outcome and required adjustments of activities to insure that outcome.

After drawing careful distinctions between play and other activities, Dewey explained the educational importance of play. He was apparently unaware of the logical inconsistency between his definition of play as an intrinsic activity and his recommendations that it be used to fulfill extrinsic objectives. Because growth proceeds from earlier activities, Dewey thought it was essential for educators to plan students' play in order that "the earlier play be of such a sort as to grow naturally and helpfully into the later, more reflective and productive modes of behavior." His statement that "the natural transition of play into work is the means and the only means of reconciling the development of social efficiency with that of individual fullness of life" illustrates that Dewey's proposals were designed to condition the child for his future industrial role.[9] According to Dewey, the good society harmonized social efficiency and individual fulfillment. Dewey did not make such a claim about a bad or unjust society, nor did he claim that American society met all the criteria for a good society. Many other educators and leaders of the play movement, however, did not make such distinctions. Few suggested that America fell short of a good or just society. And fewer still, as they echoed Dewey's call to use play as an educational force for social efficiency, worried about the possiblility that any justifiable conflict existed between social efficiency and individual fulfillment in America.

DEVELOPMENT OF PLAYGROUNDS

Although play, recreation, and amusement have a long history in this country, most early twentieth-century authorities traced the genesis of the modern play movement to the establishment of Boston's sand gar-

8. John Dewey, "Play," in *A Cyclopedia of Education*, ed. Paul Monroe (New York: Macmillan, 1914), p. 725.
9. Dewey, "Play," p. 727.

den playgrounds in 1886.[10] These sand garden playgrounds were begun under the philanthropic auspices of the Massachusetts Emergency and Hygiene Association at the request of a medical consultant, Dr. Marie E. Zakrsewska, who had been favorably impressed by such facilities in Berlin. Playgrounds began as piles of sand placed in churchyards for young children. By 1887 matrons were employed, and in 1893 a superintendent of sand gardens was appointed with kindergarten teachers as assistants at each garden. The number of gardens increased from 1 in 1885 to 21 in 1899, and the average daily attendance expanded from 15 to 4,000 during these years. In 1899, the city council began to subsidize the sand gardens with an appropriation of $3,000. The city council first subsidized playgrounds in 1888, granting $1,000 to the Charlesbank Outdoor Gym for men, which opened under the direction of the same philanthropic organization.[11]

Other cities soon followed Boston's lead. Between 1893 and 1903, sand garden playgrounds opened in Philadelphia, New York, Providence, Chicago, Brooklyn, Pittsburgh, Baltimore, Cleveland, Minneapolis, Denver, and San Francisco.[12] All of these early efforts were for young children, were located in tenement districts, and were founded by philanthropic patrons.

As the sand gardens demonstrated their value in work with young children in tenement districts, the effort was expanded to include older youths. Chicago was an early site of this expansion. In 1894, the Hull House Model Playground opened in a lot donated by philanthropist-civic reformer William Kent. It is interesting and perhaps symbolic that a kindergarten teacher from Hull House supervised the younger children and that a Chicago policeman directed the activities of the older youths. Within four years, both the Northwestern University Settlement and the University of Chicago started play-

---

10. See Henry S. Curtis, "Vacation Schools and Playgrounds," *Harper's Monthly Magazine*, June 1902, p. 24; Sadie American, "The Movement for Small Playgrounds," *American Journal of Sociology* 4 (September 1898): 159–60; Joseph Lee, *Constructive Philanthropy*, p. 125; and Clarence E. Rainwater, *The Play Movement in the United States* (Chicago: University of Chicago Press, 1922), pp. 22–44.

11. Lee, *Constructive Philanthropy*, pp. 125–26; and Rainwater, *Play Movement*, pp. 22–28.

12. See Lee, *Constructive Philanthropy*, pp. 126–219; Rainwater, *Play Movement*, p. 52; Sadie American, "The Movement for Small Playgrounds," pp. 161–64; and Walter Wood, "The Playground Movement in America and Its Relation to Public Education," *Educational Pamphlets*, no. 27 (London: Eyre and Spottiswoode, 1913), p. 5.

grounds similar to the Hull House experiment. Before the end of the nineteenth century, Philadelphia, Boston, and New York saw similar extensions of the playground movement by philanthropic organizations.[13] During the first two decades of the twentieth century, cities commonly provided recreation facilities for adults as well as for children and adolescents.[14] Phenomenal growth of the playground movement occurred in the first 20 years of this century. The first supervised playground appeared in 1885; in 1899 fewer than 15 cities boasted supervised playgrounds; 90 had these facilities in 1907; more than 330 in 1909; and over 500 by 1917. New York City alone had over 304 playgrounds in 1913, and the municipality spent over $16 million between 1903 and 1913 for the establishment of playgrounds; Chicago was a close second, spending over $11 million during the same period. The 432 cities reporting the maintenance of supervised playgrounds to the Playground and Recreation Association of America during 1915 noted expenditures totaling over $4 million for that year, while the association itself spent over $82,000.[15]

THE PLAYGROUND ASSOCIATION

An important mobilizing force in the play movement was the Playground Association of America, established in 1906. This agency was organized by Luther Gulick, its original president, and Henry Curtis, its first secretary and treasurer. The honorary president and vice-president were Theodore Roosevelt and Jacob Riis, respectively. At the fourth annual meeting, Joseph Lee was elected president, a post he retained until his death in 1937. The association's name was changed

---

13. Lee, Constructive Philanthropy, pp. 126–29; and Rainwater, Play Movement, pp. 56–66.

14. Howard S. Braucher, Developments and Opportunities in the Field of Public Recreation, pamphlet (Playground Association of America, 1900); Clarence Arthur Perry, "The Extension of Public Education, A Study in the Wider Use of School Buildings," Bulletin of the U.S. Bureau of Education, 1915, no. 28; and Playground and Recreation Association of America, The Yearbook (New York, 1918).

15. Howard S. Braucher, "Play and Social Progress," The Annals of the American Academy of Political and Social Science 35 (January–June 1910): 331; Howard S. Braucher, A Year's Work of the Playground and Recreation Association of America, pamphlet (Playground and Recreation Association of America, 1915), p. 15; Henry S. Curtis, The Practical Conduct of Play (New York: Macmillan, 1915), p. 1; Rainwater, Play Movement, p. 20; and Wood, "Playground Movement," pp. 8, 13.

to Playground and Recreation Association of America in 1912 as the movement became increasingly involved in recreation as well as play.[16]

In addition to propagandizing for increased facilities through its local associations and its magazine, The Playground, which began publication in June 1906, the national association was instrumental in organizing training programs for playground supervisors. Most contemporary leaders of the movement agreed that properly trained supervisors were the most important element in any playground. As early as 1909, a special committee of the association, chaired by Clark W. Hetherington of the University of Missouri, developed a series of course syllabi designed for the training of supervisors. By 1911, over 60 cities were offering training courses for play leaders, and 17 schools and colleges reported using the association's suggested syllabi. The University of Pittsburgh appointed George E. Johnson professor of play in 1910 and began offering a one- and a two-year curriculum in this field. Similar courses were subsequently offered at the University of Wisconsin, Cheney State in Washington, and several of the California normal schools. The secretary of the association proudly announced in 1915 that, as a result of the training efforts, "a new profession has grown up" with a reported membership of over 7,500.[17]

The play movement, like many of the educational reforms of the era, began under the auspices of private philanthropic organizations that put their resources into experimental demonstrations and then campaigned for public financial support to incorporate the innovation into some public agency. Although public support for play activities increased continually during the early years of this century, not until 1915 did more than 50 percent of the 432 cities report wholly publicly funded supervised play to the association.[18] Two different administrative structures became conduits for the public funds flowing into the play movement. New York City set one example with its board of education assuming the obligation of providing play and recreation

---

16. Wood, "Playground Movement," p. 8; and Henry S. Curtis, *The Play Movement and Its Significance* (New York: Macmillan, 1917), pp. 15–17.

17. *Proceedings of the Third Annual Congress of the Playground Association of America, Report of the Committee on a Normal Course in Play* (New York, 1909), vol. 3, no. 3; Rainwater, *Play Movement*, pp. 247–49; Wood, "Playground Movement," pp. 38–41; and H. S. Braucher, *A Year's Work*, p. 15.

18. Rainwater, *Play Movement*, p. 235.

facilities. The other type developed in New York's midwestern rival, Chicago, where five independent park commissions became primarily responsible for play and recreation facilities. While these administrative structures were quite different, the programs that each generated were remarkably similar. This reflected both the leadership capacity of the Playground Association of America and the general agreement among leaders of the movement regarding its aims and methods. Apart from the playground, a number of other play and recreation facilities emerged; these included vacation schools, evening recreation centers, social centers, and community centers.

VACATION SCHOOLS

The earliest of these facilities was the vacation school. Henry S. Curtis, a leader in the play movement and an authority on vacation schools, commented in 1902, "Vacation work as a whole naturally divides itself into two parts, the vacation school and the playground."[19] A year later, in a report of the U.S. commissioner of education, Curtis described the evolution of vacation schools. The early vacation schools, like the early playgrounds, were sponsored by philanthropic organizations. The first was held in the old First Church of Boston in 1866. New York City established one in 1894, and Chicago in 1896. By the turn of the century, such schools had appeared in Brooklyn, Hartford, Cleveland, Baltimore, Buffalo, and Indianapolis. Philanthropic societies usually cooperated closely with public schools, and public school buildings often housed vacation schools while the societies directed the program.[20] The first vacation school under direct supervision of a public school system began in Newark in 1886.[21] By 1902, at least one-third of these institutions were controlled directly by the superintendents of schools. Chicago was one of the last large cities to maintain philanthropic management. As late as 1908, the Chicago Federation of Women's Clubs operated the vacation schools, although the public board of education provided classroom space and contributed $15,000 of the total budget of $23,217. The board's

---

19. Curtis, "Vacation Schools and Playgrounds," p. 24.

20. Henry S. Curtis, "Vacation Schools," *Report of the Commissioner of Education for the Year 1903* (Washington, D.C.: U.S. Government Printing Office), 1:4–6.

21. Curtis, "Vacation Schools and Playgrounds," p. 24.

direct financial support began in 1903 with a grant of $1,000 toward a total budget of $6,869.[22] The trend, however, was toward total public support and control. By 1903, Curtis noted the existence of vacation schools in every large city, most medium-sized cities, and in over 200 smaller cities.[23]

RECREATION CENTERS

A logical extension of the playground and the vacation school was the recreation center. The purpose of these centers was to provide year-round play and recreation facilities to adolescents and young adults as well as to children. Like playgrounds, the recreation centers developed along two different administrative lines. In Chicago, the recreation centers were founded and run primarily by the park commissions. The South Chicago Park Commissioners initiated the first centers in 1905 when they opened ten play parks, each containing a field house with assembly halls, gymnasiums, shower-baths, clubrooms, a kitchen, and a public library. Beginning in 1908, the West Chicago Park Commission formed other centers. In 1905, the Los Angeles Board of Playground Commissioners opened a recreation center, and within seven years it added five more. The example was followed by Pittsburgh in 1910, Philadelphia in 1911, Minneapolis in 1912, and shortly thereafter by Oakland, Louisville, and St. Paul. Most cities, however, followed the example of New York in placing recreation centers in public schools.[24]

New York's experiment with recreation centers began in 1901 with 8 "evening play centers" in Manhattan public schools. The number was increased to 12 the following year, with the centers open from seven until ten every evening except Sunday. The average nightly attendance increased from 675 the first year to over 2,650 in 1902, necessitating the exclusion of children under the age of 14. Eleven years later, the number of centers rose to 56 and nightly attendance was over 21,000.[25] Scarcity of open land in New York forced

---

22. *Chicago Annual Report*, 1902, p. 78; and *Chicago Annual Report*, 1908, p. 281.

23. Curtis, "Vacation Schools," pp. 4–5.

24. Rainwater, *Play Movement*, pp. 93–111; Charles Zueblen, *American Municipal Progress* (New York: Macmillan, 1916), chs. 14 and 16.

25. *New York Annual Report*, 1902, pp. 64, 103; *New York Annual Report*, 1913, p. 25.

most play centers into the ground floor of schoolhouses and may have paved the way for acceptance of year-round indoor recreation. Perhaps the most important selling point of the New York example was its efficiency. In an era of efficiency consciousness, using existing facilities to their maximum capacity was an attractive possibility.[26] Accordingly, most cities followed the New York example. Nine years after the establishment of the first New York "evening play center," 201 recreation centers existed in the schools of 31 cities. By 1917, over 600 cities provided more than 3,300 recreation centers in their schools.[27]

The recreation center soon evolved into the "social center" inspired by Edward J. Ward in Rochester, New York. In 1907, after visiting both the Chicago and New York recreation centers, he convinced the Rochester school board to inaugurate a version of the New York system sufficiently different to warrant a new name. Ward proposed not only to include the users of the facilities in the administration of the program, but to make the school facility the hub of community activity and community self-regeneration. Hence, the Rochester centers were called "social and civic centers."[28] By 1913, both New York and Cincinnati began to call several of their recreation centers social centers. The Cincinnati Board of Education even allowed the discussion of political and social issues in these institutions. Within three years, the Cincinnati social centers developed experimental structures for "self-government with representatives chosen from various occupations. New York, meanwhile, organized 60 social centers during 1914, which in turn gave rise to 16 community centers the next year. The number of community centers in New York expanded to over 80 during the succeeding three-year period.[29]

By 1918, the community center idea was sufficiently entrenched that Eugene C. Gibney, an assistant director to the superintendent of schools, devoted over 100 pages of his annual report on recreation to the goals and methods of the New York City community centers.[30]

---

26. See, for example, Samuel Haber, *Efficiency and Uplift* (Chicago: University of Chicago Press, 1964).

27. Rainwater, *Play Movement*, p. 117.

28. See Rainwater, *Play Movement*, pp. 112–15; and Edward Stevens, Jr., "Social Centers, Politics, and Social Efficiency in the Progressive Era" (unpublished manuscript).

29. *New York Annual Report*, 1913, pp. 9–28; *Cincinnati Annual Report*, 1913, p. 45; and Rainwater, *Play Movement*, p. 167.

30. *New York Annual Report*, 1918; Gibney was the assistant director in charge of vacation schools, playgrounds, recreation, and community centers.

The central motif of the community center was voiced in the rallying cry "self-support and self-government." Since the size of school administrative bureaucracies had already displayed its deadening effect in many of the larger cities, one aspect of this motif was an attempt to decentralize the administrative structure of public recreation by including the clients in the new structure and by taking advantage of a smaller administrative unit, the neighborhood. This reform was viewed by recreation leaders as possessing a vital and dynamic potential for cementing client loyalties.

The advent of World War I forced recreation leaders to organize adequate facilities for armed service personnel and war industries workers. They met this demand by founding the War Camp Community Service, which eventually organized the recreational resources of over 600 communities. Like the community center, these resources were administered on a community basis. With the end of the war and subsequent demobilization, the War Camp Community Service was phased out, only to be replaced with the Community Service, Incorporated, which continued these efforts. The local orientation of the community centers, War Camp Community Service, and Community Service, Incorporated seemed designed to decentralize administration and to foster neighborhood control. Nevertheless, the influence of the Playground and Recreation Association of America and its leaders was manifest throughout the era. It was, for example, the association that received support from the Council of National Defense to organize the War Camp Community Services, and the national officers of the association occupied similar posts in the service. The same officers, Joseph Lee as president and Howard S. Braucher as secretary, served both the association and the new Community Service, incorporated after the war.[31]

PLAY AND THE URBAN WORKING CLASS

An interlocking directorate headed the major national recreational organizations, and a similar interlocking of ideas prevailed regarding the appropriate role of recreation and play in modern urban America. A remarkably consistent ideological base underlay the various forms

---

31. Rainwater, *Play Movement*, pp. 179, 180.

and agencies of play and recreation that emerged in this era. Its main tenets were: (a) left unattended in the modern American city, children would not mature into the types of adults required by corporate industry; (b) play was essential for the growth of children and the regeneration of adults; and (c) play could successfully accomplish its goals of developing the appropriate kinds of citizens only if it were adequately directed.

The play movement slogan that Joseph Lee articulated in 1902 revealed that this movement was tied to the task of developing an urban proletariat.[32] But Lee, unlike many of his contemporaries in the play movement, supported the movement for larger reasons than training an industrial working class. He was interested in what educators of an earlier period called the development of men.[33] Lee felt that without adequate play activities boys would not grow into complete men. He seemed oblivious to the possibility that the traits required by corporate industry might militate against personal fulfillment. His demands that the play movement produce sound men and good citizens who would become efficient industrial workers remains one of the paradoxes of the movement. Most of the other leaders of the play movement, interested primarily in the development of good workers, were not aware of the contradiction between efficient cogs in an assembly line and happy individuals.

Near unanimity prevailed on the primary aim of the play movement, to provide activities through which children could acquire the behavioral patterns required in the new industrial workplace. Most often, these patterns were considered synonymous with requirements for good citizenship. Sadie America, one of the early leaders of the play movement, contended that properly supervised playgrounds "would help to build up men who make good citizens."[34] Within a few years, school superintendents in Chicago and Cincinnati made similar assertions.[35] Assessing the significance of the first 30 years of the movement, Henry S. Curtis claimed, "We have not been thinking so much of health or physical development as we have of the social environment."[36]

---

32. Lee, *Constructive Philanthropy*, p. 123.

33. Lee, *Play and Playgrounds*, p. 3.

34. American, "Movement for Small Playgrounds," p. 159.

35. *Cincinnati Annual Report*, 1917, p. 37; and *Chicago Annual Report*, 1916, p. 19.

36. Curtis, *Practical Conduct of Play*, pp. 6–7; and Curtis, *Play Movement*, p. 11.

Assuming that citizenship was the primary goal of play and recreation, many leaders of the play movement argued that play was essential for the welfare and safety of the state. Michael M. Davis, Jr., who examined the commercial aspects of recreation in New York City for the Russell Sage Foundation in 1911, discovered, not surprisingly, that many unsupervised recreational facilities corrupted the development of future citizens. He found, too, that homes of many children offered no opportunities for recreation. "We are learning, in a new field," he concluded, "what was taught by the economic world a generation ago; like industry, recreation has become a matter of public concern; laissez-faire can no longer be the policy of the State."[37] Davis was not alone in urging the state to take a more positive and paternalistic role in the leisure activities of its youth.

Henry Curtis broadened the attack on the state's laissez-faire attitude toward play and recreation. Extending the rationale which had been used to support the idea of compulsory school attendance, Curtis argued for a Department of Child Welfare to guide the leisure activities of children.[38] Leaders of corporate industry agreed with Curtis that the chief concern of this guidance should be to promote social order through acceptance of the existing political economy. They, too, believed that much unrest was kindled by unrealistic working-class aspirations, perhaps the consequence of bookish training in the schools.

Significantly, the most highly praised educational aspects of the play movement were those directed toward engendering contentment, loyalty, and solidarity rather than toward raising expectations. Most of the leaders of the movement understood the importance of this emotional training for the continued success, if not the very survival, of corporate industry. While justifying his proposal, Curtis displayed the same kind of paternalism that the most enlightened corporate industrialists were developing in their employee welfare programs. Holding that the state has as much interest in the child as its parents, he proposed that the Department of Child Welfare coordinate all of the agencies and activities relating to children. Armed with unified and comprehensive administrative powers, the department, Curtis believed, would be able to "plan all of the conditions affecting the life of the child so that there

---

37. Michael M. Davis, Jr., *The Exploitation of Pleasure* (New York: Russell Sage, 1911), p. 45.

38. Henry S. Curtis, "A Department of Child Welfare," *The American City* 5 (September 1911): 119–23. Curtis expressed similar sentiments in *Play Movement and Its Significance*, p. 337.

would be a probability of securing a definite result."[39] Curtis, and others of like mind in the play movement, wished to expand state control over the children's lives.

Another proponent of public authority was John Palmer Garber, the articulate associate superintendent of the Philadelphia public schools. In a statement characteristic of those in the play movement, Garber summarized the argument for a massive intrusion of the state into the lives of individuals: "The amusements of a people profoundly affect their welfare and efficiency; hence they are a matter of grave concern to the state. This being true, all of the amusements of its people should be under the most complete and direct control of the state."[40] Whether efficiency, welfare, or both were construed as the rationale, such governmental control should be recognized as ominous in a free society.

The play movement's ultimate justification lay in its claim to protect the state. Most of its proponents believed that the greatest danger to the social order emanated from the urban immigrant slums. Allegedly the most serious source of unrest, slum children held a special interest for the play movement. Most playgrounds, vacation schools, and evening recreation centers were first started in tenement districts. In a statement typical of this concern, the Cincinnati superintendent of schools said, "The vacation school is an attempt to meet the needs of children in the crowded districts in the heated summer."[41] Like most of his contemporary school administrators, the superintendent answered the needs of children in crowded districts with programs that prepared working-class children to fulfill manpower requirements in corporate industry. Similarly, the course in play developed by the Playground Association of America in 1909 taught play leaders to study the neighborhood conditions surrounding the playground; it was unnecessary to examine the conditions of the "better communities" because "these communities are, in general, better understood, and the playgrounds are not, as a rule, located among them."[42] The Chicago Daily News in 1899 editorialized in favor of small parks designed mainly for slum areas. These

39. Curtis, "Department of Child Welfare," p. 123.

40. John Palmer Garber, Current Educational Activities (Philadelphia: Lippincott, 1912), p. 52.

41. Cincinnati Annual Report, 1911, p. 64; also see New York Annual Report, 1903, pp. 117–18; New York Annual Report, 1909, pp. 194–95; Chicago Annual Report, 1899, p. 145; and Chicago Annual Report, 1902, p. 79.

42. Report of the Committee on a Normal Course in Play, p. 137.

parks, it said, were "a work of expediency rather than philanthropy. The city is asked to do something not out of the goodness of its heart, but out of the soundness of its head. To let air and sunlight into these packed quarters, to introduce sanitary conditions, to give children an open space to play is a matter of business, of sound economics, of self-protection."[43]

Since the congested districts were the homes of the immigrants, direct consideration was given to the use of play as an Americanizing force. Pittsburgh's Playground Association president, Beulah Kennard, wrote that "wholesale immigration" and slum conditions created a "dangerously large" class of children "who fail to 'measure up' to our standard of American childhood and who seem likely to fall still farther from the standard of American manhood and womanhood." She contended that adequate playgrounds could help prevent this tendency toward degeneration.[44] An investigator sent by the British government observed that it was the general opinion of American playground supervisors that organized playgrounds were the best means for "gripping the foreign population in the western cities and civilizing them to American standards."[45] By 1912, Chicago's superintendent of schools reported that 10,565 of the 11,980 students in the vacation schools were either foreign born or had foreign-born parents, thus making them immigrants according to the official school standard.[46] In a similar vein, the critics of the Elyria, Ohio schools, chastising that system for eliminating its playgrounds and play supervisors when funds were short in 1918, predicted, "The importance of the public playground as a civic educational factor will increase with the growth of Elyria as an industrial center and with the rapid increase of the foreign population."[47] According to Evangeline Whitney, the New York City schools used its recreational facilities to help "solve the city's great problem of Americanizing its youth from foreign lands." Whitney was a district superintendent in charge of the system's playgrounds and summer schools between 1902 and her

---

43. Editorial, *Chicago Daily News*, November 13, 1899. Quoted in Michael Patrick McCarthy, "Businessmen and Professionals in Municipal Reform: The Chicago Experience, 1887–1920" (Ph.D. diss., Northwestern University, 1970), p. 89.

44. Beulah Kennard, "The Playground for Children at Home," *The Annals of the American Academy of Political and Social Science* 35 (January–June 1910): 380.

45. Wood, "Playground Movement," p. 7.

46. *Chicago Annual Report*, 1912, p. 139.

47. "Educational Survey of Elyria, Ohio," *Bulletin of the U.S. Bureau of Education*, 1918, no. 15, p. 196.

death in 1909. She remarked in her 1906 report that in each of New York's playgrounds "the march, the salute to the flag, patriotic and college songs, and drills held first place in the daily program." Her successor reminded his playground principals not to be derelict in using such devices to "awaken and maintain a proper playground spirit." His description of the vacation kindergarten boasted that songs such as "America" and games such as "Soldier Boy" effectively "aroused the patriotic impulses of our many foreign children."[48] The Americanizing power of the play movement was not restricted to the young. Curtis claimed that the Chicago experience had shown that playground systems "Americanized grown immigrants more effectively than any other agency."[49] Leaders of the play movement believed that immigrants in urban slums threatened American unity.

Concern for community highlighted the address of the governor of New Jersey, Woodrow Wilson, to the first National Conference on Social Centers held in Madison on October 25, 1911. Wilson argued that the social center movement could organize citizenship and fulfill a valuable function in society if it would bring the disparate parts of society together and forge a community. Wilson defined community as "a body of men who have things in common, who are conscious that they have things in common, who judge these common things from a single point of view, namely, the point of view of the general interest."[50] The governor reflected a widespread fear that the divergent interests, customs, tongues, and races within the American population would loose a whirlwind of social strife culminating in an anarchic, revolutionary upheaval.

An important function of the play movement was to promote the stability of the social order. Diminished class conflict was necessary to quell social unrest. Here, again, the leaders of the play movement praised its effectiveness. In his 1907 discussion of the social value of playgrounds, Lawrence Veiller asked his readers "to consider the value of the playground in reducing class antagonisms, which exist very strongly in this country, not withstanding our boast of democracy."[51] As

---

48. *New York Annual Report*, 1903 p. 161; and *New York Annual Report*, 1906, p. 359; see also *New York Annual Report*, pp. 370, 905; and *New York Annual Report*, 1910, pp. 432, 480.

49. Curtis, *Play Movement*, p. 323.

50. Woodrow Wilson, "The Need of Citizenship Organization," reprinted in *The American City*, 5 (November 1911): 266.

51. Lawrence Veiller, "The Social Value of Playgrounds in Crowded Districts," *Proceedings of the Playground Association of America*, 1907, 1:39.

if in answer to Veiller's request, five years later J. P. Garber wrote: "One of the strongest justifications for providing playgrounds and amusement centers at public expense lies in the possibility they open up for the cooperative play that trains away from the selfish individualistic bent which is the source of so much social unrest."[52] District superintendent of the New York Department of Education, Seth T. Stewart, was even more positive that the play movement had tempered social unrest and radical discontent: "Tompkins Park illustrates the difference made by a play center. The rally to the red flag years ago always occurred here, and thence rioters marched with anarchy in their train, but now this park is often the scene of games by boys and girls in flag drills and other forms of patriotic play." He concluded, "Through these broadening lines of educational work the school system is becoming more and more a social laboratory for the adjustment of the young citizen to his environment, to the end that the city itself may become the city beautiful and the citizen, sturdier in the rational enjoyment of life and happier in his loyalty to the government."[53] Few leaders of the play movement drew the doomsday potential more clearly than Henry Curtis when he prophesied, "We are sitting on the lid of an industrial volcano, that might in almost any decade rend our commercial world asunder and bring forth destructive strikes, anarchy or French Revolutions." Curtis believed that these volatile conditions were the result of the unsatisfying life which so many urban workers faced. The solution was, of course, more playgrounds. "Doubtless a playground that can furnish safety and exercise and health and fun to the children, and a family resort in the evening, can do much to improve conditions and quiet discontent. Perhaps the capitalists could afford to maintain the playgrounds for this reason alone."[54] In its fight to reduce class antagonisms, quell anarchist riots, check destructive strikes, insure adjustment of the young to their environment, and instill an eager loyalty to the government, the play movement developed many interesting educational devices.

Early in the movement, proponents believed that the salvation of slum dweller depended upon the removal of the evil influences of the street. Henry Curtis echoed the popular analysis when he stated, "At first the idea was simply to keep the children off the street and keep

52. Garber, *Current Educational Activities*, p. 68.

53. Seth T. Stewart, "Recreation Centers in the City of New York," *Proceedings of the Playground Association of America*, 1907, 1: 40–42.

54. Curtis, *Play Movement*, p. 316.

them occupied, a merely negative aim."[55] Soon, however, the play movement learned, as Walter Wood pointed out, "Four or five years' work had driven home one fact, namely, that a space in which to play does not make a playground."[56] Cincinnati's superintendent said that his vacation schools were not meant "to prolong the routine of school work," but to "counteract evil influences and develop habits of neatness, order, industry and obedience."[57] Superintendent Randall Condon, like most of the leaders of the play movement, had recognized a distinction between negative, or preventive, and positive approaches. It was often argued that evil influences could not be suppressed successfully unless one's attempts were accompanied by a positive promotion of wholesome play.[58]

The heart of the effort consisted of instilling habits of cooperation, loyalty, self-control, and teamwork. "Team games of the playground require the submission of the individual will to the welfare of the team" declared Otto T. Malley in expressing the conventional wisdom of the movement.[59] There was no dissent from the dictum that the most effective activity was group activity and the best games were team games. Luther Gulick believed that team play was essential for democracy because it taught children "that the social unit is larger than the individual unit, that the individual victory is not as sweet as the victory of the team, and that the most perfect self-realization is won by the most perfect sinking of one's self in the welfare of the larger unit—the team."[60] The association's second president concurred with and extended Gulick's analysis of the value of team play. Joseph Lee asserted that group games trained a boy in "the habitual experience of losing the sense of his own individuality in that of a larger whole; experiencing citizenship, not learning about it." The boy so engaged would learn by doing. Lee further contended that the loss of self in a common purpose actually led to self-fulfillment.[61] The ability to sacrifice individuality in a

---

55. Curtis, "Vacation Schools," p. 5.

56. Wood, *Playground Movement*, p. 6.

57. *Cincinnati Annual Report*, 1907, p. 68.

58. See Wilber Bowen, "The Moral Value of Play," *Western Journal of Education* 5 (September 1912): 309–15; Davis, *Exploitation of Pleasure*; and *Report of the Committee on a Normal Course in Play*, p. 177.

59. Otto T. Malley "The Social Significance of Play," *The Annals of the American Academy of Political and Social Science* 35 (January–June 1910): 372.

60. Luther Gulick, "Play and Democracy," *Proceedings of the Playground Association of America*, 1907, 1:11.

61. Lee, *Play and Playgrounds*, p. 27.

group enterprise was, according to Lee, essential for life in modern America.[62] In his address to the fifth annual meeting of the association in 1911, Lee made explicit the relationship between group or team play and social stability. Most work in modern society, he pointed out, was conducted by members of production groups. The adult worker must be adept, Lee said, "in holding down the part assigned to [him] in the economy of the social whole to which [he] may belong, as the boy in the school team holds down third base."[63] Team experience during youth trained the worker to hold down his assigned role in the industrial workplace.

Lee hoped to develop men who had learned to submerge their individual wills in those of a larger social group. He embraced the new social psychology that viewed the individual as an extension of his social group and the good citizen as a well-adjusted group member who contributed his share to group enterprises and who conformed to group values. Lee's interest in the efficiency of factory workers illustrates his belief that play developed good group members and hence, by his standard, good citizens. These traits incidentally, coincided with the needs of industrial capitalism. Other leaders of the play movement concerned themselves explicitly with increasing the efficiency of industrial workers through play and recreation.

Industrial conflict between workers demanding higher wages and employers responding that competitive conditions made raises impossible, arose, according to Howard S. Braucher, from the fact that "many workers at present are not worth the meager wages they receive. They must be made more efficient." Once they became efficient through the use of properly organized play, they would, Braucher assured them, be rewarded with increased paychecks. A new era was about to begin, he believed. "Society as a whole is only beginning to appreciate the increase in industrial efficiency which will come when the industrial value of play is recognized."[64] The field secretary of the Playground and Recreation Association, L. H. Weir, informed the forty-ninth annual meeting of the National Education Association that the recreation movement had grown, at least in part, because "thinking people" realized that by providing recreation "they are making workers more efficient, so

---

62. See, for example, Lee, "Play as a School of the Citizen," *Proceedings of the Playground Association of America,* 1907, 1:19.

63. Lee, *Play as an Antidote to Civilization,* pamphlet (Playground and Recreation Association of America, 1911), p. 15.

64. Braucher, "Play and Social Progress," p. 330.

that factory work and industrial work in our modern society will be better done because the workers will be more alive and better fitted for their tasks."[65] A 1920 article in *The Playground* demonstrated that the Carnegie Steel Company, although it had ignored the subtleties of Lee's argument, had captured the essential relationship between play and efficiency that Braucher and Weir had drawn. The article attributed to the company's recreation programs "a noticeable change in the physical alertness of employees"; the development of "a better spirit of true sportsmanship"; and "a closer welding of the heterogeneous groups of employees, together with a closer and more friendly relationship between workers, foremen, and superintendents." The end result of these changes, the article observed, was that "A stronger feeling of loyalty on the part of the employees now exists in the plants where recreation is fostered, which has developed efficiency and the spirit to pull together. Efficiency and the spirit to pull together are essential factors in the success of our industry."[66]

An interesting dimension of employee efficiency related to the selection and placement of potential workers. Again, the play movement was ready to accept responsibility. An important function of the vacation school was to acquaint students with the variety of jobs in the industrial economy, provide them with elementary training, and inculcate the appropriate attitudes and habits for an efficient worker. Henry Curtis noted that in addition to keeping children off the streets, the vacation school was designed to replace the disappearing apprenticeship allegedly characteristic of rural childhood. The urban child could not learn from "chores" or by following his father around the farm, so the vacation school attempted to fill the void. In 1902, the New York City director of vacation schools, Evangeline Whitney, indicated that one primary purpose of the summer programs was to help the children discover their industrial aptitudes.[67]

The vocational intent of these vacation schools is also suggested by their curriculum. Curtis was impressed with the fact that a visitor to the New York City vacation schools would have "heard no recitations" and "with the exception of the Bible" would have seen no books.[68] An

---

65. L. H. Weir, "Playground Movement in America," *NEA Addresses and Proceedings*, 1911, p. 927.

66. "Industrial Recreation," *The Playground* 14 (November 1920): 478.

67. *New York Annual Report*, 1902, p. 156; and *New York Annual Report*, 1903, p. 177.

68. Curtis, "Vacation Schools," p. 25.

examination of the curriculum in New York, Cincinnati, and Chicago reveals that all of the courses were distinctly vocational in character. Millinery, sewing, cooking, domestic science, iron working, mechanical arts, wood working, kindergarten, and nature study were the typical fare.[69]

Only after school officials became agitated over the inefficiency of the "laggards" who were repeating grades did educators introduce academic or "opportunity" classes. The main objective of these classes was to improve the efficiency rating of the schools by getting the slow students through a grade they had failed during the preceding year. This allowed the child to finish in the six-week summer session what otherwise might have cost the school system a whole semester or even a whole year. New York initiated its opportunity classes in 1913, Cincinnati began its academic classes in 1908, and Chicago started its academic review schools in 1916.[70] The primary thrust of the vacation school, however, remained nonacademic.

If one aspect of the industrial conflict was the issue of wages, another equally serious problem was the drudgery of labor. Industrial working conditions concerned many of the leaders of the play movement, who soon applied the principles learned in developing children's play programs to the problems of adult recreation, especially for industrial workers. Author and art critic Charles Mumford Robinson typically and accurately observed that for many industrial workers "life is a grind, a round of labor and a season of care." It was essential, he said, to "recreate" the laborer during his leisure hours to prepare him for tomorrow's work. Adult recreation thus provided a temporary respite from the dehumanizing conditions of the job.[71]

Hard work and long hours alone did not cause drudgery and job dissatisfaction. The problem was complex and involved elements of what modern social theorists call alienation. Of the play movement leaders, Jane Addams was perhaps most sensitive to this issue. She provided a brilliant analysis of the relation of recreation and industrial

69. See New York Annual Report, 1900, p. 70; New York Annual Report, 1903, pp. 63, 171–77; New York Annual Report, 1906, p. 353; Cincinnati Annual Report, 1907, p. 68; Cincinnati Annual Report, 1908, p. 67; Cincinnati Annual Report, 1909, p. 58; Chicago Annual Report, 1900, p. 243; and Chicago Annual Report, 1908, p. 279.

70. New York Annual Report, 1913, p. 134; Cincinnati Annual Report, 1908, p. 67; and Chicago Annual Report, 1916, pp. 13–14.

71. Charles Mumford Robinson, "Educational Value of Public Recreation Facilities," The Annals of the American Academy of Political and Social Science 35 (January – June 1910): 350; see also Curtis, Play Movement, p. 91.

alienation in her article "Public Recreation and Social Morality." Addams believed that modern industrial life imposed unnatural conditions on the worker because "when he comes to town it is his chief business not to conquer his environment, but to subordinate himself to it, to fit his activities to the conditions in which he finds himself—to obey the foreman in his factory, to manipulate prepared material which is placed in his hands." The industrial worker's duty "is no longer to subdue nature but to subordinate himself to man." This being the case, Addams asked, "What can be done to aid him in this process and to relieve it of its dullness and difficulty, to mitigate its strain and harshness?" The answer, predictably, was adequate—and carefully selected—public recreation. The worker might dissipate himself in vice and illicit pleasure unless appropriate forms of recreation were available to refine his natural impulses and channel his leisure energies into morally and socially uplifting activity.[72]

Many leaders of the play movement valued this recreative function of leisure activity because they believed it would produce happy and contented citizens able to withstand the drudgery of the factory. They saw that the specialization of labor resulting from industrial progress forced large numbers of men and women to earn their sustenance in confining and dehumanizing jobs. Boredom was an inescapable part of most jobs in corporate industry, but movement leaders hoped to mitigate some of the resulting pain and alienation with uplifting play and recreation.

Few dissented from the New York City school superintendent's opinion that "the success of the vacation schools and playgrounds depends chiefly upon the character of the teachers and conductors employed."[73] Emphasizing the point, Howard Braucher declared, "Without such a leader, a playground having most costly equipment may be a positive menace to the neighborhood. With the right leader, the smallest space may be a children's paradise."[74] Undoubtedly, one reason for emphasis upon supervision was the protection of the youngsters from neighborhood bullies and thugs who might take over an unprotected playground. Another, and more important, reason was the belief that the lower classes in general and the immigrants in particular

---

72. Jane Addams, "Public Recreation and Social Morality," *Proceedings of the Playground Association of America*, 1907, 1:22–24.

73. *New York Annual Report*, 1902, p. 65.

74. Braucher, "Play and Social Progress," p. 332.

needed guidance if they were to become functioning parts of America's corporate industry.

The playground leader, according to Mrs. Amalie Hofer Jerome, one of the founders of the Playground Association of America, had the opportunity not only to observe the development of human nature in the child, but "to direct this nature up into the forms most acceptable to society as a whole."[75] One strategy for this direction was suggested by Evangeline Whitney: "It requires much adroitness to enforce rules for cleanliness, courtesy, and good behavior, and at the same time let such freedom prevail that children are unconscious of being controlled."[76] While Whitney's comment reflected the spirit of progressive education, William Bagley, professor of education at the University of Illinois, argued for a more direct approach. After insisting that playgrounds must have adult supervision, he said, "It is because the playground, with its fascinating privileges which can be denied to recalcitrants, affords conditions which make rigor necessary and correction easy, it is for this reason, I believe, that the playground is so potent a factor in social education from the point of view of inculcating a respect for law and authority."[77] Undoubtedly, both techniques were effective in reforming the character of the lower classes.

Efforts to impose "refined" standards on music and dancing in the public playgrounds exemplified the paternalistic nature of reform in the play movement. Playground officials in both New York City and Rochester, New York, reported apparently successful attempts to gradually replace ragtime with music that appealed to more refined tastes.[78] The question of dancing, though, was more complex because many devout persons objected to any form of dancing. Michael Davis warned that the young demanded the opportunity to dance and would look to the commercial dance halls if alternatives were not provided.[79] With a typical progressive response, the pragmatic decision was made. If dancing were inevitable, then it must be channeled in acceptable outlets and forms. By 1913, dancing classes were regularly offered in New York's

---

75. Amalie Hofer Jerome, "The Playground as a Social Center," *The Annals of the American Academy of Political and Social Science* 35 (January–June 1910): 349.

76. *New York Annual Report*, 1906, p. 359.

77. William Bagley, "Do High Schools Need Reconstruction," *Religious Education* 8 (June 1913): 179.

78. *New York Annual Report*, 1903, p. 185; and Robinson, "Educational Value of Public Recreation Facilities," p. 354.

79. Davis, *Exploitation of Pleasure*, pp. 46–50.

social centers. District superintendent Edward W. Stitt was pleased because most observers agreed that the classes were "the strongest weapon with which to oppose the evils of the public [i.e., commercial] dance halls." He noted that the classes had significantly reduced "objectionable dancing typified by the Turkey-trot, Grizzly Bear, and Tango" while inculcating the social graces of polite society.[80] Clearly, much of the impetus for the play movement was an effort to uplift and guide the underprivileged. The leaders of the movement generally assumed that thay knew what standards, attitudes, and habits were appropriate for their clientele.

COMMUNITY CENTERS AND SELF-GOVERNMENT

Community centers, which evolved from social centers, were heralded as a beginning of democratic participation. The crucial difference between these agencies and their predecessors was the community center's claim to be self-supporting and self-governing.[81] The most important development of the community center ideal was documented in Eugene C. Gibney's report to the New York superintendent of schools in 1918.[82] Gibney had been trained in Luther Gulick's New York Training School for Community Workers and was subsequently appointed assistant director for vacation schools, playgrounds, and recreation and community centers in the New York City school system. Although his 1918 report was viewed an an exposition of the ideal of self-government, it characterized the mission of the community center in rather unusual terms:

> The Community Center has inherited the responsibility of the school for the civic solidarity of the nation. We have no right to use the Temples of Democracy unless we imbue the people with the creed of inspired patriotism. It is not enough to teach the young man to serve his country—he must be made to feel that he is his country, utters the voice of his country, pulses with its heart, vibrates with its aims and is inspired with its ideals. The Community Center has the special mission of transmitting corporate thought and feeling from one individual to another. It is the service of the

---

80. *New York Annual Report*, 1913, p. 28.
81. Rainwater, *Play Movement*, pp. 135–78.
82. *New York Annual Report*, 1918, pp. 9–78.

Centers that should robe the invisible body of the state, make it actual and instill an abiding faith in its reality.[83]

Gibney's description of the structure of self-government in the community is even more curious than his vision of the self-governing center's mission. Early in the evolution of each center, community groups were to draw up a governing charter. This Gibney likened to a license to operate granted by the board of education. He judiciously called it a means of "indirect control."[84] While the board could not force all centers to accept a uniform charter, it did not allow them to veer sharply from accepted standards. Gibney's wording on this point is instructive:

> If we leave neighborhood groups to blunder out their own kinds of charters we leave them free to entangle themselves so much that the real work becomes impossible. The community center must be a device for accomplishing things. It brings together groups of people. It raises and spends money. It carries out the purpose of development of the Board of Education in community work.[85]

There remains little doubt that if these representatives of immigrant and working class neighborhoods had been allowed to hammer out their own purposes that the process would have been evaluated as inefficient by men like Assistant Director Gibney. The appellation of self-governing or democratic seems somewhat of a misnomer for a group whose expressed objective is to carry out the purpose of another external authority. One cannot help but recall Plato's famous definition of the slave as one whose actions do not carry out his own ideas.

Nevertheless, Gibney continued his description of democracy with a list of six charter principles which clearly undermined the principle of self-government. Item four granted representation to all welfare, municipal, and federal agencies that cooperated with the center. Departments of the board of education and the city having contact with the center were also given a voice and a vote in the self-governing board. Although "the executive worker or leader should be nominated by the local organization," this leader "may be impeached by the Board of

83. *New York Annual Report,* 1918, pp. 18–19.
84. *New York Annual Report,* 1918, p. 42.
85. *New York Annual Report,* 1918, pp. 42, 43, 66, 74.

Education." The center had only limited power to amend its charter, and local control of the budget was "subject to the veto of the Board of Education." According to Gibney, this set of charter principles allowed the board to exercise "indirect control." Actually, the emphasis was on control. The board considered the charter a bond between itself and the people. Thus, at its pleasure the board might conclude that the self-governing center was not representative of the people. Its charter "may be revoked and the enfranchised group disbanded if the Community Center Committee does not prove competent." As Gibney observed, "self-government like self-support can not be absolute."[86]

The paternalistic approach displayed by Gibney and implicit throughout the play movement suggests a rather strange conception of autonomy, one echoed as well by the associate superintendent of public schools of Philadelphia in 1912:

> As in a democracy the people will have the amusements they want, two things are exceedingly important: first, that the people be represented in their desires by men with enlightened consciences; and second, that the people themselves be constantly educated into an enlightened condition which will make them desire the right things.[87]

The play movement, which grew from a few piles of sand in a Boston churchyard to a nationwide phenomenon by the end of World War I, began as a philanthropic effort. Like many of the other social reforms of the Progressive Era, it was an attempt by the more fortunate to bring happiness and order into what they perceived as the chaotic and dreary world of the lower classes. It was also an attempt to protect the social order by uplifting the masses, and indoctrinating them with appropriate attitudes and habits for the industrial workplace. In an important sense the play movement was one aspect of the "search for order" which permeated this era. Play and recreational facilities were the instruments of order, the play leaders were the orderers, and the lower-class children and adults were the material to be ordered. The effort, of course, was conducted in the name of democracy and for the good of those ordered.

---

86. *New York Annual Report*, 1918, p. 74.
87. Garber, *Current Educational Activities*, p. 57.

Chapter 5

Student Activities

Playgrounds and the play movement represented but one means to secure good citizenship. Similar endeavors surfaced in the new student activities movement, often referred to as extracurricular activities. It reflected the growing recognition that the most effective way to obtain social conformity and self-discipline was to train the emotions rather than the intellect. In retrospect, these efforts clearly consisted of what Jacques Ellul has since termed pre-propaganda: subtly preparing the individual's psyche to become a willing receptor of direct, active propaganda that will subsequently influence his actions.[1] These efforts were an important part of the acculturation process that attacked the preindustrial and polyglot value systems of immigrants and rural migrants and created the unified value structures required for an urban-industrial society. The essential methodology was capsulized in what became an important slogan for progressive education — "Learn by doing rather than by precept." "Doing" would implant attitudes and habits of good citizenship, but it was essential, of course, that it be directed by teachers and school authorities who understood which attitudes and habits were correct.

EXTRACURRICULAR ACTIVITIES AS A VEHICLE OF CIVIC EDUCATION

Characteristic of the often-discussed shift to nonintellectual sources of social control was a 1911 report of a NEA committee on moral education. The report advised teachers to train their students to practice

---

1. Jacques Ellul, *Propaganda* (New York: Vintage Books, 1973), pp. 15, 22, 30–32, 296, 300.

virtues "until they become fixed habits."[2] Such sentiments were found at the local school level as well as at national conventions of educators. Chicago district superintendents Harvey Cox and Edward Rositer, reviewing the 1914 Chicago school survey, noted with pride the "long list of activities" that had been "inaugurated and directed with the special purpose of encouraging initiative, teamwork, and loyalty." Activities such as student government and clubs were particularly useful in elementary schools, they argued, because children were most impressionable and hence most easily molded to correct habits during their early school years.[3] Two years later, the survey team examining the San Francisco schools similarly recognized the importance of such habit formation: "Civic education is as much a matter of habit formation as of instruction. Activity thus becomes not only the end, but also an essential means, of civic education."[4] Their report then recommended an expansion of the existing extracurricular activities as a vehicle of civic education.

By the late twenties, extracurricular activities had become an accepted part of the school program, and numerous books and articles were written describing their operation. One of the prominent leaders of the extracurricular movement, Elbert K. Fratwell, maintained that it was the school's responsibility to give children "the desire, the drive, and the ability" to become good citizens. He urged educators to use the whole school milieu, including extracurricular activities, to develop the character traits and habits which were necessary to attain this objective.[5] Some proponents claimed that these activities held special intrinsic value. L. V. Koos, for example, analyzed 40 articles devoted to these activities and found that the authors attributed several social advantages to them. Thirty-seven authors cited "training in some civic-social-moral relationship" as a value of extracurricular activities; while over half of the 40 also offered "socialization," "training for social cooperation," "training for citizenship in a democracy," "training for leadership," and

---

2. "Tentative Report of the Committee on a System of Teaching Morals in Public Schools," *NEA Addresses and Proceedings*, 1911, p. 343; see also Gilbert N. Bink, "School Publications, Literary and Music Organizations, Dramatics," *NEA Addresses and Proceedings*, 1911, p. 338.

3. *Chicago Annual Report*, 1915, p. 63.

4. "The Public Schools of San Francisco," *Bulletin of the U.S. Bureau of Education*, 1917, no. 46, p. 301.

5. Elbert K. Fretwell, foreword to *Extracurricular Activities in Junior and Senior High Schools*, by Joseph Roemer and Charles Forrest Allen (Boston: D.C. Heath, 1926), p. v.

"improved discipline and improved school spirit," as intended out-comes.[6] This belief that such activities would develop qualities of good citizenship was echoed by a junior high school teacher who contended that "through carefully directed activities a student is definitely trained to have respect for authority, for government, and for the rights of the individual and the community."[7]

The activities were appreciated by educators because they allowed school authorities to structure situations in which students would act out the desired responses until the responses became habits. When confronted with similar situations in adult life, the students would not be prey to the vicissitudes of their own intellectual processes, for they would be equipped with proper habits "learned by doing" in their earlier school experiences.

The belief that extracurricular activities could shape children's emotions and habits to make them tractable industrial workers was expressed often by educators during the early years of this century. Kansas City Junior College instructor Ruth Weeks, addressing the National Society for the Promotion of Industrial Education at its 1920 annual convention in Chicago, claimed that under present industrial and world conditions it was imperative "to keep the industrial machinery lubricated and running without friction." The major abrasive, she believed, was that "in spite of generous wages, labor is refusing to produce." She found a cure for this unrest not in teaching additional technical skills or more facts, but "in giving the child a social point of view and social habits. We must train our children so that social behavior will be habitual, subconscious, involuntary, instinctive, and not merely the self-conscious, artificial, temporary result of a stimulating crisis. We must get the social reactions out of the brain into the medulla oblongata and the spinal ganglia." Weeks then suggested student activities such as football, student government, school plays and student newspapers as the most effective way of moving these reactions from the brain to the spinal ganglia. She argued, "What is principally the matter with America is that our last generation of students are now cutting their social eye teeth on industry at an advanced and unteachable age instead of having done it long ago in the inexpensive teething ring of student activities." If

---

6. Cited in Elbert K. Fretwell, *Extracurricular Activities in Secondary Schools* (Boston: Houghton Mifflin, 1931), pp. 10–11.

7. Mary A. Sheehan, *Extracurricular Activities in a Junior High School* (Boston: Gorham Press, 1927), p. 14.

properly trained in student activities, she contended, youth would reject Bolshevism and become more obedient. For any delegates who might have missed her point, Weeks bluntly recapitulated:

> You are probably saying to yourselves "I thought you were going to talk about the present labor crisis, and here you are discussing football." So I am! But football and all it stands for is so closely related to the labor crisis, for it is through such activities, self-directed wherever possible, that the student acquires the habits necessary for social living, the qualities of social mindedness and cooperation which alone can bring human nature abreast of modern institutions.[8]

Weeks's suggestions seemed to draw heavily upon the notion of conditioned reflex. Although many other proposals were similarly grounded, American educators did not rely on this theory alone. A more common theoretical basis for student activities was the newly developing social psychology.

This reliance on social psychology appeared, for example, in the work of Phillip W. L. Cox. In arguing for "creative" school control through social activities Cox maintained that "the things boys and girls do are the things they learn." Therefore, the schools should seize the opportunities afforded by social activities to shape each student in accord with social requirements. Since the social self controls the behavior of each individual, it was the school's task to identify the social self with healthy "habits, attitudes, and impulses" for the child. Cox openly admitted the manipulation involved in this form of educational enterprise: "Doubtless, youth even at high school age are still very impressionable to indoctrination; they can, therefore, be trained to solve social problems by being drilled in correct responses to specific social situations." He was not overly concerned with this prospect because he felt certain that indoctrination would encourage those "beliefs, habits, and attitudes as all intelligent, educated men substantively agree upon."[9]

Notwithstanding minor disagreements among the supporters of such activities, Cox was correct. Most experts did agree on the broad outline of the personality type they contrived to reproduce in their

---

8. Ruth Mary Weeks, "The Educator," *Bulletin of the National Society for the Promotion of Industrial Education*, 1920, no. 32, pp. 18–22. I am indebted to David Hogan for bringing this source to my attention.

9. P. W. L. Cox, *Creative School Control* (Philadelphia: J. B. Lippincott, 1927), pp. vii, 253, 254.

students. This outline included habits and traits which would make future citizens orderly, loyal, dependable, selfless, cooperative, lawful, reasonably predictable, and, above all, self-controlled. These characteristics would subordinate the self to society and to the industrial workplace. The individual who could stand alone was not only outdated but also a menace to himself and the community. The modern American must be a team player. Edward Rynearson expressed this sentiment when he argued that out-of-class associations should lead children to realize that "each star must be a part of a constellation. The chorus spirit must govern the soloist."[10] The 1915 report of the Chicago superintendent of schools repeated this emphasis on chorus or group spirit:

> In a good school the school spirit is good; pupils respect each other and honor and admire their teachers; school impressions dominate their waking hours; happiness and joy prevail among them—an essential condition for the simultaneous, healthful development of body and mind. From school loyalty to patriotism the step is easy and natural; opportunities for encouraging it are abundant.[11]

The report went on to say that "all the activities that make for social efficiency—intelligent self-guidance and respect for law learned through the exercise of authority of pupils over pupils; team play bringing out one's best efforts while requiring self-control and self-repression—are forceful agencies for moral education."[12] The San Francisco school survey also stressed the utility of out-of-class activities for molding character and generating useful school spirit.[13] Shortly after the turn of the century, these sentiments reached the grass roots level of local administrators and classroom teachers. Paul

---

10. Edward Rynearson, "Do the High Schools Need Reconstruction for Social Ends?" *Religious Education* 8 (June 1913): 189.

11. *Chicago Annual Report*, 1915, p. 64.

12. *Chicago Annual Report*, 1915, p. 65.

13. "Public Schools of San Francisco," p. 291. The impact of the numerous school surveys upon the development of American education during the early decades of the twentieth century has yet to be adequately assessed. Such an assessment will undoubtedly examine the nature of the interlocking directory of personnel that conducted many of the surveys, the sources of support for the surveys, and similarity of the surveys' recommendations for a wide variety of school systems. It is probable that the school survey was an effective device for enforcing a surprising uniformity of educational programs and methodologies over what, in theory at least, seemed a highly localized political structure of governance.

G. W. Keller, a Wisconsin school principal, thought that schools should be concerned more with "heart training" than "mind training" because the former had a greater impact on behavior. Effective emotional conditioning, he argued, demanded that schools occupy much of the students' leisure time with extracurricular activities to stimulate self-sacrifice for the social group or the larger community.[14] Since the modern industrial laborer was usually part of a production group, his efforts formed only a fraction of the total production process. Hence, Keller and other champions of extracurricular activity realized that the student had to be trained as a self-sacrificing team player infused with group spirit. The self-assertative individualist imbued with soloist impulses was an anachronism; so schools were redesigned to minimize the chances of children developing such dysfunctional traits.

The nonintellectual determinants of behavior were an important element in the methodological framework within which this training could be effected. As early as 1907, Henry Suzzallo informed the NEA that, "in the schools' business of making men and women who will be sane and wholesome, responsive and vigorous, it is clear that the directions of control must not be restricted to the intellectual but must include the emotional as well."[15] During the following years, many educators including J. W. Carr, Franklin S. Lamar, and teachers conducting the Chicago self-survey, held that nonintellectual training imparted by public schools was more important for social stability than the intellectual training which had been the principal fare of schools in the previous century.[16] It was considered more important to do the good than to know the good; thus most innovations involved the student in activity rather than in learning concepts.

In part, this method followed the emerging concepts of social psychology, especially its emphasis on the importance of the social group in the formation of the social self. Expressing a common belief, Ellwood Cubberley said:

---

14. Paul G. W. Keller "Open School Organizations," *School Review* 13 (1905): 10–13.

15. Henry Suzzallo, "The Training of the Child's Emotional Life," *NEA Addresses and Proceedings*, 1907, p. 908.

16. See J. W. Carr, "The Treatment of Pupils," *NEA Addresses and Proceedings*, 1908, p. 452; Franklin S. Lamar, "Extracurricular Activities, " in *Readings in Extracurricular Activities*, Joseph Roemer and Charles Forrest Allen (Richmond: Johnson, 1929), p. 40; and *Chicago Annual Report*, 1914, pp. 177, 182.

The rule of the group tends to become the rule for the adolescent. To stimulate and repress and to guide and direct these adolescent tendencies is both the opportunity and the mission of the teacher. The so-called extracurricular activities. . .offer the school the most useful tool for that adaptive, directive, and corrective training of youth which it is now conceived to be the function of the school to provide.[17]

The Chicago self-survey affirmed Cubberley's view of the power of peer group pressure in its assertion that effective student self-discipline came "entirely through the influence of public opinion and the attempt on the part of the commissioners and deputies to impress upon others the fact that the school community is in opposition to anything that brings discredit upon the school body or upon an individual. Those who have handled young people know how powerful an influence this is."[18] Educators also knew that because peer influence could engender undesirable behavior, this force needed to be properly controlled and channeled.

Educators, well aware of the necessity to direct student activities toward the outcomes desired by adult authorities, frequently expressed their preference for the subtle methods of indirect manipulation over the older forms of coercion. An address before the NEA in 1910, describing the social organizations in Brooklyn's Erasmus High School, noted that the principal "believes that he has a much more intimate and personal control over the hundreds under his charge, through and by means of these organizations, than he could possibly have without them."[19] The following year, Rufus C. Bentley informed the same organization that "sharing in the control of extracurricular activities lays the foundations for adult controls. Outside activities guarantee to pupils a share in the school's control. Share in control reduces one's need for control."[20] Student participation in the governance of their activities would, it was believed, provide the opportunity for peer-group pressure to bend the psyche of the recalcitrant child. Of course, students were not to have meaningful control of these activities. Joseph Roemer and Charles Allen pointed out in their influential work, *Extracurricular Activities in Junior and Senior High*

---

17. Fretwell, *Extracurricular Activities in Secondary Schools*, p. vii.

18. *Chicago Annual Report*, 1914, pp. 178–79.

19. William R. Lasher, "School Activities as an Educational Factor in Secondary Schools," *NEA Addresses and Proceedings*, 1910, p. 448.

20. Rufus C. Bentley, "Extracurricular Activities in High School," *NEA Addresses and Proceedings*, 1911, p. 587.

Schools, that once mechanisms were developed to keep students from dominating student government, "the dangers feared by many became less hazardous to those in authority, and the new idea spread rapidly." They believed that "experience has shown that pupils may well be given a voice in 'pupil participation' in school control wherein the final authority shall remain vested in properly constituted and legal authority."[21] The tactic was to give students enough participation in the process to capture their loyalty without giving them real authority.

Franklin Lamar even suggested that "these activities should be carefully organized with the end in view of their efficiency in disciplinary training. No public school can afford to neglect them. The sponsors should be deeply concerned with behavior, and they should so unobtrusively direct the activities that the pupils forget that they are being directed." With no sense of irony, he solemnly added, "Democratic principles must prevail at all times."[22] Lamar illustrated consequences of such training by remarking that a member of a school sports team could "instantly" quiet thousands of cheering students by simply raising his hand for silence. "The training that is able to accomplish such social control is vastly worthwhile, he declared, for it is the kind that will endure throughout life."[23] American educators at the turn of the century began to appreciate the enormous potential for psychological manipulation of individuals in a mass or crowd. The remainder of this chapter will examine how these efforts to develop social control through nonintellectual training evolved in such extracurricular activities as school assemblies, music, athletics, clubs, student government, school gardens, school banks, and lunch programs.

THE SCHOOL ASSEMBLY

Keeping in mind America's tradition of religious revivalism and its penchant for political rallies, it is not surprising that educators, committed to emotional training, would sieze upon the concept of mass

---

21. Roemer and Allen, *Extracurricular Activities in Junior and Senior High Schools*, pp. 76–77.

22. Lamar, "Extracurricular Activities," p. 44.

23. Lamar, "Extracurricular Activities," p. 46.

assembly. The school assembly developed in the later decades of the nineteenth century, and by the turn of the century the Cincinnati superintendent of schools conceded that "no school building constructed on modern lines is complete unless provided with a hall large enough to seat all or nearly all of the entire enrollment of the school."[24] In the ensuing years, most cities either equipped new schools with assembly halls or added them to existing schools.[25] By 1915, 77 percent of all Chicago schools had been equipped with assembly halls.[26] In his 1935 study of extracurricular activities, Galen Jones reported, "It is difficult to conceive of a secondary school principal who is opposed to the unifying, interesting, instructive, and inspiring contributions which the modern high school assembly makes possible for the school." Only 3 of the 250 principals responding to his survey were opposed to the assembly.[27]

During the first three decades of this century, nearly all accounts agreed that the school assembly should be "the spiritual center of the school" where children could be trained to live and work together. The emphasis was usually on the value of emotional training gained in mass gathering.[28] Assemblies taught students to feel that certain kinds of situations were beautiful and noble and true. They were led to feel that a community of interest connected them with the rest of society, that what was good for society was also good for them.

Such mass psychology was often reinforced with appropriate symbols like the American flag and pictures of national heroes. The presence of the flag, according to New York associate superintendent Thomas O'Brien, would "assure them [students] of its loving protection and remind them also of that community of interest which is the heritage of all children, no matter how humble their rank."[29] School authorities were probably right in thinking that the emotional conditioning in school assemblies would yield social stability. The working-class student who had been educated to reason instead of to feel might not

---

24. *Cincinnati Annual Report*, 1900, p. 10.

25. See *Chicago Annual Report*, 1904, p. 18; and *Chicago Annual Report*, 1915, p. 14.

26. *Chicago Annual Report*, 1915, p. 135.

27. Galen Jones, *Extracurricular Activities and Their Relation to the Curriculum* (New York: Teachers College, 1935), p. 66.

28. See *Chicago Annual Report*, 1915, p. 75; "Public Schools of San Francisco,"p. 180; and *New York Annual Report*, 1910, pp. 243–51.

29. *New York Annual Report*, 1910, pp. 243–51.

respond patriotically to a flag flying over a company of troops who were smashing a strike against one of the major corporate enterprises.

SCHOOL MUSIC

During the early decades of this century, American educators developed and widely publicized a series of concepts explaining the use of music for social education. They suggested that music, which could be injected easily into school assemblies, could condition the child to respond appropriately to given social situations by its special appeal to his emotions. Arnold J. Gantvoort struck a note that echoed through the era when he informed the annual meeting of the NEA in 1900 that music "addressed itself directly to the emotions and to the soul in a language understood only by the emotions and the soul."[30]

Along these lines, a 1910 description of the assembly programs at New York City's P.S. 165 noted that the effect of "mass rhythmic movement and choral singing" was heightened by the physical structure of the building which, allowed the reverberation of the martial tread of the boys to assist the robust music of a fife and drum corps in producing "an inspiring influence." Not every school was fortunate enough to have floor beams that reverberated the resonance of marching feet or to have a principal like Mr. Giddings of New York City's P.S. 165, whose militia background allowed him to coordinate the marching with a fife and drum corps. It was suggested, though, that similar effects could be attained if the school pianist played a variety of spirited march music to accompany the entrance march of the assembled student body. The 1914 annual report of the Chicago Board of Education noted with pleasure that through its school music program "the children were obtaining an emotional education of great value. The power of music to unite the varying elements in the school in a common purpose, to arouse the emotions, and to inspire to greater effort, makes the chorus singing one of the most powerful means of Americanizing the various nationalities, and making all of the children citizens of a greater republic."[31] In a 1921 study conducted for the U.S. Bureau of Education, Osbourne

---

30. Arnold J. Gantvoort, "The Influence of Music Upon National Life," *NEA Addresses and Proceedings*, 1900, p. 148.

31. *Chicago Annual Report*, 1914, p. 189.

McConathy found that of the 359 secondary schools reporting, 322 conducted assembly singing.[32]

The belief that such emotional training would yield dividends in social education rested upon a complex of constructs somewhat similar to those that guided the play movement. Recapitulation theories were basic to both. G. Stanley Hall, addressing the NEA meeting in 1908, characterized music as "the speech of the antique, half-buried racial soul." He argued that each song "should have a moral and aesthetic justification" and should be carefully considered before admission into the school canon. Only then, he believed, would music take its rightful place in the curriculum "as a trainer of the emotions."[33] It was essential to structure the emotional sources of adult actions while the child was in the embryonic stages of human development. In basing their justifications of school music programs upon Hall's recapitulation theories, many music educators, including the renowned Arnold Gantvoort and Will Earhart, underscored the importance of the youthful years for emotional training.[34] San Francisco music educator Estelle Carpenter illustrated how this notion filtered down to the practitioner's level when she informed her colleagues that "emotions may be intensified and uplifted by the continuous use of the kind of music that will have the correct effect." If begun at an early age music training would, she counseled, have a lifetime effect on the students.[35]

The current conventional wisdom about the social value of emotional conditioning through music was embodied in the survey of the San Francisco's schools' music program: "The song is the body and in it all the members meet in intricate and perfectly balanced relation. Not only are all the members in the song, but it is there only that their meaning, their purpose, their mode of functioning can be described."[36] Clearly, this vision of the school chorus was in tune with the prevalent organic theories of society that assessed an individual's value mainly in terms of his contribution to and participation in the social order. It was

---

32. Osbourne McConathy, "Present Status of Music Instruction in Colleges and High Schools," *Bulletin of the U.S. Bureau of Education,* 1921, no. 9, p. 46.

33. G. Stanley Hall, "The Psychology of Music and the Light it Throws Upon Music Education," *NEA Addresses and Proceedings,* 1908, pp. 848–53.

34. See Arnold Gantvoort, "Influence of Music Upon National Life,"p. 146. See also "Public Schools of San Francisco," pp. 372–91.

35. Estelle Carpenter, "The Vitalizing of the Child Through Song, " *NEA Addresses and Proceedings,* 1907, pp. 858–60.

36. "Public Schools of San Francisco," p. 391.

also consonant with the needs of the emerging corporate structure of American society.

The chorus spirit reflected the function of school music to convert egotistic impulses into altruistic attachments. The chorus spirit showed each student that, although he was insignificant as an individual, his contribution to the singing group made him part of an important endeavor. "In the singing exercise the division is the unit," the Chicago superintendent reported in 1900. "The individual counts for nothing. A choir boy may have the voice of a seraph, but in school he is but one of a row of boys. Here it is all or nothing."[37] Music educators such as William L. Tomlins believed that music education could provide a new outlook and new values to suit the changing world. Life, Tomlins said, had "developed beyond community boundaries," and so it was essential for the individual's "inner life to evolve correspondingly." People were in a state of confusion because they were "out of harmony with life-at-large" and thus false to themselves. Tomlins's solution was to expand the "scope and breadth of the feelings to cosmic relations." This, he thought, could be accomplished only through music that directly affected the emotions and led to self-sacrifice, the foundation of the new social order.[38]

Closely tied to the concern for altruistic motives were ideals of school spirit, social solidarity, Americanism, and patriotism. Some educators saw a logical interconnection among these concepts in a fashion reminiscent of the notion of transfer of training that had characterized earlier school psychology, while others used these ideas and terms interchangeably. Few, however, challenged the assertion that school music implanted these qualities in the student body. Ida M. Fisher addressed the question of school spirit in a typical manner when she informed the 1911 NEA meeting that some mysterious force worked its unifying powers when school children sang together: "Through the singing of beautiful songs expressing thought common to all, the school becomes unified and the school spirit intensified. Loyalty to any school is strengthened by school spirit and anything that strengthens this spirit, which cultivates a love for one's alma mater, is worthy of our most careful and systematic consideration." Fisher considered symbolic ceremonies using mass singing, like May Day ceremonies, especially effec-

---

37. *Chicago Annual Report*, 1900. p. 227.

38. William L. Tomlins, "Music as a Moral Influence," *NEA Addresses and Proceedings*, 1909, p. 247.

tive in forging unifying bonds.[39] The school survey of Brookline, Massachusetts made a similar observation that singing developed both a "strong bond of sympathy" between teacher and pupil and a "true school spirit." The team remarked, "All can spontaneously and heartily co-operate in singing and when they do so, melody and harmony react to establish that school spirit which is so desirable in any school."[40]

The merging of school spirit, social solidarity, Americanism, and patriotism was a common feature of public school music programs such as, for example, those in San Francisco and Chicago. Earhart, in his survey of the San Francisco music program, noted that "national and state songs are kept in repertoire" and used "to develop patriotism." He specified that singing was an important method of Americanizing the city's large foreign population and for "unifying the spirit of the city's people." School singing did "not aim at or attain music values"; rather, its goal was "the elevation of the social spirit in the school and the development of fraternity of feeling."[41] During the 1907–1908 school year, Chicago music teachers compiled a 48-page booklet of "patriotic and folklore songs" to provide appropriate emotional training for the school children.[42] Ten years later, Chicago's supervisor of elementary music reported that the music program was successfully "arousing a great love of country."[43] The Chicago and San Francisco experience were duplicated in cities throughout the country.

Earhart, in a 1914 study titled "Music in the Public Schools," conducted for the U.S. Bureau of Education, found that chorus study was required in over 52 percent of the secondary schools reporting from the largest cities. He speculated that the requirement "is for the sake of that social solidarity so likely to be absent in our cosmopolitan centers; for this is not only highly desirable in school life, but on the school rests largely the responsibility of contributing it to the nation. Music is not the least agency in this endeavor."[44]

---

39. Ida Fisher, "The Relation of Music to School Activities," *NEA Addresses and Proceedings*, 1911, pp. 808–13.

40. *Educational Survey of the Public Schools of Brookline, Massachusetts* (Cambridge, Mass.: Murray and Emery, 1917), p. 295.

41. "Public Schools of San Francisco," pp. 384–85; see also Carpenter, "Vitalizing of the Child Through Song," p. 859.

42. *Chicago Annual Report*, 1908, p. 269.

43. *Chicago Annual Report*, 1918, p. 147; see also Gantvoort "Influence of Music upon National Life," pp. 150–51.

44. Will Earhart "Music in the Public Schools," *Bulletin of the U.S. Bureau of Education*, 1914, no. 33, p. 27.

Many educators maintained that school music would contribute to industrial efficiency and working-class acquiescence to the existing political economy. One side of this belief emphasized the escapist function of music: its purported ability to help workers forget or transcend their working conditions during leisure hours. P. P. Claxton, U.S. commissioner of education, defended music as one of the most practical school subjects for an industrial nation. "Music is necessary," he said, "not only for enjoyment and recreation, but for inspiration and for salvation from death in the din and dust of trade."[45] A second component of the belief pointed to music's ability to develop cooperation and self-sacrifice traits that would allow the worker to accept industrial working conditions and increase his productivity. Gantvoort insisted that "we simply *must* look to music to help us in this good work of providing soul-expansion for the masses," and music educators agreed that "when the genius of song crowns the gospel of work there will be fewer strikes, the grimy faces will be less haggard, the tense muscles will lose their rigidity: under the unconscious influence of beauty, harmony, and rhythm, labor will be more cheerfully, more faithfully performed."[46] If the grimy faces and tense muscles could be pacified by the "unconscious influence" of beauty, harmony, and rhythm, then indeed, music would prove an eminently practical school activity for an industrial nation.

Political acquiescence naturally accompanied industrial tranquility. E. W. Newton, of Ginn and Company's music division, felt that "America should become a musical nation." Reflecting the common tendency to view music as contributing to social stability, he qualified the concept "musical" to mean, "musical from the standpoint of the practical businessman, which means for the people enough music to act as an *emotional steadier*." According to Newton, the object of all education was to make good citizens, a task that required literacy and emotional training. Music answered this second demand and was thus considered "not only equal in value to other studies but distinctly superior in making citizens." Music and literacy were Newton's twin pillars of political quietude: "Present-day statistics bear me out in the statement that a singing people with illiteracy reduced to a minimum is the easiest to govern and the least liable to go off on a tangent through other

---

45. Earhart, "Music in the Public Schools," p. 5.

46. Gantvoort, "Influence of Music on National Life," pp. 151–52; see also William H. Critzer, "Chorus Work in High Schools," *Music Teachers National Association Papers and Proceedings of Its Thirtieth Annual Meeting*, 1908, pp. 185–86.

firebrand agitation." He optimistically concluded that Americans simply needed a bit more song to steady their emotions and congratulated music educators for "providing the conglomerate masses with an emotional steadier."[47]

The social and political utility of music as outlined by Gantvoort, Newton, and Commissioner Claxton may seem blunt, stark, and even callous. It is important, however, to recognize that their conclusions flowed logically from general theories about the values of music education. These principles stressed psychic reconstruction through emotional training in order to bring students into harmony with the school, the state, and society. The ideals of social solidarity embodied in the chorus spirit were not illogically extended to the configurations suggested by Gantvoort, Claxton, and Newton.

ATHLETICS

A deep chasm apparently separates the music room from the gymnasium and the athletic playing field, but closer examination of the early development of school athletics reveals that this subject, like music, was not considered intrinsically important. Both emerged because of their presumed contribution to the development of an emotional substructure conducive to good citizenship.

After a rather hesitant start at the turn of the century, athletic programs flourished in urban schools. These programs continued the work of the playground movement, responded to the same impulses, and often were directed by the same personnel. The Chicago schools formulated rules and administrative procedures for school athletics as early as 1904.[48] A year later, a committee of high school teachers in Cincinnati received replies from cities in 29 states to an inquiry regarding the advisability of high school athletics. According to the committee, "A large percent of the replies state that athletics, under the very careful supervision and direction of school authorities, may be one of the greatest aids in the building of character, the enforcing of discipline, and the improving of scholarship." In 1906, Cincinnati's Public School Athletic League was organized to stimulate interest in sports and schools began

---

47. E. W. Newton, "Music as an Emotional Steadier," *The Playground* 14 (June 1920): 170–71.

48. *Chicago Annual Report,* 1904, pp. 86–87.

awarding athletic badges to participants. The league later turned its attention to the lower grades, where it hoped to plant athletics more firmly. [49] In New York City, Dr. Luther Gulick, the director of physical training in the public school system and a founder of the playground movement, started the Public School Athletic League and initiated the awarding of athletic badges. The popularity of his program was reflected in the growing number of badge recipients. Over 1,100 students received badges in 1904, the first year they were awarded. This figure increased every year during the next decade to over 11,000 recipients by 1913.[50]

Early efforts to regulate athletics in the New York City schools show the kinds of values educators hoped to instill in the student participants. As they had in other extracurricular activities, school officials again tried to foster group loyalty and cooperativeness while reducing divisiveness, competition, and egotism. One of their tools was the intramural sports program, which encouraged widespread participation. Intramural athletics purportedly discouraged glorification of the individual athlete and promoted group loyalty. Additionally, the criteria for awarding athletic badges were changed to suppress the individualism that might arise from certain kinds of competition. The badges were given to those who met an arbitrary standard rather than to those who defeated another athlete. Superintendent Maxwell believed that intramural athletic participation would develop boys better suited to accept their positions in the modern world. As evidence he offered the endorsement of an employer of 250 young men: "When boys apply to me for employment I immediately seek out those wearing the athletic badge and consider them separately and first, and it is rare indeed that I do not find everyone of them superior to those who have not won the badge."[51]

The degree to which athletics, like music, was thought to promote moral uplift through emotional conditioning was apparent in the vigorous response of some educators to complaints about the physical brutality then prevalent in high school and collegiate football. Apologists defended football as an important moral and social exercise, even though it might cripple some of the players. Luther Gulick bluntly stated

---

49. See *Cincinnati Annual Report*, 1906, p. 461; *Cincinnati Annual Report*, 1907, pp. 50–2; and *Cincinnati Annual Report*, 1909, p.53.

50. William Maxwell, "School Achievements in New York", *Educational Review* 44 (October 1912): 288; *New York Annual Report*, 1911, p. 390; and *New York Annual Report*, 1913, p. 33.

51. *New York Annual Report*, 1911, p. 388.

that the issue was not "the number of knees sprained, or the number of hearts dilated, or even the number of lives lost," but the effect of football "upon the moral character of the general student body and the spectators."[52] Philadelphia's associate superintendent of schools, John Palmer Garnber, concurred with Gulick, alleging that athletics inculcated a desirable "corporate sensitiveness" that unified students and faculty as nothing else could.[53] He, too, felt that athletics should be judged solely by the social ends they purported to influence. The development of selfless, or corporate, spirit justified the temporary or even permanent physical damage suffered by some of the participants.

STUDENT CLUBS

A less demanding extracurricular activity fostered by most urban school systems was student clubs. Once again, the schools took a page from the settlement house handbook and borrowed a technique that the settlements had found effective. The rationale behind these clubs was that they fostered social and civic virtues through habit formation, much as athletics and music did. Urban corporate leaders quickly recognized the potential value of clubs. The Chicago Association of Commerce, for example, moved as early as 1914 to help organize clubs in the public schools. Its subsequent financial support of these clubs allowed it to exercise considerable control over their activities.[54] In most cities the familiar justification was offered: clubs were maintained by schools not because they made the students' lives more interesting or were intrinsically valuable, but because they developed what educators thought were desirable social responses.[55]

Educators were certain that school clubs would solve the "square peg in the round hole problem."[56] They feared that a "square peg" in

---

52. Quoted in John Palmer Garber, *Current Educational Activities* (Philadelphia: Lippincott, 1912), pp. 64–65.

53. Garber, *Educational Activities*, p. 65.

54. See Peter Andre Sola, "Plutocrats, Pedagogues and Plebes: Business Influences on Vocational Education and Extracurricular Activities in the Chicago High Schools," (University of Illinois, Urbana, 1972), pp. 168–208.

55. See *Cincinnati Annual Report*, 1899–1900, pp. 50–51; *Chicago Annual Report*, 1914, p. 184; and Laura Blackburn, *Our High School Clubs* (New York: Macmillan, 1928), pp. 5–9.

56. Blackburn, *High School Clubs*, p. 9.

school might not fit in adult occupational roles. Educators showed how far they were prepared to carry their campaign against square pegs in their distrust of high school fraternities and sororities. They accused these "secret" societies of perverting the social spirit that ought to characterize schooling. In many ways, fraternities were to the school what the gang was to the settlement. Both groups were beyond the beneficent control of constituted authorities.

The attack against fraternities was begun by Gilbert B. Morrison, who led the crusade to eradicate their so-called bad influence. He informed the 1904 annual meeting of the National Education Association that a "fraternity problem" existed in the public high schools.[57] At first, he held that only those fraternities deviating from acceptable standards were evil, but the following year, writing in School Review, Morrison took a much harder line, condemning most secret societies. He began with the observation that man's natural tendency toward social organization placed upon the school the responsibility "of meeting and guiding the social tendency of our children." He then catalogued numerous fraternity evils, most of which were reiterated by school authorities in the ensuing decade. Fraternities are "unnecessary," "factional," "selfish," "snobbish, " and "narrow." Moreover, they "form premature and unnatural friendships," "dissipate energy and proper ambition," "set wrong standards of excellence," "lessen frankness and cordiality toward teachers," "inculcate a feeling of self-sufficiency," "foster a feeling of self-importance," and, significantly, "weaken the efficiency of, and bring politics into, the legitimate organization of the school."[58] Any selfish or factional organization that developed in the students a sense of self-importance or self-sufficiency that interfered with legitimate school organizations was to be transformed or abolished.

The attack did not take long to materialize. Within two years after Morrison's first efforts, the Chicago school system ruled against secret societies. The superintendent's 1907 annual report was largely a justification for outlawing secret societies, which he thought were maladaptive for adult responsibilities. He argued that the basic purpose of American schools was to provide "equal opportunities for all pupils to get a preparation for the responsibilities that come with maturity," but

---

57. Gilbert B. Morrison, "Secret Fraternities in High Schools," NEA Addresses and Proceedings, 1904, pp. 484–85.

58. Gilbert B. Morrison, "Social Ethics in High School Life," School Review 13 (1905): 363–67.

his criticisms of fraternities, similar to Morrison's earlier catalog, indicated the kind of "preparation" the Chicago schools had in mind. Teachers had testified that "idleness, expense, trivial conversation, indulgence, love of display, and the spread of gossip all go with fraternity." Fraternities "work against anything like a 'genuine school spirit,'" an objection that the superintendent found "so fundamental that we might act upon it alone." For good measure, he added that they inhibited scholarship and were "centers of rebellion against school regulation." Fraternity members were excluded from many extracurricular activities during the following year, including the publication of their high school periodical. In March of 1908, the school board passed a resolution recommending that members of secret societies be suspended from school. Interestingly, the resolution also provided that each school set aside a room to be used for organized social purposes, an apparent attempt to offer sanctioned alternatives to fraternities.[59]

The Chicago response typified developments in other cities. In December of 1912, the Denver school board passed a fraternity resolution which provided for the dismissal of any teacher or principal who failed to cooperate in the effort to prevent secret fraternities.[60] By 1915, over ten states had passed statutes outlawing public school fraternities.[61] Because secret societies were outside the realm of legitimate authority school officials feared that these organizations would develop unhealthy habits, emotions, and loyalties. They accurately perceived that effective socialization for industrial America required uniformity of purpose in agencies molding the emotional substructure of citizenship.

STUDENT SELF-GOVERNMENT

Although educators thought that students could not be trusted in secret societies, they professed that students should be self-governing. Concurrent with the campaign to eradicate the fraternities was a groundswell of rhetoric and support for a variety of self-governing

---

59. *Chicago Annual Report*, 1907, pp. 132–34; and *Chicago Annual Report*, 1908, pp. 20–21, 230–31.

60. Quoted in *New York Annual Report*, 1913, p. 217.

61. William R. Hood, "Digest of State Laws Relating to Education," *Bulletin of the U.S. Bureau of Education*, 1915, no. 47, pp. 591–93.

schemes in the public schools. The need to replace corporal punishment with a more effective form of discipline and to combat the effects of municipal corruption were the impetus for student government, projected as a remedy for both problems. In a sense, both were really part of a single problem. At issue, educators believed, was the development of student habits and emotions in accord with disciplined citizenship. The corruption which Lincoln Steffens called "the shame of the cities" arose, in the opinion of many teachers and administrators, from the failure of the older forms of coercion. Traditional discipline was predicted on the physical presence of authorities who dispensed retribution for each infraction of regulations. Since it was impossible in modern urban America to have a policeman on every corner, professionals suggested a new type of discipline, one that would put him in the soul of each child. These internalized policemen were termed habits and character. The new "self-discipline" would require long and careful nurturing before the children would develop safe social habits. Extracurricular activities in general and student self-government in particular were seen as devices to condition this new self-disciplined citizen.

One of the earliest efforts along this line was William R. George's Junior Republic, a self-governing village for young people founded at Ithaca, New York in 1885. The Junior Republic received widespread publicity and inspired several modified facsimiles such as School City, established by Bernard Crosant, principal of P.S. 125 in New York. It was, however, the proselytizing efforts of Wilson Gill, who had earlier founded the American Patriotic League, that alerted educators throughout the nation to the potential disciplinary effects of student self-government and promoted many experiments in the field during the second decade of this century. Gill's sanction of student government stressed the character-building potential of the emotional training and learn-by-doing pedagogy that were central to the play movement, athletics, and music. His arguments were a litany chanted by numerous other advocates of student government.[62] By the end of the twenties, such experi-

---

62. Wilson Gill, "Child-Citizenship and the City School," *NEA Addresses and Proceedings,* 1908, pp. 285–89; see also Richard Welling, "Pupil Self-Government as a Training of Citizenship," *NEA Addresses and Proceedings,* 1911, p. 1106; A. O. Bowden, "Student Self-Government," *School and Society,* July 27, 1918, p. 99; and M. Channing Wagner, "Extracurricular Activities—A Training for Democracy—Abstract," *NEA Addresses and Proceedings,* 1931, p. 594.

ments had been institutionalized in most city schools and had evolved into the now familiar student council.[63]

At least one contemporary observer objected to the contradiction between student self-government and democracy. In response to Wilson Gill's 1908 speech to the Department of Superintendence, Oliver P. Cornman, a district superintendent in Philadelphia, complained that School City existed simply for ends imposed by teachers: "Many of our plans of pupil self-government, it seems to me, do not sufficiently concentrate upon the problem of realizing the best possibilities of the individual pupil, but are suggested or controlled by the ulterior consideration of finding a remedy, or panacea if need be, for the admitted and deplored ills of the body politic." Cornman argued that the plan was paternalistic because it required constant "surveillance and control by school authorities. " He suggested that even a return to the old-fashioned "frank paternalism" would be more desirable than the present "thinly disguised one."[64] One might think that Cornman's criticism, coming as it did from a district superintendent, represented the practitioner as opposed to the theoretician. In reality, though, his was an atypical view, for an examination of student government in the New York schools shows that actual school practice closely approximated the theory.

During the 1904–1905 school term, the discipline problem moved the New York City schools to investigate the use of student self-government to elicit appropriate behavior from the students. Superintendent Maxwell remonstrated that the praiseworthy abolition of corporal punishment "has left the schools, in the judgment of many persons, without adequate means of securing the discipline that is necessary for the welfare for either the individual pupil or of the entire student body. With this view, I am disposed to coincide. What is to be done?" The answer was to be found in student self-government. A committee consisting of associate superintendents Andrew W. Edson and Edward L. Stevens was appointed in January of that year to examine the operational systems of pupil self-government in Philadelphia and Syracuse.[65]

---

63. Paul W. Terry, *Supervising Extracurricular Activities* (New York: McGraw-Hill, 1930), pp. 14–16; see also William R. George, *The Junior Republic* (New York: D. Appleton, 1910); William George and L. B. Stowe, *Citizens Made and Remade* (Boston: Houghton Mifflin, 1917); and Jack M. Hall, *Juvenile Reform in the Progressive Era: William George and the Junior Republic* (Ithaca: Cornell University Press, 1971).

64. Oliver P. Cornman, "School Cities," *NEA Addresses and Proceedings*, 1908, pp. 289, 290.

65. *New York Annual Report*, 1905, pp. 120, 451.

The committee isolated two systems of student government: the School City plan in Philadelphia and the Ray system in Syracuse. The main difference between the two was that the Ray system had less intricate machinery and thus greater flexibility than the School City plan, although both seemed to deliver the desired results. In Syracuse's Franklin School the "spirit of the kindergarten" emanated from every class. The committee reported that as a result of the Ray system of government, "profanity and obscenity have been eliminated, the conduct of pupils in classrooms, halls, yards, and on streets in going to and from school has been improved in a remarkable manner." Their report included the following Citizen's Pledge from the Franklin School: "As a citizen of this school, I pledge that I will try at all times to do right myself and to influence others to do right. I will faithfully assist the teachers and tribunes in securing good order and right conduct in the school." With obvious pleasure the committee said, "Everything observed in this school led your committee to feel that a fine *esprit-de-corps* prevailed, which made bad conduct unpopular."[66]

The committee found the School City plan in Philadelphia to be a much more complicated system with many more offices, functions, and formal duties requiring constant attention and guidance from teachers. At the Hollingsworth School, where it seemed to work best, "the teachers are about the rooms and hallways to advise the officers what to do, so that much of the government is government of the teachers second-hand. Little real authority is delegated to the pupils. The problem of discipline is easy." Although the committee believed that the plan was a thinly veiled projection of teacher authority in the guise of student government, it conceded that "it works well as long as the fiction holds." It recommended that some form of student government, preferably the Ray plan because of its simplicity, be implemented in the New York City schools as a more effective way to eliminate bad conduct than the older "repressive and coercive measures."[67]

Superintendent Maxwell, agreeing with the general conclusions of the committee, urged his principals to begin experiments with pupil self-government at the earliest possible time. The most nagging issue, it seemed, was not major offenses that would justify expulsion from

66. *New York Annual Report*, 1905, p. 452.
67. *New York Annual Report*, 1905, pp. 453, 456.

school or internment in the truant schools, but minor infractions—casual insubordinations and the like—that required a denial of privilege. Maxwell was convinced that teacher-enforced sanctions would simply result in the glorification and martyrdom of the offender. The beauty of self-government, according to Maxwell, resided in the fact that punishment was, in a sense, self-inflicted:

> If, however, the same punishment were inflicted by a jury of his peers the consolation of strutting as a hero or posing as a martyr would be entirely removed. The efficacy of the punishment would be reinforced by the whole strength of the public opinion of the class or the school. The ridicule or the pity of his fellows is what the child finds hardest to endure and what he will strive most earnestly to avoid. In this psychological fact lies the chief reason for the success, such as it is, that has attained the different forms of pupil self-government that have been tried at various times in the history of education.[68]

The following year Maxwell reported, "The principals are beginning to turn their attention to some plan of pupil self-government as a means of lightening the burden of discipline which now rests on the shoulders of the teachers, and as a means of training in the duties of citizenship." To stimulate further development in this area, he suggested that through student government teachers and principals could instill self-control in students, teach them to organize themselves for public duty, and control the wayward and recalcitrant.[69]

Within four years, New York's associate superintendent, John H. Walsh, attributed the dramatic reduction in the number of misconduct expulsions directly to the institution of student self-government. The authority of both teachers and principals was a pronounced feature in his description of the student government in P.S. 109. The program began in the lowest grades by preparing the students "in the simple forms of pupil cooperation" and expanded in scope and complexity through the upper grades. The resolutions passed by the legislative branch of the student government could take effect only when "signed by the principals, who exercise a final veto." The court could impose a range of penalities, but all had to "be approved by the teacher."[70]

---

68. *New York Annual Report,* 1905, p. 121.
69. *New York Annual Report,* 1906, pp. 126–27.
70. *New York Annual Report,* 1910, pp. 273–75.

The New York City program for student self-government had been organized to entrench the authority of teachers and administrators. The program began as a disciplinary device, and educators were convinced that it had salutary immediate and future effects on student behavior. It purportedly improved offensive school behavior, a current problem, and would ultimately diminish social deviance among their graduates. There is little direct evidence to suggest that either of these beliefs was actualized.

SCHOOL GARDENS

Student self-government, athletics, and music are probably the most recognizable present descendents of the extracurricular activities initiated at the turn of this century. A more curious ancestor was the school gardening program. Like its sister activities, school gardening manipulated nonintellectual levers in order to encourage proper behavior for the new urban-industrial society.

Urban schools often sponsored gardens on school property or on vacant lots donated for this purpose by interested private individuals and companies. Some schools even supervised gardens in the students' homes. The gardens varied in size from large plots to window boxes and single flower pots, with crops of vegetables, berries, fruits, and flowers. The school garden originated at Roxbury, Massachusetts in 1890 and within 26 years the concept had spread to over 1,220, or 78 percent, of the city school systems responding to a U.S. Office of Education questionnaire. The growth was internal as well as external. Cincinnati's work in this field, for example, grew from a meager beginning in 1908. By 1911, it had expanded to include a staff of 40 specially trained teachers who made over 4,340 visits to children's gardens.[71] The Cincinnati visitations mushroomed to over 13,000 in 1913, when 3,600 of the participating students were awarded "buttons" for meritorious work. Similar growth occurred in New York City after 1908, when teachers and administrators organized the School Garden Association of New York. Within three years, the New York superintendent could boast of

---

71. J. L. Randall, "School and Home Gardening," *Report of the Commissioner of Education* (Washington, D.C.: Government Printing Office), 1: pp. 216, 262.

over 162,700 garden plots and 6,512 window boxes.[72] One might question the relevance of an apparent rural or agrarian-oriented effort in an urban setting. One might also ask why, in an era when school finances were usually stringent, urban systems like Philadelphia and Los Angeles each spent over $19,000 in 1916 for school gardening.[73] An obvious answer was that it added some beauty and joy to an otherwise drab and somber urban scene. In part this was accurate, but only as a fragment of a much larger answer.

The NEA devoted a general session of its 1903 annual meeting to the topic of school gardens. The speeches of two participants, Orville T. Bright and Henry Lincoln Clapp, anticipated the rationale for school gardens that surfaced in the subsequent decades. After his glowing summary of the history of school gardening in Europe, Bright offered three justifications for school gardens. First, he said, they would relate school lessons to life; presumably the classroom lessons would be translated to the garden experiences. The gardens would also provide an avenue into the home and interest parents in school activities. Finally gardening would instill responsibility and self-motivation, for the students would be confronted with obvious consequences of their care or neglect of the plants.[74]

Emphasizing Bright's concern for responsibility, Henry Clapp, a Boston school principal, extended the rationale for school gardens. They would, he counseled, give city school children physical exercise, a sense of responsibility, and a respect for manual labor. Clapp believed further that gardening experiences would help Americanize foreigners and generally produce good men and women. He assured his audience that gardening would redirect the aim of education away from its traditional emphasis on intellectual matters, which he believed had denigrated manual labor and fostered disobedience.[75]

Writing after the campaign for school gardens had already achieved considerable success in city schools, J. L. Randall voiced a similar rationale in the U.S. Commissioner of Education's 1916 report. He recalled an observation by the president of the National Cash Register Company

---

72. *Cincinnati Annual Report*, 1912, pp. 93–96; *Cincinnati Annual Report*, 1913, p. 275; and *New York Annual Report*, 1911, p. 191.

73. Randall, "School and Home Gardening," p. 263.

74. Orville T. Bright, "School Gardens, City School Years and the Surroundings of Rural Schools," *NEA Addresses and Proceedings*, 1903, pp. 78, 79.

75. Bright, "School Gardens," pp. 85–88.

that all of his successful executives had done farm work or garden chores as boys. The president supported gardening as an aspect of his company's welfare program because he concluded that it nurtured the self-motivation, tractability, and sense of responsibility needed for success in corporate America. His conclusion was supported by many teachers who claimed that "children engaged in gardening are more easily taught and governed." Randall pointed out that other innovative corporations such as the Carnegie Steel Company and the Tennessee Coal, Iron and Railway Company also supported gardening as part of their welfare work.[76]

Patterson's endorsement of gardening was included in the report of the school survey team at Elyria, Ohio. In similar investigations of the Elyria businessmen the team found that 27 out of the 29 successful businessmen studied performed such chores during their boyhood. On the basis of this finding, the team strongly recommended the expansion of the school gardening program in Elyria.[77]

The popularity of gardening programs in city schools was assured by its agreement with the aims of other educational innovations and by its roots in traditional American beliefs. Gardening was part of the larger plan to extend the school's influence in the lives of the students. The effort to penetrate the family and direct the child's out-of-school activities was important to most of the new programs developed at the turn of the century. Gardening programs, like the playground movement, assemblies, and school music, aimed to teach through activity rather than precept. Gardening, it was hoped, would show the child his "place in life's plan" and equip him with the habits to fulfill the functions appropriate to that place. In addition to its compatibility with other reforms, school gardening reflected well-defined and long-established American beliefs. It was a manifestation of a traditional reliance on the moral value of work and a national faith in rural virtue.[78] These values also inspired the charity "sunshine" summer vacations and camps that took underprivileged city youth to rural areas.

76. Randall, " School and Home Gardening," pp. 259–64.

77. "Educational Survey of Elyria, Ohio," *Bulletin of the U.S. Bureau of Education*, 1918, no. 15, pp. 16, 220. Similar recommendations were articulated in "Public Schools of San Francisco," pp. 608–20, 645.

78. For interesting and ably documented descriptions of this faith see Peter Schmitt, *Back to Nature: The Arcadian Myth in Urban America* (New York: Oxford University Press, 1969); and Leo Marx, *The Machine in the Garden* (New York: Oxford University Press, 1964) .

SCHOOL SAVINGS BANKS

While school gardening harmonized traditional beliefs with the newer psychological principles evident in other curricular innovations, the school savings bank concept derived more exclusively from earlier beliefs. The traditional Protestant equation of frugality with virtue needs little elaboration. A correlate of this ethic, which has received increasing attention from social historians, is that the propertyless have no real stake in society and therefore constitute a threat to it.[79]

The first school savings bank was instituted at Beloit, Wisconsin by Sereno F. Merrill in 1876 and lasted until 1881, when Mr. Merrill's successor abandoned the enterprise. Three years after the Beloit experiment began, Captain R. H. Pratt initiated a similar program at the Carlisle Indian Training School. Following these pioneering examples, John Thiry successfully launched the movement in New York City and Long Island in 1885, when he interested bankers and school officials in the project. By the 1890s, savings banks existed in over 52 schools representing 12 states and had over 27,000 student depositors. By 1914 the movement had spread to almost every state, and over 216,000 students deposited an aggregate total of at least $1,256,335.40. Most of the depositors and deposits were concentrated in the highly urbanized and industrialized North Atlantic and North Central sectors of the nation.[80] These areas also contained the highest percentages of immigrants, a group that supposedly needed special attention to uplift them to the American standard of citizenship.

School officials and backers of the school savings bank movement often voiced its aims, but it was John Thiry who set the tone of the movement:

> Surely the masses need education in thrift. This is the providence of the school savings banks system. It is an educational factor. It claims to teach virtue because all virtues require self-control and husbanding of strength and resources, and these things invariably lead to thrift. The saving of time, of strength, of health, of intellectual force, of moral integrity, are all allied to the saving of money.[81]

---

79. See Joan W. Scott, "The Glassworkers of Carmaux, 1850–1900," in *Nineteenth-Century Cities: Essays in the New Urban History*, ed. Stephen Thernstrom and Richard Sennett (New Haven: Yale University Press, 1969).

80. Sara Louisa Oberholtzer, "School Savings Banks," *Bulletin of the U.S. Bureau of Education*, 1914, no. 46. pp. 13–17.

81. Quoted in Oberholtzer, "School Savings Banks," pp. 9–10.

Variations on this theme were sounded by numerous school officials from Augusta, Maine to Cincinnati, Ohio.[82] School savings banks,
like most of the other activities discussed in this and the preceding
chapter, were valued not for their own sake, but as a means to create a
more reliable working class and thus a more stable social order.

Sara Oberholtzer, writing for the U.S. Bureau of Education, affirmed
the frequently cited correlation between social stability and such training for working-class students. Underscoring the important training
aspect of school savings relative to postal savings, she said, "School
savings banks are needed to prepare young people, especially those
who have no careful home training, to profit by the postal savings
opportunity." The phrase "those with no careful home training" was a
common contemporary synonym for working-class and immigrant children. The dangerous and nonproductive classes, she contended, were
those who had no stake in society because they did not own property.
Before the working class could own, they would have to be taught to
save. The school savings program would train the children to thrift and
enable them to purchase a share of society. Such proprietorship, in turn,
would blunt the cutting edge of social conflict. The working class would
have more to lose than their chains; they might very well lose a house, a
small business, a modest investment, or a savings deposit.[83] This prop
for social stability was to be built not by the education of the working-
class intellect, but by habit formation. It was part of the nonintellectual
training that dominated contemporary urban schooling.

PENNY LUNCHES

The emotional training aspect of urban education was so prevalent that
it even permeated programs designed for seemingly altruistic and lauda-
tory purposes. The penny lunch program, which, like so many other
school programs, originated in the settlement houses, became a means
of helping children to function better in the urban-industrial order. The
idea of low-cost lunches for hungry children spread to many urban
schools by the end of the first decade of this century. While few could
fault the notion that hungry children should be fed, a companion belief

82. See Oberholtzer, "School Savings Banks," p. 8; *New York Annual Report*, 1910, p.
203; and *Cincinnati Annual Report*, 1915, p. 129.

83. Oberholtzer, "School Savings Banks," pp. 7–10.

of many educators may, upon examination, appear less sound. This was the understanding that the poor suffered from malnutrition because of ignorance and indolence regarding food selection and preparation rather than because of poverty. Superintendent Maxwell, in his 1906 recommendation for school lunches in the New York City schools, asserted that although malnutrition was a major cause of poor health and school retardation, "It is not so much that the children of the tenement house have not sufficient food, but that their food is often badly cooked or is of such a character that it does not afford the requisite sustenance."[84] Maxwell expressed this sentiment simply as an aside, but six years later it became a central theme in the New York City school lunch program. In his 1912 annual report, Maxwell noted that physical examinations administered to one-third of the school children had detected malnutrition in nearly 10,000 of them. He continued to believe that the cause was ignorance rather than poverty, envisioning the school lunch program as a substitute for the "wretched pickles, candy, and cakes with which they are tempted in the streets."[85]

At a deeper level, though, it was an attempt to alter ethnic and cultural eating habits and tastes in order that the working classes might more adequately survive upon the meager economic rewards of the corporate wage structure. Benefits undoubtedly accrued to the worker accustomed since school days to the type of diet that low wages could sustain, especially when the alternative was to suffer malnutrition because his traditional foods were not available at prices he might afford. Nor did it require excessive acumen to recognize the benefit accruing to the employer whose workers had been domesticated to live within their meager salary. In this way the school lunch program, and even more so the cooking classes that foreshadowed the domestic science curriculum, was interestingly similar to the Jeanes teachers who scurried about the South training little black girls to "make do" with the returns of share cropping.

New dietary habits taught in the school lunch room were expected to influence present as well as future homes of the students. "Poverty is usually the direct result of wasteful habits," said Harriet A. Tupper, principal of New York's P.S. 107. "The mothers are urged to come in and try the food. Then they begin to ask questions about how such food can be served for the price. This leads to a little advice as to food values and

---

84. *New York Annual Report*, 1906, pp. 110–11.
85. *New York Annual Report*, 1912, p. 180.

the good seed is sown. I have no data to prove direct results, but I am confident that there are results and that they are good."[86] Of course the gentle art of persuasion and example was not always as successful as Tupper claimed. In some cases, the resistance to change of long-standing cultural habits must have been enormous. In Chicago, for example, the superintendent reluctantly conceded in 1918, after a long battle: "Principals must necessarily cater to local food tastes based upon nationality if the prime purpose of the lunch room is to be achieved, the feeding of hungry children. One might be led to believe that a hungry child will eat anything that will allay the gnawing pangs of hunger, but *experience has proven this to be untrue.*"[87]

A second kind of external consideration that became prominent in the penny lunch program was the effort to use it to inculcate values, attitudes, and habits. Again, a nonintellectual approach was initiated by school officials. Children were taught by example and by doing rather than by precept. Educators soon discovered that the school lunch table offered an opportunity to instill in lower-class children an habituated acceptance of the value of cleanliness, order, regularity, patience, and an appreciative response to school authority. "Soup is served at 12 from a counter, and ladled out by the cook," reported Ms. Kittredge, director of the New York Lunch School Committee. "A line of children wishing to buy is formed and they march up to the counter, receiving tray, spoon, and soup for one cent. If any child wishes to make further purchase he passes on to the penny table where a variety of at least a dozen articles of food can be bought for one cent each."[88] The principal of New York's P.S. 120 observed that all the students were required to consume their food in a socially approved manner that would develop better habits in the children of the urban poor. He said, "This habit of setting down to a table decently and in order is valuable, as it is in many instances the only place they do sit down to eat, as ordinarily they eat what they may find when they are hungry."[89] Superintendent Maxwell listed the development of "patience and politeness" as educational values of the program. The ability to wait in line patiently and politely was surely an important characteristic for citizens of an urban, industrial, and bureaucratic social order. The school lunch was structured to stimu-

---

86. *New York Annual Report*, 1912, p. 186.
87. *Chicago Annual Report*, 1918, p. 103 (emphasis added).
88. *New York Annual Report*, 1912, p. 181.
89. *New York Annual Report*, 1912, p. 185.

late this response, with the bowl of soup being what later theorists might term the positive reinforcement for hungry children. It was an interesting device that benevolently blended the needs of the student with the requirements of the social order.[90]

The lunch program also enabled the teacher to interact with students in ways that would develop in them an appreciation for the benevolence of school authority. Harriet Tupper suggested one way in which the "splendid feeling of being comrades among children" might be achieved and then used to establish the correct relationship between students and authority. Teachers were aware of some hungry pupils without adequate means to purchase even the penny lunches. Tupper believed that the teachers could use this information and a small amount of their own money to ease the natural suspicion that poor children displayed toward school authority: "And when one shyly slips that child a sandwich or an apple on his tray, then adds the required sum from one's own pocket, a bond of real sympathy is established which goes far toward eliminating friction in the class room." She noted that in the lunch program, "the training in ethics is so constant that a day never passes without some example of it."[91] Tupper did not, however, comment upon the ethics of patronizing the helpless in order to purchase loyalty.

The school penny lunch program began for seemingly intrinsic and altruistic reasons—the necessity for humans to express their humanism by feeding hungry children. It was, however, quickly seized upon as an effective means to accomplish other ends. The lunch program demonstrates how urban reformers merged benevolence with moral training. This moral training was designed to make its recipients more effective members of the society that was responsible for their plight. The refusal of reformers and educators to examine the social order led them to blame the victims and attempt to reshape them into citizens who more nearly met the needs of industrial America. This seems to have been the inevitable result of any school reform designed to meet the needs of a particular class or group of children. The needs were usually understood to mean the ways these children could fit into the reformers' vision of society. At the turn of the century, the training method increasingly involved emotional conditioning and habit formation.

---

90. This was also characteristic of the Chicago Penny Lunch Program. See, for example, *Chicago Annual Report*, 1911, pp. 129–30.

91. *New York Annual Report*, 1912, pp. 187, 188.

Chapter 6

Vocational Education I - Rationale

Although compulsory attendance, the play movement, Americanization, and organized extracurricular activities made some impression on American schooling, it was not as deep as that created by vocational training, which fundamentally transformed American urban schools during the early decades of the twentieth century. In 1907, Frank M. Leavitt, the president of the Manual Training Department of the National Education Association, announced that industrial training was the single most important and widely discussed topic in educational circles during the preceding two years. From these deliberations, he reported, emerged a unanimous opinion that a large scale system of industrial training was essential for the welfare of the nation.[1] The centrality of the vocational training movement issued not only from its concrete impact on school reform. The movement also emphasized in sharp relief the various features of progressive education ambiguously or incompletely embodied in many of the other innovations discussed in the preceding chapters. More precisely than any other innovation it demonstrated the relations between corporate industry, progressive ideology, and schooling.

The present chapter explores the rationale behind the programmatic aspects of vocational education. The rationale arose from the varied arguments developed by educators attempting to enunciate policy and defend emerging programs. An early argument distinguished between manual training and industrial education, the latter

---

1. Frank M. Leavitt, "The Relation of Industrial Education to Public Instruction,"*NEA Addresses and Proceedings*, 1907, p. 778.

being a response to the organization of work in modern capitalism. The labor force now required workers with habits, values, and personality patterns conducive to assembly line techniques. From most workers, however, it required little skill. The massive "skill dilution" and the subordination of the worker to tasks and production schedules over which he had little control resulted in widespread worker alienation and industrial unrest. The rationale for industrial education maintained that such learning would develop in the future industrial worker psychic structures that would increase his productivity and diminish his alienation. The old curriculum was considered too abstract, too general, and too bookish to have the desired impact on children destined to become the rank and file of the hierarchical and highly specialized urban-industrial army. The traditional unified public school curriculum would have to give way to a differentiated one, even though varied curricula would yield different and unequal education.

Early justifications of this resulting unequal education were based upon a starkly realistic appraisal of the variegated life possibilities among the different economic classes in America: lower-class children should be trained for factory work simply because that was their vocational destiny. When it became apparent that this explicitly class oriented-rationale contradicted traditional American beliefs in individual opportunity, educators quickly developed a more democratic justification for unequal education. Assuming the Platonic belief that humans have dissimilar abilities, the experts advised that students having neither the capacity nor the desire to study the traditional curriculum be given an equal opportunity to study industrial subjects more adapted to their taste and abilities. A related issue in the vocational education movement concerned the age at which children should be tracked according to their intellect and interest. This widely debated topic constituted one of the more interesting questions because it disclosed the extent to which the industrial education movement was committed to the interests and needs of corporate industry.

MANUAL TRAINING

The forerunner of the vocational training movement of the early twentieth century was the curriculum innovation called manual training, which began soon after the Civil War.[2] The manual training movement received its impetus partly from reform-minded educators who, following the pedagogic tenets of Pestalozzi and Rousseau, believed that education should do more than train the mind or the intellect. These educators did not deprecate intellectual training or the principles of faculty psychology that supported the classical curriculum. They merely wished to add to the curriculum certain manual activities—drawing, leather work, clay modeling and wood working, for example—that they believed would give the child a practical understanding of the world around him. Initially, these activities were meant to benefit all children, for reformers sought not to differentiate the curriculum but to diversify it. Their innovations did not aim at developing specific skills or producing workers for specific occupations, but at enlarging the educational experience of students so that each could function as a whole person in the modern world.

The efforts of these reform educators received strong support from businessmen and industrialists in the decades following the Civil War. The commercial community saw the manual training movement as a means of producing more efficient employees. Entrepreneurs had predicted that the skills and principles learned from manual training activities would have specific transferability to the industrial and commercial workplace, but in the 1890s they began to question this transferability. By the turn of the century their support had changed to opposition against what they called educational frills, and the magnates began to support a more strictly vocational type of learning called industrial training.[3] When advocates of industrial training spoke of manual activities, they now generally referred to the newer industrial training exercises. Older training activities taught the general principles underlying manual endeavors without reference to special occupational competence. The new industrial or vocational training, on the other hand, was designed to be occupationally specific. The purpose of manual training, said the New York superintendent of

---

2. For a more complete analysis of the manual training movement see Marvin Lazerson, *Origins of the Urban School* Cambridge, Mass.: Harvard University Press, 1971), chs. 3, 4, and 5; Edward Chase Kirkland, *Dream and Thought in the Business Community 1860-1900* (Ithaca: Cornell University Press, 1956), chs. 3 and 4; and Dennis Robert Herschback, "Industrial Education Ideology, 1876–1917" (Ph. D. diss., University of Illinois, 1973).

3. The commercial or mercantile interests also turned from manual training and began a drive to diversify the public school curriculum in order to introduce business or commercial education. Although commercial education had objectives and used methodologies similar to those of industrial training, the latter is the focus of this chapter.

schools in his 1906 report, was "the general development of the elementary school pupil." Industrial training, however, "aims to prepare boys for a vocational life. It does not look toward the general development of the pupil but to his specific training in the field of the arts and crafts."[4]

INDUSTRIAL TRAINING AND INDUSTRIAL EFFICIENCY

Industrial training was not simply regarded as an addition to the classical curriculum; it was a replacement for it. The new industrial army was specialized and hierarchical. Consequently, different types of training was deemed necessary to fit children for the different vocational levels. Those slated for the lower ranks could not receive the same education as those headed for the "officer corps." The latter type of education, it was believed, would not fit the "rank-and-file" child for his appropriate work and would be beyond his mental capacity. The unified curriculum was seen as an anarchronism, irrelevant to the industrial needs of the twentieth century.

By the end of the first decade of the twentieth century, many educators considered it their patriotic responsibility to train students to fit the requirements of a hierarchical work force. "The industrial pursuits of life upon which the whole fabric of society rests must be taken in account," a Toledo, Ohio principal noted in 1901, as he proposed that the purpose of American education should be to prepare youth for manual labor.[5] The 1907 annual report of the New York City schools bluntly asserted that "the purpose of industrial training—considering it as a part of our educational process—should be primarily, to increase the industrial efficiency of the nation. To improve the conditions of individuals, or to provide means whereby individuals may increase their earnings, should not be its purpose, although industrial training may effect such results."[6] Two years later, the United States commissioner of education expressed similar senti-

---

4. *New York Annual Report,* 1906, pp.310–11; see also Chicago Association of Commerce, *Industrial and Commercial Education in Relation to Conditions in the City of Chicago* (Chicago, 1909), p. 4 (hereafter cited as *Industrial and Commercial Education*).

5. Virgil G. Curtis, "The Relation of Manual Training to Technical Education," *NEA Addresses and Proceedings,* 1901, p. 659.

6. *New York Annual Report,* 1907, p. 465.

ments to a national gathering of school superintendents.[7] American industry, they agreed, could not meet the rising tide of foreign industrial competition, especially from the Germans, until the public schools increased the productive potential of future American industrial workers. The Cincinnati school superintendent cited recent consular reports to prove that "the prestige of American industries will rapidly decline unless our educational systems are expanded." Superintendent Dyer left little doubt regarding the direction he thought that expansion should take: "Better for the submerged half of our youth an education that will produce intelligent and competent artisians than no education."[8] The supporters of vocational education usually assumed that the only alternatives for "the submerged half" was industrial training or no education. The term "submerged half" was understood by Dyer's colleagues to mean working-class children.

Implicit in the rationale for schooling to fit the worker to industrial manpower requirements was the notion that it was ultimately in his own best interests, as defined for him by educators and intellectuals. Industrial education involved an acceptance of the inevitability of industrial progress. This fatalism was captured in the response of the Ohio commissioner of common schools to a 1909 speech calling for industrial education in elementary schools. "We are living in an age of intense industrial and business activity," stated Commissioner Jones. "The lines of work now open to those who leave our schools are very different from what they were a quarter of a century ago. We cannot change these things if we would. It remains for our public-school system to adapt itself to existing conditions."[9] If these conditions were inevitable, many educators reasoned that the students were best served by learning to adjust to industrial requirements.

A more optimistic and more frequently articulated line of reasoning followed the "percolate down" notion of sharing economic benefits. A more efficient and productive work force yielded higher profits, which in turn allowed employers to increase wages. Gifts from the Knapp and Stout manufacturing company had enabled Menomonie, Wisconsin to become a recognized leader in turn of the century industrial education. Menomonie's superintendent, Lorenzo D. Harvey, argued that labor should not oppose the establishment of

7. Elmer Ellsworth Brown, "Industrial Education as a National Interest," *NEA Addresses and Proceedings*, 1909, p. 288.

8. F. B. Dyer, "The Need for Special Classes," *NEA Addresses and Proceedings*, 1907, p. 315.

9. Edmund A. Jones, "Discussion," *NEA Addresses and Proceedings*, 1909, p. 386.

trade schools for children still in elementary school.[10] In an address to the 1907 annual meeting of the NEA he identified the interests of the laborer with those of the manufacturer, saying that "whatever can be done to dignify labor and make it more effective is the course of wisdom for both the employer and the employee. It is the sons and daughters of the rank and file in the army of labor who are to benefit personally by the establishment of this class of schools."[11] Defenders of industrial education assumed that the general welfare of the community coincided with the manpower needs of corporate industry.

Vocational education was not, however, merely an attempt to secure skilled workmen for the nation's factories. The movement was a complex attack against a knot of social and economic problems, most of which stemmed from the new organization of work in corporate industry. By the 1890s, the structure of this new organization had become apparent. The older "shop," which had housed skilled artisans, was supplanted by the modern factory with its efficiency-oriented assembly line mode of production. The production process was repeatedly analyzed and subdivided into component parts so that machines could replace more expensive artisan labor. As the assembly line became more efficient, the factory worker turned out increasingly fragmented parts of the total product and brought increasingly less skill to the process. Where it had taken the artisan years to master his trade, the factory hand could now literally learn his job overnight. Although the new factory with its sophisticated machinery and refined articulation of tasks, was far more complicated than the old shop, this did not mean that the production worker had to possess a high order of skill or knowledge. A small corps of technicians, engineers, and maintenance men could keep the factory operating. This small segment of the industrial work force required both the skill and technical aptitude. Vocational education, adapted to the task of equipping this group for particular competencies, was usually offered in the trade schools.

The production worker, on the other hand, needed training but not much knowledge or skill. More important than craft requirements were general social and personality traits suited to corporate industrial organization. Since the new production process consisted of a series

10. See Judson E. Hoyt, "Manual Training in the Menomonie Public Schools." *NEA Addresses and Proceedings*, 1901, pp. 261–72.

11. L. D. Harvey, "The Need for Special Classes," *NEA Addresses and Proceedings*, 1907, pp. 312–13.

of interdependent operations, it was necessary for the worker to be loyal, dependable, punctual, and cooperative, qualities best obtained through appropriate habit formation. As industrial tasks continued to subdivide into increasingly minute and simple operations, worker boredom and alienation became more acute. Hence, the educational problem posed by most industrial laborers involved personality adjustment, habit formation, and value conditioning. Advocates of vocational education often grouped these attributes under the amorphous rubric of "industrial intelligence." The vocational education movement must be seen as a complex development because it was designed to develop a wide range of personnel to man the corporate industrial structure, not simply the production worker but workers at all levels in the industrial hierarchy.

Many perceptive proponents of vocational education recognized the implications that these changes in factory work had for schooling. In 1901, Charles F. Warner, principal of a Springfield, Massachusetts high school, after suggesting that educational systems "ought to be adjusted to industrial needs," informed the annual convention of the NEA that "the wonderful development of machinery and machine methods, especially in this country, and the realization of the immense profitableness of rapid production thus made possible, have led to such a degree of specialization in the trades, through the principle of the division of labor—to such a development of trades within trades—that many of the original, all-round trades of our fathers have been lost."[12] Six years later, a vice-president of General Electric Company repeated this theme in a speech before an NEA symposium on "The Relation of Industrial Education to Public Instruction." While he remarked upon the skill dilution resulting from corporate industrialism, the General Electric vice-president was more interested in educating the minority who would act as mid-range officers in the industrial army than he was in training privates and corporals.[13]

Other educators were vitally interested in those destined to fill the lower ranks. "America is in the front rank of the nations in her education of leaders in industry," claimed the founder of the Chicago Manual Training School. "Her engineering schools are second to none in the world, superior to most. But while the training of the

---

12. Charles F. Warner, "Education for the Trades in America—What Can Technical High Schools Do For It?" *NEA Addresses and Proceedings*, 1901, p. 670.

13. Magnus W. Alexander, "Industrial Training as Viewed by a Manufacturer," *NEA Addresses and Proceedings*, 1907, p. 797.

officers of her industrial army is secured, preparation for filling the ranks is largely neglected."[14] Professor George H. Mead also expressed concern regarding the fate of the machine tenders who no longer seemed to require skill. He observed that the older apprentice system had disintegrated because "the very skill of the artisan stood in the way of his adapting himself to the new regime. The skilled artisan was no more but rather less valuable than the untrained man." The laboring classes should fear above all else the division of labor that was becoming so prominent in industry. The result of such specialization would be "that our community will conceive that it can fulfill its industrial functions with an elite of trained workmen and a proletariat of ignorant and unskilled."[15] Interestingly, Mead did not suggest any practical ways to alter the work structure that seemed to demand the very outcome he feared. Indeed, less than three years later, he chaired a committee for the City Club of Chicago that recommended industrial education programs insuring this very division of the industrial work force.[16]

Charles W. Hubbard, addressing the Harvard Teachers' Association, displayed none of Mead's hesitation regarding the division of the working class: "It is therefore not a question of converting all workers into skilled workers, but of selecting those who have the greatest natural ability; to educate these properly to fill the places to which they have the ability to rise; and to give to the rest such education as will fit them to fulfill such civic and family duties as may fall to their lot."[17]

The shifting structure of industrial work, and its impact on the American working class, received formal acknowledgement in an influential 1910 *Report of the Committee on the Place of Industries in Public Education to the National Council of Education*. As an introduction to the report's policy and programmatic recommendations, Charles R. Richards, the well-known director of New York's Cooper Union, reviewed the history of vocational education in the context of the industrial transformation of the workplace:

---

14. Henry H. Belfield, quoted in *Industrial and Commercial Education*, p. 14.

15. George H. Mead, "Industrial Education, the Working-Man, and the School," *The Elementary School Teacher* 9 (March 1909): 371, 381.

16. City Club of Chicago, *Report on Vocational Training in Chicago and in Other Cities* (Chicago, 1912). These programs will be analyzed in the next chapter.

17. Charles W. Hubbard, "Industrial Education,"*The School Review* 15, (May 1907): 392.

During these past sixty years the course of industrial development in this country has been marked by a tremendous increase in the size of productive units and attendant quantity production; by extraordinary division and subdivision of labor; by the steady introduction of machinery, and by the proportionate lessened need of the highly skilled worker. At the same time the methods of the industries have become immeasurably more dependent upon the principles of exact science, and more and more have come to require some need of specialized knowledge on the part of the skilled worker. This development has left but few industries untouched, has changed the industrial organization from comparative homogeneity to a situation in which a minority of workers requires even greater skill and intelligence than formerly, and a majority which need skill only in a narrow range of operations.[18]

The Massachusetts Commission on Industrial and Technical Education remarked in its 1906 report that industry everywhere faced a shortage of skilled workers. However, "this lack is not chiefly a want of manual dexterity, though such a want is common, but a want of what may be called *industrial intelligence*," reported the commission.

By this is meant mental power to see beyond the task which occupies the hands for the moment to the operations which have proceeded and to those which will follow it, power to take in the whole process, knowledge of materials, ideas of cost, ideas of organization, business sense, and a conscience which recognizes obligations. Such intelligence is always discontented, not with its conditions but with its own limitations, and is wise enough to see that the more it has to give the more it will receive.[19]

The first part of this statement refers to the "big picture" notion of worker discontent. As work became increasingly subdivided and centrally controlled, workers, doing a fraction of a job at the behest of a foreman, experienced deepening alienation. They could neither plan nor execute this work in its entirety, so their creativity and satisfac-

---

18. Charles R. Richards, "Some Notes on the History of Industrial Education in the United States," *Report of the Committee on the Place of Industries in Public Education to the National Council of Education* (National Education Association, 1910) (hereafter cited as *Report of the Committee on the Place of Industries in Public Education*), p. 25. See also Ralph Albertson, "The Decay of Apprenticeship and Corporation Schools," *Charities and the Commons,* October 5, 1907, pp. 814–20; and Walter E. Weyl and A. M. Sakolski, "Conditions of Entrance to the Principal Trades," *Bulletin of the U.S. Bureau of Labor,,* 1906, no. 67, pp. 681–780.

19. *Report of the Commission on Industrial and Technical Education* (Boston, 1906) pp. 4–5.

tion were stifled. Many analysts, perhaps the most sensitive being Jane Addams, believed that if the worker was shown how his work contributed to a total process, he would experience the satisfaction of the older artisan.[20] The latter part of the commission's statement implies that discontent with job conditions or meager rewards was unacceptable and misguided. If his industrial intelligence could convince the worker that the only obstacle to his satisfaction was his failure to contribute to the industrial process, vocational education would have gone a long way toward meeting the needs of industry.[21]

The problem of industrial discontent informed the thought of many proponents of vocational education, and their defense of this concept often suggested ways to relieve this frustration. "One of the purposes of industrial education held, more or less consciously, by its advocates relates directly to the contentment of the masses," wrote Frank M. Leavitt, professor of industrial education at the University of Chicago and former president of the NEA's Manual Training Department. "It is one of the most subtle and far-reaching aspects of the movement. That social discontent exists no thoughtful observer will doubt, whether he can assign the cause or not. It has been claimed that the schools are partly to blame because of the false ideals of pleasure which they have engendered." He argued that the false ideals emphasized consumption while ignoring "the finer pleasures to be derived through creative work or even the sterner joy of useful productive labor."[22] Leavitt thought that the schools, through industrial education, ought to develop a taste for the "sterner joys" in future workers.

Vocational educators often asserted that "industrial intelligence" cultivated in industrial training courses would greatly modify industrial discontent as it prepared working class youth to accept industrial life. They believed that these youths avoided factory work because of false pride.[23] Many agreed with Professor C. R. Richards, a prominent leader

20. See Jane Addams, *The Spirit of Youth and the City Streets* (New York: Macmillan, 1909), p. 127; and Jane Addams, *Democracy and Social Ethics* (Cambridge, Mass.: Harvard University Press, 1960), pp. 213–19.

21. See Richard Sennett and Jonathan Cobb, *The Hidden Injuries of Class* (New York: Vintage Books, 1973) for a penetrating analysis of the effect of this kind of lesson on the American working class.

22. Frank M. Leavitt, " Some Sociological Phases of the Movement for Industrial Education," *NEA Addresses and Proceedings*, 1912, p. 925.

23. See, for example, H. Stanley Jevons, "The Causes of Unemployment," *Contemporary Review* 95 (May 1909): 548–65.

of the industrial training movement, when he informed a group of Chicago businessmen that the training received in public schools was one of the chief obstacles to recruitment of working-class youth into the factories because the traditional emphasis on intellectual subjects had taught them to reject the dirty hands common in industry.[24] The task of vocational education was to enoble the image of industrial jobs so that future workers would see beyond the dirty hands and understand the importance of their particular contribution to the industrial progress of the nation.

The supporters of the new industrial training argued that the curricula should be designed from a pragmatic and instrumental viewpoint. Superintendent of schools at Passaic, New Jersey, O. I. Woodley, touched a responsive chord when he recommended that "the relative importance of the various subjects in the curriculum should be determined by the amount they contribute to the correct interpretation of modern life."[25] The components of the "correct interpretation of modern life" become clear when one examines contemporary educational literature. In addition to the elimination of allegedly false pride among potential industrial workers, it included those ideals and habits that made workers amenable cogs in corporate machinery.

An illustrative list of acceptable ideals was presented by Professor Monin. His other three R's—inculcated through industrial training—would help combat boredom and alienation resulting from the tedium of industrial work. As he put it, "Most of us must do in life that which is not interesting in itself. We must learn to do the common thing well, that which is uninteresting, and in doing this we learn to like it, to be interested, and will learn restraint, respect, and reverence."[26] In a similar vein, the vice-president of General Electric Company advised the Manual Training Department of the NEA that "to awaken in the boy a respect for, and an interest in, useful work is the great responsibility of the teacher."[27] Another industrialist, speaking to the Harvard Teachers'

---

24. Quoted in "Industrial Education—Industrial Supremacy," *Chicago Commerce*, January 24, 1908, pp. 20–21. I am indebted to Peter Sola of Howard University for bringing this source to my attention.

25. Quoted in "Industrial Education—Industrial Supremacy," p. 21.

26. O. I. Woodley, "Industrial Education," *NEA Addresses and Proceedings*, 1909, p. 312.

27. Alexander, "Industrial Training as Viewed by a Manufacturer," p. 802; see also Weyl and Sakolski, "Conditions of Entrance to the Principal Trades," p. 682; John F. Tobin, "Response," *Bulletin of the National Society for the Promotion of Industrial Education*, September 1907, p. 53; and Alberston, "Decay of Apprenticeship and Corporation Schools," pp. 814–20.

Association, suggested that the "education for life" slogan had a special meaning for working-class children: "a boy or girl who is to be a manual worker should early learn the habit of work."[28]

Industrialists were not alone in the belief that schools should shift their efforts from opening students' minds to accommodating them to industrial work. In his 1909 report on the progress of education for the year, John W. Cook informed the NEA that "the leading function of the school, so far as our industrial population is concerned, is to aid them in acquiring the greatest efficiency possible in earning their living by furnishing specific instruction in arts and crafts, by inculcating habits of cleanliness, industry, and sobriety,"[29] The belief that most working-class children should be trained for factory work also appears in the writings of Augusta, Georgia's school superintendent, Lawton B. Evans; the principal of Manhattan's Trade School for Girls, Mary Schenck Woolman; settlement worker, Robert A. Woods; and Louis L. Park.[30]

The accompanying belief that working-class children could be better trained for the factory through an industrial curriculum than through traditional studies rested in part upon racist vestiges of Darwinism and the eugenics movement. Certain categories of students were considered inherently inferior and thus incapable of mastering the intellectual content of the traditional curriculum. Since the newer branches of psychology taught that nonintellectual levers were more effective for the control of human behavior, industrial training relied more heavily on conditioned reflexes than on intellectual appeals. In fact, many supporters of industrial training explicity justified their proposals with references to psychological theories that stressed instinctive conditioning.[31]

The supposed dichotomy between precept and action, between knowing and doing, thought and practice was central to many discus-

28. Charles W. Hubbard, "Industrial Education," *School Review 11* (May 1907): 393.

29. John W. Cook, "The Progress of Education for the Year,"*NEA Addresses and Proceedings*, 1909, p. 396.

30. Lawton B. Evans, "The Factory Child," *NEA Addresses and Proceedings*, 1904, pp. 245–49; Mary Schenck Woolman, "Private Trade School for Girls," *Charities and the Commons*, October 5, 1907, pp. 839–48; Robert A. Woods, "Industrial Education from the Social Worker's Standpoint," *Charities and the Commons*, October 5, 1907, pp. 852–55; and Louis L. Park, "Preparing the Boy for Industry,"*NEA Addresses and Proceedings*, 1918, pp. 259–61.

31. See J. H. Trybom, "A Report on Manual Training in the Detroit Elementary Schools, with a Discussion on the Disciplinary Value of Manual Training," *NEA Addresses and Proceedings*, 1901, pp. 251–55; J. L. McBrien, "Discussion," NEA Addresses and Proceedings, 1907, pp. 381–82; and Jesse D. Burks, "Can the School Life of Pupils be Prolonged by an Adequate Provision for Industrial Training in the Upper Grades?" *NEA Addresses and Proceedings*, 1907, p. 794.

sions of industrial education. Some of the movement's apostles maintained that intellectual appeals were inadequate, if not positively dysfunctional, in training future industrial workers. Frank Hall endorsed this view by illustrating that too much intellectual training could be "positively harmful" for the working-class child: "Personally I would rather send out pupils who are lopsided and useful, than those who are seemingly symmetrical and useless," said the superintendent of the Illinois Farmers Institute. "A bent back is symmetrical if a bent back is best adapted to carrying the burdens one ought to carry. Symmetry takes second place; efficiency, the first. And life-efficiency involves vocational efficiency. A man without a vocation is more to be pitied than 'the man without a country.'"[32]

The Dayton, Ohio superintendent of schools told his NEA audience that American society was in danger of failing "not on account of intelligence [but] because of a lack of moral fiber." He cautioned: "It is more important that our pupils be taught truth, honesty, and justice and obedience than that they should be taught the principles of arithmetic and grammar, though these things are important." He concluded, "We should train the pupils in our public schools in right habits of living and morality. Precept is not enough."[33] Most educators agreed that these habits could be inculcated only by replacing the intellectual curriculum with concrete activities in which "learn by doing" would be the watchword. They recommended that in-school activities be supplemented with concrete out-of-the class experiences that would build the proper emotional substructure for the future factory worker. Ruby M. Hodge, a Los Angeles teacher of manual training, offered specific suggestions: "The child's experiences must be enlarged. This may be done through visits to mills, factories, parks, beaches, chambers of commerce, and commercial centers. In these places he will learn the value of community work, the results of law and order, and the outcome of obedience. His ambitions may be aroused, his ideals of life raised."[34] Educators thought that the more closely school experiences resembled later industrial experiences, the more completely the responses developed in school would control the adult worker's behavior in the factory. Their proposals, then, were designed to protect the established economic

32. Frank H. Hall, "The Ethical Value of Vocational Instruction in Secondary Schools," *NEA Addresses and Proceedings*, 1909, pp. 492–94.

33. J. W. Carr, "Discussion," *NEA Addresses and Proceedings* 1907, pp. 380, 381.

34. Ruby H. Hodge, "Relation of Primitive Handicraft to Present Day Educational Problems," *NEA Addresses and Proceedings*, 1907, pp. 817, 818.

order. Two proponents of vocational training even went so far as to claim that their program, because it resulted in earlier marriages, diminished opposition to the established order. "That young man who is planning to become an efficient wage-earner, and to save a part of his earnings to make a home for himself and somebody's sister," wrote one of the supporters, "is about as safe—ethically safe—so far as plans for the future can make one so, as any young man in the community."[35]

DIFFERENTIATED CURRICULUM AS CLASS EDUCATION

Ellwood Cubberley, in his widely read and influential work, *Changing Conceptions of Education*, captured the mood and intent of the movement with his observation that city schools would have to abandon "the exceedingly democratic idea that our society is devoid of classes" and begin to educate the various classes according to their special needs.[36] Cubberley was not only a leader in educational circles, but an astute analyst of contemporary trends as well. He saw that the older notions of democracy and equality were not appropriate for corporate industrialism. In concert with many of his colleagues, he urged the schools to adjust their conceptions of democracy, equality, and education to fit the requirements of the modern order. Significantly, the U.S. commissioner of education reported in 1906 that "industrial training is offered in most of the negro [sic] schools, reform schools, and schools for defectives."[37] Once this experiment was declared a success in institutions for society's castoffs, it was proposed for large-scale introduction into public schools to "meet the needs" of working-class children. The important Massachusetts *Report of the Commission on Industrial and Technical Education* noted that enlightened educational experts "see that this sort of training is used in the education of the feeble-minded, in reformation of wayward and viscious children at reform and truant schools, and that it is being used to elevate the colored race in the south; and they ask why

---

35. Hall, "The Ethical Value of Vocational Instruction," p. 493; see also H. W. Stebbings, "Industrial Education as a Social Force," *Educational Review* 23 (May 1902): 462–67.

36. Ellwood P. Cubberley, *Changing Conceptions of Education* (Boston: Houghton Mifflin, 1909), pp. 56–57.

37. *Report of the Commissioner of Education for the Year 1906* (Washington, D.C.: U.S. Government Printing Office, 1906), 1:1044.

it may not be used equally efficient in stimulating and directing the higher orders of mind, in preventing as well as curing juvenile delinquency, and in improving the social conditions of white as well as black children."[38] Many leaders saw industrial education as a tool to suppress black demands for social justice. A 1909 article in the *Chicago Daily Tribune* reported that President Taft, in conference with Booker T. Washington, expressed his support for Negro industrial education because too many of the students at black liberal arts colleges had become professionals and were agitating for political rights of the Negro.[39] Implicit was the belief that Negro graduates of industrial institutions would work with their hands and shun such agitation.

In the larger world of public education, where this successful experiment was now to be tried on a grander scale, it was also believed, for similar reasons, that traditional education was inappropriate. "How can a nation endure that deliberately seeks to rouse ambitions and aspirations in the oncoming generations which in the nature of events cannot possibly be fulfilled?" asked James E. Russell, professor at Columbia University Teachers' College. "If the chief objective of government be to promote civil order and social stability," he continued, "how can we justify our practice in schooling the masses in precisely the same manner as we do those who are to be our leaders? Is human nature so constituted that those who fail will readily acquiesce in the success of their rivals, especially if that success be the result of 'cuteness,' rather than honest effort? Is it any wonder that we are beset with labor troubles?"[40] Sheep and sheep dogs obviously should have different training, especially if order and stability are the objective. Similarly, the Columbus, Ohio superintendent of schools conceded that the introduction of vocational training meant a commitment to class education. In his defense of a differentiated curriculum he pointed out "in life, men do not quibble about class distinctions. What they want is a job, and school is preparation for life."[41] Although Superintendent Shawan, like so many American educators and intellectuals, presumed to speak for working men, laborers frequently bridled at accepting class distinctions.

---

38. *Report of the Commission on Industrial and Technical Education*, p. 4.

39. "Thinks Negro Should Use Hands," *Chicago Daily Tribune*, June 5, 1909, p. 1. Quoted in John Edward Erickson, "Newspapers and Social Values: Chicago Journalism, 1890–1910" (Ph.D. diss., University of Illinois, Urbana, 1973).

40. James E. Russell, "The Trend in American Education,"*Educational Review* 32 (June 1906): 39.

41. J. A. Shawan, "Discussion," *NEA Addresses and Proceedings*, 1909, p. 386.

Most evidence suggests that the American working class took factory jobs with reluctance; it apparently had to be taught that dirty hands were as noble as clean ones—at least according to those supporting vocational education.

The right of the public schools to harden class lines and funnel one segment of the population into the industrial proletariat was bound to be questioned. Responding to this challenge, L. D. Harvey maintained that "the state has a right to do whatever is necessary for its well-being and perpetuity; good citizenship is essential for such well-being and perpetuity." According to Menomonie, Wisconsin's superintendent of schools, "The fundamental factor of good citizenship is a trained intelligence which enables the individual to support himself and those dependent upon him; a school which provides such training and sends out individuals so trained may be supported legitimately by public funds." Borrowing an argument used earlier in defense of compulsory attendance, he admonished that "if a large number of the children of any given community are not having opportunities furnished for the training which enables them to meet this necessity, then the state is failing in its duty to itself."[42] Within the following two years, Harvey's classical justification, reiterated by both the NEA and the New York State commissioner of education, was generally accepted among educators.[43]

With the development of vocational training, especially in the form of industrial education, the states, through the public schools, officially sanctioned the emerging class structure of corporate industrialism; in fact, some evidence suggests that the schools actively recruited new members of the industrial proletariat from working-class children. To the extent that professionals subverted the tradition of equal education, a new ideology would be needed to replace the older American faith in unlimited upward mobility exemplified in the Horatio Alger stories. In part, this justification was found in the substitution of "equal educational opportunity" for the older ideal of "equal education."

---

42. Lorenzo D. Harvey, "Is There a Need for Industrial Schools for Pupils Unlikely to Complete the Regular Elementary School Course and Go on to High School? Should It Provide Trade Instruction?" *NEA Addresses and Proceedings*, 1907, p. 312. This rationale was repeated by Harvey several times during the preceding years. See, for example, "President's address; The Need, Scope, and Character of Industrial Education in the Public School System," *NEA Addresses and Proceedings, 1909*, p. 59.

43. "Declaration of Principles," *NEA Addresses and Proceedings*, 1907, p. 29; and Andrew S. Draper, "The Adaption of the Schools to Industry and Efficiency," *NEA Addresses and Proceedings*, 1908, p. 69.

Few quarreled with the idea that industrial education was designed to produce an industrial working class. A more difficult issue to resolve, however, was the source of this working class. Only during the early years of the movement did the proponents explicity discuss the class origin of the recruits. Later, as the ideology of "equality of educational opportunity" replaced the ideal of equity, the social background of vocational education students became an implicit consideration.

An early and widely disseminated proposal to recruit the industrial proletariat from the urban poor was William Maxwell's 1900 plan to place trade training in elementary schools in tenement districts. Traditional education, he allowed, might give the tenement child tastes and desires "higher and better than those which he finds in his sordid surroundings," but it would not give him "any art by which he may earn a living." The superintendent proposed that "trade schools to take the place of the last two years of work in the elementary schools should be established in tenement-house neighborhoods."[44]

The following year, Charles A. Richards, of Columbia Teachers' College, endorsed Maxwell's proposal at a meeting of NEA. Richards's attempt to identify the children who would form "the army of trade workers" amounted to a plea for class education, for he, too, concluded that public schools should recruit the proletariat from those children too poor to attend high school. This departure from the older ideal of equal education put the public schools in the business of not only training the industrial proletariat, but also of selecting it from the poor segments of society. Schools were asked not to facilitate intellectual development and social mobility, but to replicate the class structure. "Such a plan is, of course, capable of only limited application under special conditions of population," said Richards in recognizing its enormous import, "and I am not sure that even then it is a plan that would fit into American ideas of education or prove practical in operation; but it has the virtue at least of aiming directly at a class that actually needs and will profit by training for the trades, and in a way that would make it economically possible for this class to be reached."[45]

Calvin M. Woodward, the director of Washington University's Manual Training School and a seasoned leader of the older manual training movement, spoke directly after Richards and minced few words attacking both Richards's and Maxwell's proposals. While addressing

---

44. *New York Annual Report*, 1900, pp. 89, 91.

45. Charles A. Richards, "Discussion," *NEA Addresses and Proceedings*, 1901, p. 674.

the issue of class education only obliquely, Woodward clearly saw the proposals as an imposition on the freedom and mobility of immature children and thus as a threat to older American educational ideals. Woodward's major concern was that the new industrial programs would deny many children the self-fulfillment derived from a traditional high school curriculum. The prospect of the school tracking a pupil into a lifetime occupation was repugnant to the St. Louis educator, a champion of older notions that schooling should stimulate ambitions, open avenues otherwise closed, and develop capacity for independent choice.[46]

The opposition of Woodward and others eventually forced a modification in the arguments for industrial training, but its impact was not immediately felt in the New York system. In 1907, industrial training in elementary schools was still justified along class lines. George S. Davis, associate superintendent in charge of division I, the "most thoroughly foreign" of all the systems divisions, noted that industrial training in elementary schools was "a matter of special consideration for this division." He proposed to give some of the children industrial training "during the last two years of the elementary schools, and perhaps even earlier."[47] The Davis plan represented a partial shift from the strictly economic rationale expressed earlier by Maxwell and thus foreshadowed a new kind of justification. He felt that children should not receive industrial training simply because they were poor; he added the provision that poor children who were not progressing satisfactorily in the school curriculum should be given the new training.

Eugene Davenport, dean of the University of Illinois College of Agriculture, emphasized the relationship between the working class and industrial education when he pointed out that questions surrounding industrial education entered school policy considerations only after the extension of compulsory attendance laws. Masses of working-class children entering the public schools necessitated the development of industrial education. Davenport expressed two assumptions commonly held by proponents of industrial training, namely, that working-class parents expected industrial training to enable their children to follow parental occupational trails, and that unless the schools moved children along

---

46. Calvin M. Woodward, "Discussion," *NEA Addresses and Proceedings*, 1901, pp. 676, 677.

47. *New York Annual Report*, 1907, p. 166.

certain occupational paths at least some of those occupations would be abandoned by the future generation.[48]

Davenport was not alone in identifying industrial training with working-class children. The class nature of industrial education was evident in the NEA's 1910 report on the place of industries in public education. The prestigious report cautioned that the kinds of education children received between the ages of 14 and 16 "must be determined by the economic conditions and the capacities of the children concerned" in harmony with the conditions of industry.[49] A similar class bias marked the survey of Brookline, Massachusetts schools. Although the survey team found that children of working-class immigrants in that city were not significantly different from upper-class children in scholastic achievement, it concluded that too high a proportion of the working-class students hoped to attend college. "A system of education in which school aims chiefly to prepare for high school, and high school to prepare for commercial work or college, will not fit these children for their life work. A large proportion of them must enter the industrial field and the schools they attend should offer practical, industrial and homemaking courses related to their general academic training."[50]

This assumption that working-class children should be trained by the public schools to stay in their proper class appeared repeatedly in the official records of the Chicago school system. Leslie Lewis, a district superintendent, complained in 1900 that the schools had motivated too many children to seek the "genteel occupations" when society needed mechanics and artisans. He recommended more industrial training to prepare children for their station in life rather than lift them out of it.[51] Thirteen years later, this sentiment was expressed by Rufus M. Hitch,

---

48. Eugene Davenport, "Unity in Education and Its Preservation While Meeting the Demands for Industrial Training," *NEA Addresses and Proceedings*, 1909, p. 486.

49. "Report of Subcommittee on Intermediate Industrial Schools," *Report of the Committee on the Place of Industries in Public Education*, p. 64; "Report of Subcommittee on Industrial and Technical Education in the Secondary School," *Report of the Committee on the Place of Industries in Public Education*, p. 84.

50. *Educational Survey of the Public Schools of Brookline, Massachusetts* (Cambridge, Mass.: Murray and Emery, 1917), p. 398; the 1917 survey of San Francisco schools expressed similar assumptions regarding the student following parental occupational lines, although in comparatively muted terms. Discussing an information form that asked, among other questions, the occupations of parents and siblings, the survey stated: "Information concerning the occupation of fathers, brothers, and sisters, and the occupations which the pupils themselves expect to enter is significant in any study of a program for vocational education." "The Public Schools of San Francisco," *Bulletin of the U.S. Bureau of Education*, 1917, no. 46, p. 508.

51. *Chicago Annual Report*, 1900, p. 230.

also a district superintendent. He admitted the students in his largely immigrant district were exceptional, but he nonetheless recommended that they be given more industrial training to prepare them for life. Hitch then outlined the changes he had instituted since 1911, changes that in some schools, especially Jackson and Gladstone, had students spend half their time in industrial training classes during the last two years of elementary school. This innovation was not aimed at slow learners, problem students, or truants, but at pupils of working-class parentage. The schools seemed determined to go along with what the district superintendent called " a movement to fit elementary school programs more nearly to the probable life career of the boy or girl." Hitch, like many other educators, assumed that children of the working class would become the industrial proletariat.[52]

In most cities, industrial training classes were aimed at the children of the urban poor, and most of the available evidence indicates that this type of recruitment was successful. The superintendent of schools in New York City, for example, justified the selling of millinery and other garments made in the city trade school for girls. This was done, he said, to cover the cost of materials that the schools had initially bought because "girls who come to the trade school are usually too poor to purchase their own material for the kind of garments they ought to make."[53] The industrial training classes in Columbus, Georgia were also for working-class children. Accordingly, G. Gunby Jordan said of the system, "We have a primary industrial school which white children (mainly children of the working-class) attend."[54]

EQUALITY OF EDUCATIONAL OPPORTUNITY

The slogan "equality of educational opportunity" was a particularly fortuitous one for those seeking to advance an educational innovation designed to produce an industrial working class from the urban poor. The initial rationale had been unacceptable because it suggested that industrial education was training poor children to take their place at or near the bottom of the industrial economy. This new slogan contained

---

52. *Chicago Annual Report*, 1913, pp. 157–59.

53. *New York Annual Report*, 1912, p. 345.

54. G. Gunby Jordan, quoted in "Industrial Education and the Future: Progress in Columbus," *Charities and the Commons*, October 5, 1907, p. 769.

the magic words in the American democratic lexicon: "equality," "opportunity," and "education." Who could challenge the notion of giving every child an equal opportunity in education? Unfortunately, the slogan actually meant less than equality or opportunity and probably less than education, at least less than what had been formerly understood by that term. In actual practice the new slogan meant little more than the earlier justification for industrial education: an opportunity for the children of the poor to be trained by the public schools for efficient service as industrial proletarians. The new formulation obviously attempted to overcome the explicit class nature of the earlier rationales, a strategy evident in George H. Mead's disclaimer:

> Our great contention is that vocational training be introduced into our school system as an essential part of its education in no illiberal sense and with no intention of separating out a class or working-men's children who are to receive trade training at the expense of academic training. We are convinced by what we have found elsewhere in America, as well as in other countries, that such a division is unnecessary. We are convinced that just as liberal a training can be given in the vocational school as that given in the present academic school. Indeed, we feel that the vocational training will be more liberal if its full educational possibilities are worked out.[55]

Mead did not deny that working-class children were to be segregated, but he insisted that the training they received would not slight the academic or cultural aspects of education. This claim, increasingly advanced by advocates of industrial education, will not withstand close investigation.

One argument for equality of educational opportunity maintained that it was democratic for working-class children to receive training designed to place them in the industrial proletariat because the state had long provided schools to educate wealthy children for upper-class vocations. Industrial education, those proponents claimed, was simply an equal chance for working-class children to gain a free training for their destined vocations. James E. Russell of Columbia Teachers' College early formulated this specious argument for educational equality. He condemned the nation's school system because:

> It does not give equality of opportunity to all. This may seem surprising, particularly as we have been boasting for over a century of our American

---

55. City Club of Chicago, *Report on Vocational Training*, p. 9.

liberty, fraternity, and equality. It is the boast, too, of most Americans that our great public-school system—the greatest thing on earth—provides alike for every boy and girl taking advantage of it. This is half true—and dangerous, as are all half-truths. The fact is, the American system of education grants equality of opportunity only to those who can go on to college and universities. It takes little account of the boy—and still less of the girl—who cannot or does not wish for a higher education. Those who "drop out" at the age of twelve or fourteen, compelled to earn a livelihood, have missed their opportunity. But why? Do we in America have need only of professional men and "men of affairs"? Are those who pay taxes and do the rougher work of life to be denied the opportunity for self-improvement? Are only those who can afford to stay in school to reap the advantages of education? In a word, what are we doing to help the average man better to do his life work and better to realize the wealth of his inheritance as an American citizen?[56]

The belief that equality meant the opportunity for members of each class to become efficient in their class labors negated the traditional American ideal of equality. Indeed, those who embrace this rationale made little effort to conceal the class nature of their proposed educational system. Whether this notion conceded the real obstacles to economic mobility in early twentieth-century America or simply reflected a belief that poor children should naturally comprise the new industrial proletariat is difficult to discern. Nevertheless, many proponents of the new training continued to call, in the guise of democratic opportunity, for a class-replicating educational system. In 1908, responding to the older ideal of equal education, Edward C. Eliott cautioned his readers in the *Journal of Education* that such equality was perhaps not an ideal capable of fulfillment. He recommended instead Aristotelian distributive justice. "An equilibrium of opportunity," he stated, "implies that grade of reward commensurate with capacities, whether those capacities could be heredity or the result of present circumstances." He contended that the first responsibility of industrial education was to "fit the square worker into the square industrial hole, the round worker into the round hole, and the triangular worker into the triangular hole."[57] More accurately put, industrial education was to find the child's general capacity and then mold him, in harmony with that capacity, to fit the needs of the industrial labor market. This purportedly by democratic rationale

---

56. Russell, "The Trend in American Education," pp. 33–34.

57. Edward C. Eliott, "The Place of Industries in Public Education," *Journal of Education*, March 12, 1908, pp. 290, 291.

was endorsed by numerous educators, including Eugene Davenport, Andrew S. Draper, and the Maryland legislature's Commission on Industrial Education.[58]

The initial rationale for industrial education and its subsequent reformulation yielded a system of class education. Both justifications provided that working-class children should receive a different kind of education because of their social and economic status. From such premises and plans a new rationale, based on the notion that children of different social groups were not equal, soon evolved. Only a few students, it was asserted, possessed the intellectual capacity to negotiate successfully the traditional curriculum designed to produce leaders. Others possessed the ability to work with their hands rather than their minds; they would be the modern equivalents of the hewers-of-wood and drawers-of-water once the public school had identified and properly trained them for their particular futures. They would be chosen not because they were poor, but because they were different. An early expression of this notion can be found in the 1901 report of the superintendent of Chicago:

> Our educational scheme must recognize the whole boy and girl, must recognize the active as well as the receptive side of their natures. It must provide work for both hands and head. As Dr. Dewey says, "The simple fact in the case is that in the great majority of human beings the distinctive intellectual interest is not dominant. If we were to conceive our educational end and aim in a less exclusive way, if we were to introduce into educational processes the activities which do appeal to those whose dominant interest is to do and to make, we should find that the hold of the school upon its members would be more vital, more prolonged." In giving further reason for adding to our traditional course of academic instruction Dr. Dewey says, "The school should not be an institution that is arbitrary and traditional, but must be related to the growing evolution of society. One of the social changes most prominent at the present time is the industrial one. It is absurd to expect that a revolution shall not affect education. Correlated with these industrial changes is the introduction of manual

---

58. See *Report of the Commission to Make Inquiry and Report to the Legislature of Maryland Respecting the Subject of Industrial Education, 1908-1910* (Baltimore, Md.: Geo. W. King, 1910), p. 12; Davenport, "Unity in Education," p. 486; Draper, "Adaption of the Schools to Industry," p. 74; Charles F. Warner, "Education for the Trades in America," *NEA Addresses and Proceedings,* 1901, p. 665; Charles R. Richards, "Discussion," *NEA Addresses and Proceedings,* 1901, p. 675; and H. M. Rowe, "To What Extent May Commercial and Industrial Training be Properly Included in the Grammar School Course?" *NEA Addresses and Proceedings,* 1908, p. 888.

training, shop-work, household arts and cooking. The school must not remain apart, isolated from forms of life that are affecting society outside. The impulse to create, to produce, whether in the form of utility or art, must be recognized. This impulse or tendency is just as real and important in the development of the human being as something that appeals simply to our desire to learn, to accumulate information and to get control of the symbols of learning.[59]

This concept emphasized the idea that nature made the great majority of mankind doers and makers rather than thinkers. This assertion cleared the state and its agents, the educators, of the charge that they were creating working-class adults by denying working-class children opportunities for continued intellectual advancement. Educators could now believe that they trained each student according to his natural abilities. If most children were "motor minded," as educators began to refer to those removed from the traditional academic curriculum, then the school should develop their motor abilities rather than force intellectual training upon those unsuited by nature for higher forms of thought. The ideology, dressed in the garments of democratic phrases, developed into a modern version of the Platonic vision—to each according to his mettle. Nature, often genetically defined by the new science of eugenics, not the educational system, was responsible for shunting many children into the industrial proletariat. This ideology, generally accepted by 1910, enabled school officials to claim that they were not engaged in class education. Industrial education was hence forth not explicitly for the children of the poor—it was for children endowed with limited mental capacities. Interestingly, these children generally continued to be working-class children.

By 1910, educational journals were filled with demands for "equality of educational opportunity" through industrial training for those "unable" to profit from the traditional academic program. The NEA's

---

59. *Chicago Annual Report*, 1901, pp. 104–5. Although the Chicago superintendent used Dewey's idea as a support for what he called manual training rather than industrial training, it is easy to discern that the logic of the argument was more appropriately suited to industrial training. Industrial training was designed as part of a differential curriculum in which different children would experience different educations while the older manual training had been designed as an addition to a unitary curriculum in which every child would experience the same education. Dewey thought that most humans were not intellectually oriented and therefore that the majority should have a less intellectual education than the small minority in whom intellectual interests were dominant. Dewey's ideas lent credence to the arguments for a differentiated curriculum and thus to industrial training as one component.

1909 "Declaration of Principles" included a statement that in the name of democracy the schools "must provide equal educational opportunities for all." Reflecting its sensitivity to the new rationale that eschewed the class orientation of industrial training, the statement continued, "Although they must give practical preparation not only for the professions, but also for commercial life, the demands of any part of the business world that courses of study be subordinated to particular interests is not in accord with the proper aims of a national system of common schools."[60] The latter part of this formulation was probably intended to calm the fears of organized labor that industrial training could be used by business interests to flood the labor market with cheap workers. Organized labor was initially reluctant to relinquish their last vestige of control over entry into the workplace, the apprentice programs.

Eventually, though, labor accepted the notion of equality of educational opportunity as a means of adapting to the conditions of industrial employment. The following recommendations of the American Federation of Labor's Committee on Industrial Education, chaired by John Mitchell, were approved at the 1909 annual convention.

> It is believed that the future welfare of America largely depends on the industrial training of our workers and in *protecting* them. The inquiries of the committee seem to indicate that if the American workman is to maintain the high standard of efficiency, the boys and girls of the country must have an opportunity to acquire educated hands and brains, such as may enable them to earn a living in a *self-selected* vocation and acquire an intelligent understanding of the duties of good citizenship.
>
> No better investment can be made by the taxpayers than to give every youth an opportunity to secure such an education. Such an opportunity is not now within the reach of a great majority of the children of wage-workers.[61]

While this statement advocated protection of the worker and self-selection for vocational choice, it still subscribed to the Davenport notion of equality based on giving wage workers' sons training to fit them to follow their fathers into the factories. It stressed that economic rather than intellectual limitations determined educational training and vocational possibilities.

---

60. "Declaration of Principles," *NEA Addresses and Proceedings*, 1909, p. 34.
61. Quoted in *Report of the Commissioner of Education for the Year 1910* (Washington, D.C.: U.S. Government Printing Office), 1: 229.

Within the next six years, the AFL leadership would march more in step with the prevailing educational rationale for industrial training. "To assure every child equal free opportunities for the kind of education which meets his needs and talents is the only basis for genuine equality of opportunity," wrote Samuel Gompers in 1916 in *The American Federationist,* "the only condition upon which democracy will function." The AFL leader supported industrial training because "the old cultural ideals of education, dealing with the abstract only, denied to the great majority of children adapted to their· minds and natures, and hence failed to fit them for the duties and possibilities of the work of life."[62] Gompers, claiming that working men were in favor of industrial education for their children, was in line with the new ideology, which held that most children were incapable of intellectual training. The belief in the inherent inability of many children was basic to the equality of educational opportunity ideal.[63] An important corollary of this rationale was expressed by Chicago's superintendent, who supported segregation as a means of educating the brightest for leadership and the rest for subordination. This was necessary, he maintained, because "individuality belongs to the genius, and when it is preached that everyone is free to exercise it, then is given expression to a high-sounding phrase which in practice becomes a menace."[64] Although the Chicago superintendents was perhaps a bit more blunt than many of his contemporary educators, he did suggest one value of the new ideology for the emerging corporate industrial structure. It allowed educators to dispense with the older ideal of education for self-governing individualism. Such a character trait would certainly be a defect in the industrial army, where only generals could safely exercise autonomy.

The belief in varying abilities was used not only to recommend that the majority of children be directed into industrial training but also to

---

62. Quoted in *Report of the Commissioner of Education for the Year 1916* (Washington, D.C. : U.S. Government Printing Office), 1: 162.

63. See Woods, "Industrial Education from the Social Worker's Standpoint," p. 855; Katherine E. Dopp, "Equality of Opportunity Can be Served Only by a Systematic Recognition of Individual Differences in Native and in Prospective Capacity Career," *NEA Addresses and Proceedings,* 1908, pp. 746–50; Burks, "Can the School Life of Pupils be Prolonged," pp. 789–93; William Esterbrook Chancellor, "Democracy in Education," *NEA Addresses and Proceedings,* 1908, p. 741; Augustus S. Downing, "The Meaning of Industrial Education to the Elementary Schools," *NEA Addresses and Proceedings,* 1909, p. 381, 384; W. E. Striplin, "Dangers and Advantages of Specialization Prior to the High School Age," *NEA Addresses and Proceedings,* 1911, p. 199; Ben W. Johnson, "Industrial Education in the Elementary School," *NEA Addresses and Proceedings,* 1910, pp. 254–56.

64. *Chicago Annual Report,* 1909, p. 18.

support the notion that many of these children should be denied any education irrelevant to their development as efficient factory workers. While calling for a more practical and relevant training, C. A. Prosser, one of the leading proponents of industrial training and secretary of the National Society for the Promotion of Industrial Education, cautioned teachers not to waste valuable school time trying to develop "the power of artistic or aesthetic expression" in children headed for industrial life.[65] The peculiar value of the doctrine of dissimilar mental capacity was that it justified all manner of exclusions. Indeed, by 1910, the idea that inherent intellectual inequalities should be the basis for differential, i.e., unequal, education disguised as equality of educational opportunity had become the conventional wisdom in education. This position was ratified when, in the same year, the prestigious and influential NEA Committee on the Place of Industries in Public Education issued its report. The committee, chaired by Jesse Burks, lamented the restraints that the older democratic ideals had placed on implementation of educational differentiation. It charged that, in trying to keep the doors to professional careers open to all aspirants, American schools in reality had denied any training to children destined for working-class jobs.[66]

American education needed a justification for differentiation that would not seem to cut children off from opportunities for careers open only to those who had completed the higher course. This required some kind of self-selection of future vocations, or at least selection based on objective criteria. The obvious question educators had to face involved the timing of the selection. Logically, the report moved directly to this issue:

> From the point of view of the development of the child the age at which this process of experimentation toward a calling should be definitely initiated corresponds fairly well with the beginning of the seventh school year. Its external symptom is the high rate of elimination from school at that time, and its internal sign is the unrest, the questioning of values, the beginnings of "storm and stress" that characterize the commencement of the age of independence, of adolescence. It would seem that at this time the secondary phase of education should begin.[67]

---

65. C. A. Prosser, "Discussion," *NEA Addresses and Proceedings,* 1912, pp. 929–30.

66. Jesse D. Burks, "Introduction by the Chairman," *Report of the Committee on the Place of Industries in Public Education,* p. 7; and Ernest N. Henderson, "The Industrial Factor in Education," *Report of the Committee on the Place of Industries in Public Education,* p. 22.

67. Henderson, "The Industrial Factor in Education," p. 22.

The committee proposed that the first six years of schooling, elementary education, should cover the "essentials and fundamentals" and precede any attempt at specialization. In the seventh year the child should enter the secondary stage, where differentiation would begin. A few talented students would be separated into the traditional curriculum to be trained for the professions and positions of leadership. Most though would be tracked into a variety of programs in which they would be given "experimental work along the line of industrial training" in order to determine their special aptitudes. Once these aptitudes had been discovered, the students would begin "higher education" and receive special training to fit them for their place in the world of work.[68] This theory of schooling would turn all education into vocational training. Education would serve to prepare the student to carry out his function in the stratified industrial society. Public schools would act to sift and sort children into the appropriate strata of that economic order.

Precisely when specialized vocational training should enter the curriculum had troubled educators from the beginning of the twentieth century. In 1901, for example, this issue of timing had raised Woodward's ire against Maxwell's program of replacing the last two years of elementary school with an industrial training curriculum for tenement district children. The New York superintendent and other proponents of industrial training wanted to start the training during the last two years of elementary school because further delay meant that most working-class children would no longer be in public school. Most states did not legally compel children to attend school beyond age 14. If most working-class children were to receive industrial training, it would have to begin at least by the seventh grade.

This proposal, however, raised two problems. The elementary curriculum had provided the minimum cultural and intellectual education required for all children. Further, many educators believed that age 12 was too young to require a vocational choice that might determine the child's future life chances. When proponents developed the rationale of equality of educational opportunity based upon the child's intellectual capacity, they discovered, fortuitously, that those differential capacities surfaced during the last two years of the compulsory attendance age. In his 1907 NEA address, Burks supported equality of educational opportunity based on capacities.[69] He also proposed that secondary education

68. Henderson, "The Industrial Factor in Education," p. 23.
69. Burks, "Can the School Life of Pupils be Prolonged?" p. 793.

be marked by a differential curriculum introduced at the beginning of the sixth year of the elementary school. One of Burks's fellow New Yorkers, Augustus S. Downing, an assistant state commissioner of education, affirmed the rationale before the National Council of Education of the NEA.[70]

These proposals did not pass unchallenged. During the heated discussion that followed Downing's address, two supporters of industrial training attacked its introduction in the elementary years. E. E. Bascomb supported the general concept of vocational training insofar as it related education to life, but he opposed the introduction of such education in the sixth grade because he felt that pupils were too young at this stage of their lives to have such a choice made for them.[71] Carroll Pearse, Milwaukee's superintendent of schools, reiterated Bascomb's argument and expressed concern that the issue might be decided by organizations like the National Association for the Promotion of Industrial Education. A speech delivered to that organization's previous meeting had called for legal sanctions against children refusing to train for the vocations chosen for them by the schools.[72] Pearse and Bascomb appealed to older notions of democracy and individualism, notions that placed the free development of the individual above social stability or economic efficiency. Because these priorities seriously conflicted with the requirements of corporate industrialism, they did not receive serious consideration. Although many educators may have shared the concerns of Bascomb and Pearse, they were resisting a force too strong to be opposed by the rhetoric of nineteenth-century democratic individualism.

The advocates of early differentiation soon carried the educational field. Their ideas were disseminated in journals and at professional meetings, and their policies were swiftly implemented in the schools. The U.S. commissioner of education reported in 1915 that the issue had been settled. Although he expressed surprise that "so radical a departure from traditional procedure" had been rapidly accepted, the commis-

---

70. Downing, "Meaning of Industrial Education," pp. 381, 383.

71. E. E. Bascomb, "Discussion," NEA Addresses and Proceedings, 1908, p. 385.

72. Carroll G. Pearse, "Discussion," NEA Addresses and Proceedings, 1908, pp. 387–88; Pearse was referring to a speech by Harvard's Eliot which said in part: "I assert that it is perfectly proper to enact laws which will give the teachers the authority to sort out the boys and girls, assign to each the trade at which he or she seems best adapted, and the law should then compel these children to be trained for these trades." Eliot quoted in "Report on the NSPIE," Journal of Education, February 13, 1908, p. 175.

sioner found that the discussion had shifted to the means of implementing the plan.[73]

It is important to underscore the fact that these attempts to justify vocational education occurred in conjunction with experimental efforts to develop such educational programs in the urban public schools. Whereas this chapter has examined the rationale for vacational education, the next will focus upon the programmatic features of the movement that were implemented in the urban public schools early in this century.

---

73. *Report of the Commissioner of Education for the Year 1915,* (Washington D.C.: U.S. Government Printing Office, 1915) 1: 30–31.

Chapter 7

Vocational Education II - The Programs

Vocational education was one of the most widely discussed educational issues during the early twentieth century. Attempts to implement manual training in public school curricula led to perhaps the most revolutionary change those curricula have ever undergone. This chapter, which analyzes the development of industrial education, begins with an examination of programs to introduce differentiation in the elementary grades in four representative cities: New York, Chicago, Cincinnati, and Los Angeles. The focus then shifts to a study of committee reports and survey teams that both described and recommended programs in many city school systems across the nation. Next, programs for vocational education for females and blacks are examined. The chapter concludes with an investigation of characteristic vocational curricula and their impact on the academic subjects.

VOCATIONAL TRAINING IN ELEMENTARY SCHOOLS

The idea of differentiating the curriculum prior to secondary schooling generated a great deal of discussion during the years 1900–1910. In New York City, Superintendent Maxwell's 1900 program for industrial training in the tenement districts started much of the controversy regarding early specialization in the elementary school. Woodward's stinging rebuke, perhaps, helped make Maxwell's subsequent proposals for early specialization increasingly less "radical" than those tried in some other cities. One of these subsequent proposals, offered by

Maxwell in 1904 in a speech before the Congress of Arts and Sciences, suggested that the board of education consider closing the elementary course of study at the end of the sixth year. Maxwell believed that educators, recognizing that "childhood closes at 12" and youth begins at 13, should reorganize schools so that secondary education started at the latter age; a new "preacademic school" would be developed for pupils in grades seven through nine. Those students who continued past the ninth grade would then enter the academic high school.[1] Maxwell did not at this time add to his proposal the idea of differentiation at the seventh-grade level in order to begin industrial training at that point.

The proposal was not adopted, but it resurfaced four years later in somewhat altered form. The superintendent, in his annual report noted that the 1908 NEA "Declaration of Principles" called for change in educational viewpoints with respect to vocational training. Accordingly, he again suggested modification of the last years of elementary schooling: a differentiated curriculum beginning in grade seven would provide a vocational track for those students destined to enter industry after completion of grade eight.[2] This proposal, like the one of 1904, failed, and Maxwell subsequently joined those who opposed introduction of industrial training before age 12. Maxwell's alternative to differentiation in the elementary grades was represented by the opening, in 1910, of a vocational school for New York City boys. Admission was limited to those boys who were at least 14 years old and who had passed an examination equivalent to the working permit test. Although it accepted students with "higher attainments," the school was designed for the pupil who had not finished elementary school.[3]

During the next three years, Maxwell faced increasing demands for addition of vocational training to the seventh and eighth grades. "It is now quite evident that if the demand for the engrafting of vocational training continues to grow, your board must pursue one or the other of two policies," he told the board of education in 1911. "Either establish an elective course of vocational work in the seventh and eighth grades of the elementary school, or else establish many more trade schools of which the Manhattan Trade School for Girls

---

1. *New York Annual Report*, 1904, p. 138.
2. *New York Annual Report*, 1908, p. 459.
3. *New York Annual Report*, 1910, pp. 182–85.

and the Vocational School for Boys may be taken as types." Maxwell urged the latter course. Among his reasons for this choice he included Woodward's arguments against his 1900 program, namely, that children were not ready to choose a life career at age 12 and needed the "cultural" work of grades seven and eight.

In response to continued agitation for differentiation in the seventh and eighth grades, Maxwell repeated his objections the following year, insisting that the seventh and eight grades were critical school years for vocational choice. They were the years when students took those traditional academic subjects "which enable their teacher to discern special aptitudes." On completion of these years, the pupil's progress, according to Maxwell, would "furnish clear indications of his special aptitudes, which may lead to the literary course, the commercial course, or the manual training course in the high school. There is no danger to which our children's education is exposed at present so imminent as that of early specialization." In 1913, after presenting the board of education with a plan for greatly expanded trade schools, the superintendent again cautioned against substituting "industrial tasks" for the "time-honored studies" before the child reached adolescence.[4]

It is clear that Maxwell did not oppose industrial training; by 1914 he simply disapproved of the introduction of a differential curriculum into the last two years of the elementary school. In reality this was modest resistance, restricted, as it was, to preventing any change in the existent elementary school structure. Maxwell's trade schools for adolescents who had not graduated from elementary school accomplished nearly the same end as did the differentiated elementary or junior high schools that were developed in other cities. Maxwell's mild protest made New York the only city of our four examples to display any reservation over early specialization.

The other cities closely followed the recommendations for early specialization that came out of the 1906–1909 NEA discussions. The 1912 report on vocational training, chaired for Chicago's City Club by George H. Mead, recommended a six-year elementary school followed by a two-year differentiated middle school; it also included a separate industrial school for "over-aged" children who would not finish their regular elementary education before they were 12. Mead, in his introduction to the report, said the recommendations were

---

4. *New York Annual Report*, 1911, p. 194; *New York Annual Report*, 1912, p. 122; and *New York Annual Report*, 1913, pp. 116–17.

made "with more confidence because they seem to us to be in harmony with the present policy of the Board of Education of Chicago and of its superintendent of schools, Mrs. Ella Flagg Young."[5]

Surprisingly, Superintendent Young's policy in this respect differed markedly from her predecessor, Edwin G. Cooley, who is most remembered for his support for industrial training. In 1908, however, Cooley had strenuously objected to industrial training in elementary years saying that "the child should not be robbed of the opportunity to acquire this power and culture [provided by the traditional elementary curriculum] by over-anxiety to fit him in some particular groove where he will become a producer."[6] Nevertheless, by 1911 Superintendent Young could report:

> The experience during the year has brought into the foreground the necessity for a division into two lines in the upper grades [of elementary school] so that provision may be made for those children whose power lies in the practical rather than academic lines, no less than for those children who are going to the high school. . . . It is important that the administration of the course includes a recognition of variations in individuals.

The division began with the sixth grade and continued into the eighth grade. A general course channeled some students into the regular high school curriculum, and an industrial course led others into the two-year vocational course in the high schools. It was expected, though, that many from the industrial course would not enter the high school.[7]

Superintendent Young's 1914 report also reflected the debate over early specialization. After outlining the progress made in the years since the revision of the elementary curriculum, the report cautioned against specific trade training. Because a major objective of the Chicago program was to separate those children destined for manual vocations from those headed for professional and white collar occupations, it did not aim to develop specialized skills for particular trades.[8] This lack of specialization was, of course, in line with the

---

5. City Club of Chicago, *Report on Vocational Training in Chicago and in Other Cities* (Chicago, 1912), pp. 11–15.

6. *Chicago Annual Report*, 1908, pp. 221–22.

7. *Chicago Annual Report*, 1911, pp. 88, 90.

8. *Chicago Annual Report*, 1914, p. 314.

thrust of industrial training—to stimulate tractable psychological pre-
dispositions, habits, conditioned responses, and personality traits
rather than to impart technical skills. Writing in 1915, the superintendent noted: "The demands of society for some degree of skill in hand
work, together with the fact that many children fail to profit from the
purely academic has led to the introduction of industrial work in
twenty-three of the elementary schools of Chicago and the formation
of prevocational classes for the elementary children in some of the
high schools." Organized in 1912 on Mead's recommendation, these
prevocational classes for students not yet finished with elementary
work, showed signs of obsolescence by 1918. Their decline, according to the superintendent, was due to the greatly expanded industrial
training given in the elementary schools.[9]

Like Chicago schools, the Cincinnati school system lowered the
age at which vocational training could begin. From the beginning of
the century until 1913, elementary school pupils received one hour
of manual training per week. In 1913, however, prevocational education was introduced. This program, similar to Chicago's in being
aimed at elementary pupils 12 years of age and older, offered an
additional four hours per week of manual work along with the modification of academic subjects to coordinate more closely with the
"industrial work of the manual training and domestic science departments." The program apparently reached as far down into the schools
as the second grade. In 1914, the elementary curriculum of Cincinnati's Lincoln School District, a "downtown area" that is, a working-
class district, was reorganized. "Retarded" pupils were segregated by
age, more industrial work was added to the fifth and sixth grades,
academic courses were differentiated to take account of the "needs"
of those students not destined for high school, and emphasis was
given to homemaking classes for girls. During 1915, one junior high
school for seventh through tenth grades was founded in Cincinnati. Its
program was devoted to industrial, commercial, and household arts.[10]

Examples of the trend in school and curriculum reorganization
were not limited to the East Coast and the Midwest. Los Angeles public schools, too, underwent restructuring designed to increase efficiency and lower the beginning age of vocational training. In 1911, a

---

9. *Chicago Annual Report*, 1915, p. 85; and *Chicago Annual Report*, 1918, pp.
90–91.

10. *Cincinnati Annual Report*, 1914, pp. 69–70; *Cincinnati Annual Report*, 1915, p.
251; and *Cincinnati Annual Report*, 1916, p. 48.

junior high school encompassing grades seven through nine was started, and within a year four similar schools were added. The elementary school was cut back to six years because, as Superintendent J. L. Francis phrased it, "Six years is sufficiently long for the mastery of the arts." Each of the junior high schools offered a diversified curriculum with three uniform courses—general course, an elementary industrial course, and a commercial course. These had been planned "with two classes of students in mind: (a) those intending to enter the high school and (b) those electing to leave school at the end of the ninth year." One of the primary advantages projected by the superintendent for the new organization was the opportunity for children to discover their vocational futures.

The Los Angeles plan called for the general outlines that would lead to this discovery to emerge at the end of the sixth grade, when it was determined if the child would aspire to a high school education or elect one of the junior high school's vocational training courses. Francis justified an early choice, claiming that "the young people of this country must know earlier what they are to do in life and prepare to do it. Whether they afterward do it or not is of minor importance compared with what they become in preparing to do it."[11] This last statement asserted that whether a child actually worked as a carpenter, a plumber, a foundry worker, or a production line assembler mattered less than how his schooling made him perceive those vocations. Francis' justification substantiates my contention that industrial education was relatively unconcerned with the development of skills for most of the industrial proletariat; it actually aimed to instill habits, values, and psychological traits. If the school could produce the right sort of person, then the school would have done all that the industrial system required of it.

The invention of the junior high school was indeed fortunate for the proponents of industrial education. Their problem had been to reach the working-class child before he became 14 and escaped the compulsory public school. It was, moreover, necessary to reach him without incurring the charge of too early specialization and premature delineation. The insertion of the junior high between the elementary and high schools allowed educators to carve two years from the elementary curriculum. Professionals claimed that the elementary curriculum was inefficient for those children designated as future

---

11. J. H. Francis, "A Reorganization of Our School System," *NEA Addresses and Proceedings*, 1912, pp. 371–75.

working-class adults. All the necessary elementary school work could be completed in six years; then, at approximately the end of the sixth grade, the child's intellectual gifts surfaced, awaiting guidance into the proper school channel.[12] Industrial training in junior high school, as opposed to elementary school, could circumvent the charge that a premature choice of life work was being forced. Educators argued that junior high school students were not children but adolescents, and that industrial training in junior high was not geared for specific job training but offered an opportunity for the student to explore different vocational possibilities that were suited to his capacities. As the manually inclined student, now separated from the academically inclined student, was matched with courses designed to meet his special needs, the industrial training program processed his personality and habit patterns into the types required by corporate industrialism. In the traditional elementary curriculum, if the child dropped out of school at age 14, he would have "wasted" two years.

THE DROPOUT PROBLEM

The problem of the school dropout has long concerned educators and social reformers. It led to the passage of relatively effective compulsory attendance laws at the turn of the century. As school reformers began to search for a rationale for a differential curriculum that would not seem too out of step with the rhetoric of democracy, they turned to the problem of the child who left school soon after the compulsory age of 14. It was usually held that many children could not achieve in the academically oriented curriculum of the upper elementary school. These children, it was urged, soon fell behind in their school work, repeated grades, and eventually became what Leonard Ayers termed "laggards." They quit school because they had little interest in the work offered and saw no relevance in it for their future life's work. This analysis, which could be found in literally hundreds of journal articles and speeches advocating industrial training, usually stated that the motor-minded child would not drop out if the school offered him a practical curriculum that met his special needs. Once the schools offered industrial training, this line of argument continued, the truant officer would become

---

12. Calvin O. Davis, "Secondary Schools, " *School Survey, Grand Rapids, Michigan* (Grand Rapids, Mich.: White Printing Co., 1916), p. 230.

obsolete. Children would happily remain in school until they were equipped for their role in the world of work.

One of the early contributions to this argument came from Calvin M. Woodward. In his role as president of the St. Louis Board of Education, he issued a report entitled, "When and Why Pupils Leave School: How to Promote Attendance in the Higher Grades." This report was later reprinted in the 1900 report of the U.S. commissioner of education.[13] Woodward noted that the dropout rate greatly accelerated after age 12 and the retention rate fell sharply after the fourth and fifth grades: of every 100 children who began the second grade, the Boston schools retained 75 by the fifth grade; the Chicago schools, 71; and the St. Louis schools only 49. The decline was much sharper for the retention of sixth grade pupils: Boston kept only 49; Chicago, 26; and St. Louis, 14. The causes of this disgraceful record could be, Woodward believed, easily remedied. A peculiar problem for St. Louis was that its schools, unlike Boston's and Chicago's, did not provide free books for the students and thus posed a financial hardship for poor pupils. More important, he said, was the fact that the schools did not directly address the interests of students unattracted to bookish education. Woodward declared that these children needed more manual training high schools. Although the superintendent had argued only for free texts and the addition of a rather broadly gauged manual training component to the school curriculum, the possibilities of Woodward's line of analysis were not ignored in arguments developed by the proponents of a narrower type of industrial training.

The most influential of these arguments was voiced by Susan M. Kingsbury, special investigator for the Massachusetts Commission on Industrial and Technical Education, in 1906. Her conclusions served as a justification for the conclusions of the commission and were included as a special section of its report. Kingsbury's ideas were given additional publicity in *Charities and the Commons* the following year.[14] She began with the announcement that 25,000 children between the ages of 14 and 16 were not attending school in the state of Massachusetts. Five of every six in this group had not completed the grammar grades, one-half had failed to complete the seventh grade, and one-fourth had not even

---

13. *Report of the Commissioner of Education for the Year 1899–1900* (Washington D.C.: U.S. Government Printing Office), 2: 1364–74.

14. *Report of the Commission on Industrial and Technical Education* (Boston, 1906), pp. 25–93; and Susan Kingsbury, "What Is Ahead for the Untrained Child in Industry?" *Charities and the Commons*, October 5, 1907, pp. 808–13.

finished the sixth grade. These untrained children, destined to become industrial workers, portended ill for the future of American industry. The future was equally bleak for the children, since her research indicated that they tended to enter the "undesirable" industries that required little skill and presented almost no opportunity to learn a trade. These industries offered what she called "dead-end" occupations that paid a small beginning wage and held slight hope for advancement. Of 354 employers she surveyed, only 86 said that children under 16 were of value as employees.[15] During the "wasted years" between 14 and 16, children not in public school could expect low wages and periodic unemployment.

Why, then, did so many children leave school at age 14? Kingsbury confessed that the answer to this question was difficult to determine: "It is only by going into the home and getting into touch with the parents that we can approach the truth. Even then only a certain range of facts, mostly negative in character, are easily secured." Nevertheless, with only this narrow range of "facts," and without respect for the ambiguity that social scientists have since learned to attach to data garnered by interview techniques, she was able to discover the answer. Not surprisingly, it was precisely the answer required for the commission's proposed solution. Kingsbury found that most parents wanted their children to remain in school, especially if an in industrial curriculum was provided. She claimed that less than one-fourth of the dropouts were caused by financial hardships. The basic reason, in most cases, was because the work of the school did not interest students. This disinterest occurred when they reached the age at which their characteristic tendency was "to do and not to study." Schools, with their bookish curriculum, did not meet this need. The solution, according to Kingsbury, was to provide children who wished "to do" with an industrial training curriculum that would meet their interests. Kingsbury's survey work was significant because it offered "objective proof" that the cause of the dropout problem was the traditional course, which excluded industrial training. She maintained that poverty was not a significant factor and that teachers might contribute to, but were not fundamentally responsible for, the widespread withdrawal of working-class children.[16]

Kingsbury's conclusions were generally accepted as empirical facts and soon became the conventional wisdom of those supporting indus-

---

15. Kingsbury, "What Is Ahead for the Untrained Child?" pp. 808, 812.
16. Kingsbury, "What Is Ahead for the Untrained Child?" pp. 809, 811.

trial training.[17] Her conclusions offered a timely, convenient, and tidy rationale for the new programs. It was the children's rejection of the traditional curriculum, not economic hardship, not parental desire for the addition of the child's wage to the family income, not personality or social class differences between teachers and working-class students, that caused the high dropout rate. If industrial training could be added to the curriculum, parents would encourage attendance and students would willingly remain in school until their training was completed. But this argument was perhaps too tidy and convenient. Several nagging questions beg for a closer examination of the facts that Kingsbury and her successors offered.

The first question concerns the assertion that a large percentage of parents wanted their children to stay in school and would have kept them there if an industrial curriculum had existed. Kingsbury and her staff, interviewing dropouts' parents, may have elicited the kind of response they wanted. One must remember that at this time the interview survey technique was in its infancy, and even the fallible reliability safeguards since developed were then unknown. It is also the case that many of these working-class parents may have been reluctant to admit to college-educated ladies that they had allowed their children to quit school. Any suggestion that the school was at fault because it had failed to offer the appropriate course for the child may have been a welcome refuge for the harried parents. At the very least, one must view with suspicion the claim that many working-class parents wanted their children to continue in school only if an industrial training program were available.

Similarly open to challenge is the claim that curriculum problems rather than teacher-pupil friction caused the working-class child to leave school. From what is known of the difficulties that conscientious teach-

---

17. See Charles F. Warner, "Industrial Training in the Public School," *Charities and the Commons*, October 5, 1907, p. 823; Paul Hanus, *Beginnings of Industrial Education* (Boston: Houghton Mifflin, 1908), pp. 3–52; F. B. Dyer, "Need for Special Classes," pp. 313–15; Andrew S. Draper, "The Adaption of the Schools to Industry and Efficiency," *NEA Addresses and Proceedings*, 1908, p. 68; Joseph M. Frost, "Industrial Training in High School," *NEA Addresses and Proceedings*, 1909, p. 317; Theodore W. Robinson, "The Need of Industrial Education in Our Public Schools," *NEA Addresses and Proceedings*, 1910, p. 370: Chicago Association of Commerce, *Industrial and Commercial Education* pp. 6, 14, and 46; Robert W. Selvidge, "A Study of Some Manual Training High Schools with Suggestions for an Intermediate Industrial School," *Manual Training Magazine* 10 (June 1909): 373–87; Charles DeGarmo. "Relation of Industrial to General Education," *School Review* 17 (March 1909): 145–53; and City Club of Chicago, *Report on Vocational Training in Chicago* (Chicago, 1912), pp. 2, 6, and 37.

ers presently have with children of different ethnic, religious, and social class backgrounds, it is hard to believe that such problems did exist in the past. Indeed, it was known even then that they did not exist. Superintendent Maxwell, for example, reported that one serious cause of children leaving school was that many teachers "froze out" certain students.[18] Alfred Guillo of Throop Polytechnic Institute in Pasadena, California, an advocate of industrial training, was "satisfied that election as to vocational subjects is not in itself a satisfactory preventive of children leaving school." He felt that:

> . . .the element of first importance is the personality of the teacher. Again and again I have known children to elect a subject because of their eagerness for it, and before their selection was made final by announcement, throw the subject overboard, because of the teacher assigned to the particular class. I have known children who had taken a subject for a year and were anxious to continue it decide not to do so, because of the personality of the teacher. This is, of course, a large subject. Nor is it a very cheerful subject, but none the less it is true and it is vital. . . . My boy of fourteen assures me confidently, "a great many more kids leave school because the teachers are cranky and no good, than because they sour on the things that are taught."[19]

Indeed, the children were their own most eloquent spokesmen on the influence of the teacher on the dropout rate. A touching statement appeared in Helen M. Todd's 1913 article, "Why Children Work—The Children's Answer," which appeared in the widely read *McClure's Magazine*. Todd, the factory inspector in Chicago investigating the conditions of child labor relative to the state child labor laws, was astonished that 412 of 500 children she questioned in the factories stated that they would rather work in a factory than attend school. One major reason involved the fear of the teachers, particularly "the . . . fear and dread [of] corporal punishment." Her report of a conversation with one underaged factory worker she had herded back to school represented many of the responses she recorded:

> "What," I said in despair, remembering the dark, damp basement in which I had found him, "what is it you like so much about your job?"

---

18. *New York Annual Report*, 1902, p. 91; see Edith Abbott and Sophonisba P. Breckenridge, *Truancy and Nonattendance in Chicago Schools* (New York: Aron Press, 1970), p. 61.

19. Alfred Guillo, "Discussion," *NEA Addresses and Proceedings*, 1907, pp. 803–4.

"The boss," he answered, "don't never hit me."

"Did they hit you at school?"

"Yes."

"What for?"

"They hits ye if ye don't learn, and they hits ye if ye whisper, and they hits ye if ye have a string in yer pocket, and they hits ye if yer seat squeaks, and they hits ye if ye scrape yer feet, and they hits ye if ye don't stand up in time, and they hits ye if yer late, and they hits ye if ye forget the page."

According to Todd's count, 269 children said they preferred the factory to the school because they did not get hit in the factory.[20] Not all of the vast numbers of children who swelled the ranks of dropouts quit school because of physical abuse or other teacher-related problems, but Todd's evidence makes Kingsbury's disclaimer of this factor ring hollow.

The contention that many families of dropouts could afford to keep their children in school was apparently important to Kingsbury's argument. This had to be factually established to strengthen the conclusion that these children left school primarily because they objected to the traditional curriculum. Only thus could proponents of industrial training pose the issue in terms of industrial training or no education for these children. Kingsbury discovered that 76 percent of the dropouts were not caused by economic necessity. This figure must have seemed suspicious to contemporaries familiar with Robert Hunter's *Poverty* (1904), John Spargo's *The Bitter Cry of the Children* (1907), Charles B. Spahr's *America's Working People* (1900) or R. W. Deforrest's and L. Veiller's *The Tenement House Problem* (1903). Nevertheless, the claim that economic necessity was not a factor, essential to the argument for industrial training, was accepted as true. Citing the Kingsbury survey as evidence, George H. Mead's introduction to the Chicago City Club's report on vocational training asserted that "the prevailing reason for leaving school is not to be found in the financial need of the family of the 14 year old child," but in lack of interest in school. In fact, "other investigations have been so conclusive on this point that this committee has not felt that we needed to undertake a special study of the motives of

20. Helen M. Todd, "Why Children Work—The Children's Answer," *McClure's Magazine*, April 1913, pp. 75–76.

Chicago children for dropping out of school as soon as the law permits, or those of their parents in allowing this elimination." Mead must have been uneasy with this assertion, however, for he included a rather unusual explanatory footnote suggesting that even if poverty was a factor in the Chicago dropout problem, educators should not allow it to hinder the development of industrial training programs.[21]

Todd's experience with working children in the factories of Chicago suggested a far different set of facts regarding the contribution of poverty to the dropout rate. "Ask any 20 children in a factory this question: 'Why are you working?' " said the factory inspector. "The answer will show you that the greater part of child labor comes from the premature death or disability of the father through industrial accident or disease, or the unemployment of the father through being engaged in an industry which occupies its people only a portion of the year, at low wages." Of 800 working children she queried regarding the cause of their employment, 381 responded that it was due to "death of the father through some industrial accident, or his sickness from some industrial disease contracted in the course of his work."[22] Undoubtedly, some of the children whose fathers were not ill also cited financial hardship at home as a contributing cause to their choice of factory work over school. In 1913, the Illinois Bureau of Labor Statistics conducted a survey of conditions among the state's employed children between the ages of 14 and 16. It found that 76.15 percent of the 2,365 children who left school for gainful employment reported they had done so to help support themselves or their families.[23] Interestingly, this statistic did not receive the wide publicity of the Kingsbury finding.

The claim that most children did not drop out of school because of family poverty was probably not essential to the assertion that these same children would have chosen to remain in school if industrial training had been available. It did, however, apparently strengthen that argument enough to warrant its acceptance by champions of industrial training. These proponents had raised the dropout question principally to advance the claim that industrial training was the only educational program that would keep these children in school. The data compiled

---

21. City Club of Chicago, *Report on Vocational Training*, p. 4.

22. Helen M. Todd, "Why Children Work," p. 69.

23. Luke D. McCoy, *Seventeenth Biennial Report of the Bureau of Labor Statistics of the State of Illinois* (Springfield, Ill.: Schnepp and Banes, 1915), p. 708. I am indebted to David Hogan for bringing this source to my attention.

by Kingsbury strengthened that claim by declaring invalid other purported causes of student attrition.

The claim that industrial training would appeal to children and keep them in school was often accompanied by a plea to raise the compulsory school attendance age, a qualifier that disputes the validity of the argument. The suggested limit varied: the Chicago club's report and Cincinnati's superintendent proposed 16; Harvard's President Eliot and Andrew Draper called for age 18.[24] In a characteristic plea for the extension of school attendance laws in order to accommodate industrial training, Eliot said bluntly, "It is perfectly proper to enact laws which give the teachers the authority to sort out boys and girls, assign to each the trade at which he or she seems best adapted, and the law should then compel these children to be trained for these trades."[25]

Such pleas might have challenged the alleged holding power of industrial training programs. Speculation might have focused also upon compulsory attendance in the traditional as well as vocational curriculum. This possibililty bothered some of the proponents of industrial training. Lorenzo D. Harvey, president of the Stout Institute, contended in his "presidential address" before the NEA's 1909 general session that students should be compelled to attend school beyond age 14 for the good of the state and for their own benefit. Coercion, however, was to be applied to industrial training rather than the traditional curriculum because in the older program "a large number of them would fail to secure any large benefit from the school work, and in many instances, their presence would be a positive damage to others who might benefit from it, because of their lack of interest or capacity to master the kind of work the schools offer and of the interference with the work of other pupils in the school resulting from these conditions."[26]

In addition to legal means, some school officials actively sought the compulsion of the marketplace to secure attendance in industrial training classes. These educators rightly understood that once employers demanded certificates of schooling as a condition of employment, the holding power of industrial training programs would be greatly enhanced. In 1906, the Cincinnati superintendent called on the city's

---

24. Dyer, "Need for Special Classes," p. 315; Draper, "Adaption of the Schools to Industry and Efficiency," p. 76; Eliot, quoted in Chicago Association of Commerce, *Industrial and Commercial Education*, p. 15; City Club of Chicago, *Report on Vocational Training*, pp. 11 and 25.

25. Eliot, quoted in "Report on the NSPIE," p. 175.

26. Harvey, "President's Answer," p. 57.

businessmen to follow the example of businessmen in Worcester, Massachusetts, where it was public knowledge that only applicants who had been certified by the schools would be hired. Such a policy, he promised, would aid retention in vocational classes.[27] Undoubtedly he was correct, but this preoccupation with proof of school training ultimately contributed to a general overemphasis on the credentialing function of schools, described by Ivar Berg as "the great training robbery."[28] Moreover, the rise of credentialing was not entirely accidental, for many school officials actively promoted its ascendency.

Interestingly, there seemed little systematic examination of the actual holding power of industrial training programs. Most of the evidence supporting their retention capabilities consisted of casual observations that increased attendance coincided with the inauguration of an industrial training program in a city. Woodward made one such observation in his statement regarding the increase in Kansas City's high school attendance after the establishment of a manual training program.[29] Another was made by W. J. Bogan, principal of Chicago's Lane Technical High School, who boasted that over 50 percent of the students who enrolled in his school graduated, while the average for high schools in the United States was only about 10 percent.[30] One of the few systematic efforts to test the relative holding power of industrial training occurred in New York City during 1914, when Superintendent Maxwell responded to agitation for New York to institute a "Gary-type" platoon system in its upper elementary grades. The Gary system, which had a differentiated curriculum featuring industrial training, was most noted for its space-saving technique of having students move in platoons from one learning station to another. This allowed the school to schedule more students per square foot, as each station was in constant use. Maxwell was committed to the prevocational type of industrial training program, and his "experiment" attempted to demonstrate its superiority over the Gary structure. Three types of schools were tested: Gary-type, prevocational, and control schools (which were the regular, or traditional, type of elementary school). It did not surprise Maxwell

---

27. *Cincinnati Annual Report*, 1906, p. 43.

28. Ivar Berg, *Education and Jobs: The Great Training Robbery* (Boston: Beacon, 1971).

29. *Report of the Commissioner of Education for the Year, 1899–1900*, 2: 1364–74; pp. 1364–74; see also Frost, "Industrial Training in High Schools," p. 319.

30. Quoted in Chicago Association of Commerce, *Industrial and Commercial Education*, p. 13

that his prevocational schools not only were more effective in teaching the "fundamental subjects," but also demonstrated a slightly higher holding power than did the Gary-type schools. What did come as a surprise, however, was that the traditional elementary schools not only taught the fundamental subjects on a par with the prevocational institution, but that they also demonstrated a holding power superior to either of the other two types of schools.[31]

Maxwell's investigation, however, evoked few calls to action or reform. In fact, compared to the response given to the Kingsbury investigations, this experiment went relatively unnoticed. Educators, like social and political experts and officials, often respond to the implications of any study not on the basis of its plausibility or the probable validity of its conclusions, but on the basis of how well its conclusions buttress the argument they are advancing. We have seen, for example, how the dropout problem was frequently cited by advocates of industrial training programs. While many of these proponents were genuinely concerned with the low retention rate in the public schools, an analysis of their discussion of the problem reveals that the dropout issue rationalized rather than caused support for industrial training. Most often arguments justifying such training were weakly constructed and lacked empirical data; nevertheless, they were accepted as facts in the campaign to change the American school structure.

INDUSTRIAL TRAINING AND INDUSTRIAL NEEDS

If the dropout problem and the question of equal education opportunity served as rationales for industrial training, so, too, did the slogan "education for individual needs." Embedded in all the arguments for industrial training was the notion that the monolithic and singular traditional curriculum did not and could not meet the needs of the diverse types of students the schools were intended to serve. These students, the argument continued, needed a curriculum with options that would satisfy their individual differences and needs.

Given this purported purpose of the new programs, the instruction, not the child, should have been modified. Even a cursory perusal of the industrial training movement literature, though, discloses repeated

---

31. *New York Annual Report,* 1915, pp. 118–30.

declarations that the schools had to be concerned with industrial efficiency and that their purpose was to develop students who would contribute to that efficiency. While advocating commercial education before the 1900 meeting of the NEA, H. M. Rowe, a Baltimore physician maintained that "all education, when considered in relation to the great masses of the people of our country, must be measured finally by the single test of usefulness and utility."[32] Students were often characterized as economic units to be trained for efficiency. The Indiana state superintendent of public instruction typically implored that "no impractical thing, nothing that raises impossible ideals and false hopes, nothing that belittles honest work and lessens efficiency should have time and place in the schools."[33] Although the new industrial programs were ostensibly designed to meet the "individual needs" of children, educators asserted that the focal point of the programs must be industrial requirements and that the finished products should be efficient economic units adjusted to their industrial environment.[34]

Perhaps the easiest way to reconcile these apparently contradictory aims of industrial training would be to call them paradoxical. But, as is often the case with purported historical paradoxes, further analysis may remove some of the confusion. Deeper examination shows that advocates of industrial training usually put the priorities of industrial capital above those of self-fulfillment. For example, the influential 1910 NEA *Report of the Committee on the Place of Industries in Public Education* cautioned that industrial training must meet the "needs" of diverse students but that it should not attempt to meet individual "wants."[35] This

---

32. H. M. Rowe, "The Advantages and Difficulties of Introducing the Commercial Branches in Grammar and High Schools," *NEA Addresses and Proceedings,"* 1900, p. 565.

33. Indiana Department of Public Instruction, *Twenty-Fourth Biennial Report of the State Superintendent for the School Years Ending July 31, 1907 and July 31, 1908* (Indianapolis: Wm. B. Burford, 1908), p. 419. See also William Barclay Parons, "The Practical Utility of Manual and Technical Training," *NEA Addresses and Proceedings*, 1905, p. 134; Frank A. Vanderlip, "The Economic Importance of Trade Schools," *NEA Addresses and Proceedings*, 1905, p. 141; W. T. Bogan, "Discussion," *NEA Addresses and Proceedings*, 1912, p. 927; and "Declaration of Principles," *NEA Addresses and Proceedings*, 1905, p. 42.

34. See A. C. Thompson, "Conditions Which Demand Industrial Training in Elementary Schools," *NEA Addresses and Proceedings*, 1909, p. 317; Harvey, "President's Address," p. 65; Clifford B. Connelley, "The Effect of Industrial Environment," *NEA Addresses and Proceedings*, 1910, p. 242; Frank T. Carlton, *Education and Industrial Evolution* (New York: Macmillan, 1908), p. 47.

35. Report of Subcommittee on Intermediate Industrial Schools, *Report of the Committee on the Place of Industries in Public Education*, 1910, pp. 68–70.

distinction permitted educators to claim that they were developing individualized programs and then to define what different groups of students should need. Predictably, the professionals' definition of student needs corresponded closely with the manpower requirements of corporate industry, for the paramount individual educational need was deemed to be the ability to earn a living. This entailed the development of habits and personality traits that would be saleable in the industrial labor market.

Examples of the nexus between the needs of students as defined by educators and the manpower requirements of corporate industry proliferate in the literature of the industrial training movement. In his writings and speeches Lorenzo D. Harvey formulated important concepts in this relationship. In a 1905 address to the NEA, Harvey argued that if the schools equipped the student to do useful work, they would meet the student's educational needs.[36] Later in his NEA "presidential address," he stated, "The educational process involves knowing, not for the sake of knowing, but for the sake of doing because of knowing, and for what one may come to be as a result of doing because of knowing. Knowledge is useful only as it affects conduct—conduct in its broadest sense, not merely moral conduct but physical and mental conduct as well."[37] Once it was accepted that the child's needs were met by equipping him for useful work and that no core of knowledge contained intrinsic value, then industrial training programs could be based on the demands of industry while claiming to meet the needs of the child.

The Massachusetts report of 1906 defended a position similar to Harvey's when it concluded that "the latest philosophy of education reenforces the demands of productive industry by showing that that which fits a child best for his place in the world as a producer tends to his own highest development physically, intellectually, and morally."[38] The same year, James E. Russell of Teacher's College, Columbia, echoed the Massachusetts doctrine by arguing that education should make students "good for something." More specifically, it should "contribute to the greater efficiency of the workingman" and lead him to "take more pride in his work."[39] The following year, the NEA dutifully included in

---

36. Lorenzo D. Harvey, "Manual Training in the Grades," *NEA Addresses and Proceedings,* 1905, p. 121.

37. Harvey, "President's Address," p. 49.

38. *Report of the Commission on Industrial and Technical Education,* p. 19.

39. James E. Russell, "The Trend in American Education," *Educational Review* 32 (June 1906): 35, 40, 41.

its "Declaration of Principles" the following: "We believe that it is the duty of the state not only to qualify its children to be good citizens but also as far as possible to be useful members of their community. Hence, wherever conditions justify their establishment, trade schools should be maintained at public expense to fit children as far as possible for a chosen career."[40] Thus it became the duty of the state to provide for the individual needs of working-class children by training them to fit the requirements of industry. During the ensuing years many proponents of industrial training returned to this theme.[41]

The key to the new industrial programs was to provide "the right kind of education" for various kinds of children. Like the men in the tale of Plato's noble lie, the economic station for which each individual was trained by the state was to be determined by his capacity. It was considered inefficient to develop a child's potential simply because potential existed. Such development was justified only if there was an economic demand for it; a major function of industrial training, in fact, was to match the inherent capacity of the child with the labor demands of corporate industry. This function was implicit in most industrial training literature, surfaces in many school programs, and was graphically portrayed in the City Club of Chicago's report on vocational training. The report contained a "diagram showing articulation of proposed schools and courses with the existing schools and with occupations." This diagram illustrated how each school or industrial training course would funnel students into the stratifies layers of corporate industry. (See diagram page 172–73.) Following the consensus of the industrial training movement, the report projected that the high school would train the noncommissioned officers of the industrial army while the lower schools, the elementary and trade schools, would process the rank-and-file:

---

40. "Declaration of Principles," *NEA Addresses and Proceedings, 1907,* p. 29.

41. See Clifford B. Connelley, "To What Extent Does Manual Training Aid in Adjustment to Environment," *NEA Addresses and Proceedings,* 1911, p. 715; Joseph Blair, "Cooperative Schools," *Atlantic Educational Journal* 7 (February 1912): 211; Charles A. Bennett, "Vocational Training—To What Extent Justifiable in Public Schools?" *Vocational Education,* March 1912, p. 258; Robinson, "Need of Industrial Education," p. 370; James J. Joyner, "The Tendencies in Industrial Education," *Journal of Education,* July 14, 1910, pp. 31–32; Edward A. Rumely, "Our Public Schools as Preparatory Schools for Practical Life," *NEA Addresses and Proceedings,* 1910, p. 603; and Virgil G. Curtis, "The Relation of Manual Training to Technical Education," *NEA Addresses and Proceedings,* 1901, p. 665.

It is the distinctive opportunity of the high school, and therefore, its duty, to take advantage of the superior academic attainments of its pupils by training mainly for the positions above that of the actual mechanic for the directive positions in the industries. . . . On the lower academic levels the industrial courses should provide for the actual mechanic of the future the training in skill which is needed in the industries, and should give as much of the technical instruction in applied sciences, mathematics, knowledge of materials, etc., as the academic attainments of the pupils will permit. Such elementary courses should give that all-round training in skill which is not generally obtainable in the industries, and should endeavor to develop such a degree of industrial intelligence and adaptability as will make rapid advancement possible after work is begun.[42]

Although every student was a potential recruit for the manpower requirements of corporate industry, each supposedly trained to fit his particular niche in the industrial work force, the case of industrial training for blacks and women is especially instructive. Though the effort to fit women to their places reached across class lines, it was considered particularly significant for girls of working-class parents who were to become wives and mothers in working-class homes. For blacks, the attempt to fit individuals into niches was more narrowly a class-oriented training, for it was understood that blacks would "naturally" reside at the lowest social, economic, and intellectual levels. Children in both groups were trained for a specific kind of future determined for them by an agency of the state, the public school.

INDUSTRIAL TRAINING FOR BLACKS

Some of the earliest experiments with industrial training had been tested on black and American Indian children under the direction of General Armstrong at Hampton Institute, Virginia. Armstrong's primary aim was to "tame" and "civilize." The movement for black industrial training received strong impetus when corporate industrialists, working through their foundations, heavily financed Booker T. Washington's efforts at Tuskegee Institute. They did so in order to create an alternative nonunion black work force to counter the effects of increased labor organization. By the early years of the twentieth century, black industrial training

---

42. City Club of Chicago, *Report on Vocational Training*, facing page 14, 40. To emphasize this theme it was restated on page 98.

Diagram showing articulation of proposed schools and courses with existing schools and with occupations

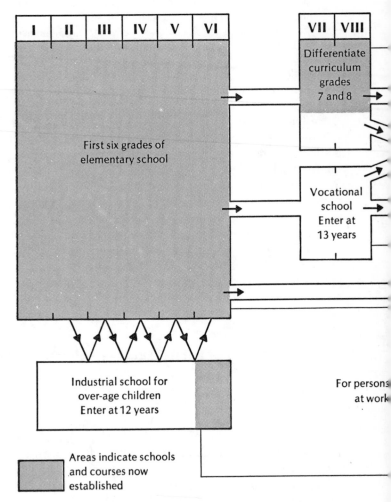

Source: City Club of Chicago, *Report on Vocational Training* (Chicago, 1912), opposite page 14.

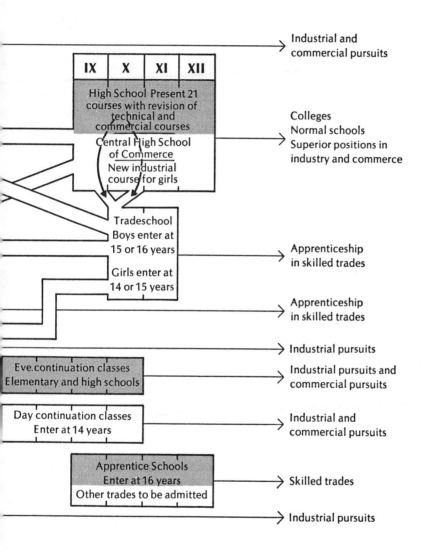

Industrial and
commercial pursuits

IX   X   XI   XII

High School Present 21
courses with revision of
technical and
commercial courses

Central High School
of Commerce

New industrial
course for girls

Colleges
Normal schools
Superior positions in
industry and commerce

Tradeschool
Boys enter at
15 or 16 years

Girls enter at
14 or 15 years

Apprenticeship
in skilled trades

Apprenticeship
in skilled trades

Industrial pursuits

Eve.continuation classes
Elementary and high schools

Industrial pursuits and
commercial pursuits

Day continuation classes
Enter at 14 years

Industrial and
commercial pursuits

Apprentice Schools
Enter at 16 years
Other trades to be admitted

Skilled trades

Industrial pursuits

was well established in the South, and many urban school systems in the North had opened industrial schools for black children.[43]

The report of the Maryland legislature's Commission on Industrial Education in 1910 revealed the objectives and ideology of the movement for black industrial training. A special section devoted to "Industrial Schools for the Negro" praised the civilizing efforts of missionaries using industrial training among "primitive" people in Africa and lauded the exploratory endeavors at Hampton and Tuskegee.[44] The report insisted that blacks needed civilizing and moral uplift which could be accomplished only through manual labor. Accordingly, it proposed industrial training as the only educational device which would prepare the race for diligent and loyal service with the dishcloth, plow, and broom. It offered this advice for teachers of black children:

> Let them read to their pupils the printed recommendations of the Superintendent and insist upon their learning to do well and thoroughly whatever useful service their hands find to do, as the surest means to their advancement.
>
> Teach them that mere book learning will avail them but little in the battle of life, that they must expect to fulfill the ordinance of the Creator, who declared that "in the sweat of thy face shalt thou eat bread"; teach that ease and rest and pleasure are good things only when they come as the reward of work well done; that agriculture is a great industry and that farm labor is honorable; that domestic service is indispensable in every household and that its performance faithfully, honestly and efficiently is not only commendable but contributes to the sum of human happiness; that as they expect to dwell permanently in close neighborhood to their white brethren, they should strive to gain the good will and respect of these white brethren; that they must not depend upon any mere statute law to make them better or more respected citizens, but that they must work out their own advancement; . . . If the masses of the negro [sic] race can be taught to take a sensible and practical view of things in accordance with the teachings of their sincere well-wishers, a good beginning in

43. For a more complete discussion of this aspect of black industrial training in the South see James Douglas Anderson, "Education for Servitude: The Social Purposes of Schooling in the Black South" (Ph.D. diss., University of Illinois, 1973); for a discussion of industrial training for black children in the urban North see Judy Jolley Rosenbaum, "Black Education in Three Northern Cities in the Early Twentieth Century" (Ph.D. diss., University of Illinois, 1974).

44. *Report of the Commission to Make Inquiry and Report to the Legislature of Maryland Respecting the Subject of Industrial Education, 1908–1910* (Baltimore: Geo. W. King, 1910), pp. 36–40.

the right direction will at least be made. And the teachers in our public schools may, so far as practicable, teach the children how to do many useful things to their advantage.[45]

The paternalism permeating the industrial training literature asserted that the school should determine the best kind of future for black children. "Your committee [has] kept in view the fact that the colored people," stated the Maryland report, "in a sense, are still wards of the state and that it is the duty of the state to teach them with patience and kindness the things that will fit them for their mission in life and at the same time promote their own true and substantial welfare and happiness."[46] This same paternalism was reflected in Elizabeth Holt's description of the Augusta, Georgia public schools' program for black industrial training. Here, where students were given certificates at the end of their training period, Holt noted that "by this certification it is the purpose of our school system to supply the city with duly authorized and certified cooks, laundresses and seamstresses." She "believ[ed] that the best friend to the Southern negro [sic] is the Southern white man who realizes his limitations, sympathizes with his needs and deals with him fairly and wisely for his greatest good in the community in which he must continue to live."[47] Northern school supervisors preached essentially the same message regarding working-class white children. These educators began with a statement of the inherent weakness or limitations of the child, then took cognizance of the inevitability of the socioeconomic conditions which the child would face as an adult, and ended by asserting that only someone with superior insight and benevolence could really determine the child's best interests.

INDUSTRIAL TRAINING FOR WOMEN

Like those programs designed for blacks, industrial training programs for girls aimed to fit them for a particular place in society and equip young women with reality principles appropriate for their station in life. The blacks were relegated to the bottom of the socioeconomic structure, and

---

45. *Report of the Commission to Make Inquiry*, p. 38.

46. *Report of the Commission to Make Inquiry*, p. 39.

47. Elizabeth G. Holt, "Negro Industrial Training in the Public Schools of Augusta, Georgia," *The Journal of Home Economics* 4 (October 1912): 317, 323.

women were trained for domesticity. Without exception, the literature on industrial training for girls emphasized that woman's natural role was as wife and homemaker, so programs for girls focused on courses in the household arts, especially sewing and cooking.[48] "No girl can be considered properly educated who cannot sew," John D. Philbrick observed in analyzing city school systems for the U.S. commissioner of education.[49]

By 1900, nearly three-fourths of Chicago's seventh-and eighth-grade girls were enrolled in household arts courses.[50] Ten years later, almost half of New York's girls of the same grade levels entered these programs, and the superintendent announced that all girls in high school and in the upper four grades of elementary school must receive domestic instruction.[51] The NEA's report said that one of the two aims of industrial training for girls was to prepare them for homemaking.[52] The chairman of the woman's branch of the Farmers' Institute of North Carolina, Mrs. W. N. Hutt, endorsed this policy when she reminded the 1910 NEA convention that, regardless of what other vocation a woman might adopt, "she will, with it all, wake up some fine morning and find herself in some man's kitchen, and woe be unto her if she has not the knowledge with which to cook his breakfast."[53] Similarly, Mary E. Williams, New York's director of cooking, argued that every girl should study domestic science as part of her vocational training because it would equip her to follow the "natural vocation" of every woman. Once a woman heard the "God-given call of her mate," Williams claimed that she would desert all other vocations to assume the "position of the highest responsibility and holiest duties of human life, those of homemaking and motherhood; upon which the progress of civilization and of human society depend."[54]

48. See, for example, City Club of Chicago, *Report on Vocational Training*, p. 16.

49. John D. Philbrick, "City School Systems in the United States," Bureau of Education, *Circulars of Information* (Washington, D.C.: Government Printing Office, 1885), p. 89.

50. Henry S. Tibbets, "The Progress and Aims of Domestic Science in the Public Schools of Chicago," *NEA Addresses and Proceedings*, 1901, p. 258.

51. *New York Annual Report*, 1910, p. 131.

52. "Report of Subcommittee on Industrial and Technical Education in the Secondary Schools," *Report of the Committee on the Place of Industries in Public Education*, 1910, p. 110.

53. W. N. Hutt, "The Education of Women for Home-Making," *NEA Addresses and Proceedings*, 1910, p. 128.

54. *New York Annual Report*, 1909, p. 531.

Williams' defense of domestic training offers a clue to another perspective on household arts. The girl, properly trained in school, could provide something apparently lacking in contemporary urban working-class families: she could regenerate the working-class home and provide the stability needed by industry for its workers. Household arts would equip the girl to keep the industrial worker off the street, out of the saloon, and away from temptations of the whorehouse. The principal of Chicago's Spry School informed fellow educators, "The evening meal of the factory hand may be made more tempting than the lunch counter, and the clothing of the family, as well as the arrangement and tidiness of living room at the home may be attractive as the gilded home of vice. Domestic science may become the unsuspected, and yet not the least efficient, enemy of the saloon."[55]

No less ambitious aspirations appeared in New York City's household arts program. The superintendent's 1910 report informed the public that this program attempted "to ally our work with municipal reform in all its branches." It indicated that there was particular concern to reach the "tenement dwellers" through homemaking courses. The section outlining the work in household arts concluded grandiosely:

> This work has been called the panacea for all evils, laying, as it does, the foundation for the support and betterment of the home. We have been a factor during the past years in helping to solve the economic questions of the nation. Not only has it been a question of careful marketing, and the saving of foods in the kitchen, but the girl's taste in being trained in the proper selection of furniture, and of inexpensive but artisitic fittings and furnishings. The woman is the buyer. She uses the wage of the American citizen and expends it wisely and well, or is ignorant and foolish in such expenditure. Therefore, it goes without saying, the home, for which a large portion of the nation's money is expended, is closely connected with the public question of city reform and the nation's need. As is the home so is the nation.[56]

Such household programs, if successful, were also strategically important to accommodate the urban masses to the grossly unequal distribution of wealth that characterized American society. This maldistribution saw the amassing of enormous wealth among a tiny percentage of the nation's population and the bitter impoverishment of a large share of

55. Tibbets, "Progress and Aims of Domestic Science," p. 259.
56. *New York Annual Report*, 1910, p. 131.

those at the bottom of the economic structure. Wealth gathered through financial and industrial manipulations came partly through the payment of inadequate wages to industrial workers. The militant response of the working class to their penury surfaced in violent industrial labor conflicts which made many capitalists fear a socialist, anarchist, or syndicalist revolution. If household arts courses could train the future working-class wives and mothers to manage their homes on the available income, then once again industrial training would establish its claim to satisfy the needs of industry.

If the girls were to reform the working-class family, it was essential that they accept their role as wives and mothers. Hence, socialization for domesticity became a fundamental goal of the industrial training program for girls. The method of conditioning was similar to that used for training working-class boys to adopt the industrial worker as their model. The curriculum was designed to point to the ultimate vocation, and no subject was presented apart from its relevance to the future vocation of the students. Two examples from the NEA's report of 1910 suffice to demonstrate the method. In its section devoted to industrial training for girls, the report described programs at the Boston Girls' High School of Practical Arts and the Cleveland Technical High School. The principal of the Boston school noted that a major aspect of the girls' mathmetics course involved solutions to simple problems like the maintenance of household accounts. "Our academic work, as well as the drawing, correlates with the shop," he declared. "Descriptions of various processes, with materials in hand, are required as lessons in good English. The chemistry deals with the questions of food, clothing, and shelter. The aim of these courses is to set before the girl the highest ideals of home life; to train her in all that pertains to practical housekeeping."[57] The description of the industrial training department for girls in Cleveland's Technical High School revealed similar orientation in that program. Domestic science topics were assigned in the English classes, chemistry revolved around food composition, and mathematics was devoted to adding household accounts and dividing cooking recipes. "In short, all technical subjects involving homemaking are taken as the basis of the course for girls, and the rest of the studies are grouped around these."[58] It is a little wonder that young girls subjected to this

---

57. Weaver, quoted in "Report of Subcommittee on Industrial and Technical Education" p. 112.

58. "Report of Subcommittee on Industrial and Technical Education," p. 113.

king of training would think that they had aborted the divine order of the universe if they did not find husbands and make homes for them. The only normal role for women, in this scheme of reality, was wife, homemaker, and mother.

Nevertheless, because industry needed female labor, justifications had to be found for training girls to meet this demand. The justifications were based on the woman's role in the home. In "exceptional" cases the woman might work outside the home. Four such cases readily come to mind, although only two of them were usually cited in the literature. The first instance occurred during the waiting period, "the three, six or eight years after leaving school and prior to marriage." This instance was apparently common for most working-class girls. Because of the high rate of industrial mortality, the second case, a wife forced to work "when a family loses its male head" was more common than might now be imagined.[59] The third situation, not often discussed by educators, occurred when the husband's wages were too low to support the family. The last case, which was also frequent, but apparently so distasteful or abnormal a possibility that it was rarely mentioned at all, arose if the girl should fail to hear that "God-given call of her mate" and thus was unsuccessful in her search for a husband.

Clearly, industrial training for girls was designed to put them in aprons and behind brooms. Even occupations outside the home for which the programs trained girls were specifically not to detract from the girl's potential as a homemaker. As stated by the NEA report, the second aim of industrial training for girls was to "train for work in *distinctly feminine occupations*."[60] Contemporaries understood what "distinctly feminine occupations" meant. The Massachusetts report had earlier recommended that if a woman was obliged to work, and many were, industrial training should "fit her so that she can and will enter those industries which are most closely allied to the home."[61] Ideally, girls were to be trained for jobs containing some of the functions of homemaker, wife, or mother, or for vocations connected with domestic service, such as maid, cook, and child care. Training for the garment industry was also considered an excellent preparation for family life, for the use of the needle was associated with the role of homemaker. Secretarial practice, bookkeeping, and general office work were often seen as

---

59. "Report of Subcommittee on Industrial and Technical Education," pp. 110–11.

60. "Report of Subcommittee on Industrial and Technical Education," p. 11.

61. *Report of the Commission on Industrial and Technical Education*, p. 19.

the office equivalent of the wife. Girls in these positions were expected to do the routine and household chores of the office. The definition of household-allied occupations was generally elastic enough to meet particular needs of industry. For example, some schools trained girls for upholstering, handbag making, and paper box construction. In most cases, though, the occupations for which girls were trained ostensibly met their needs by preparing them for domesticity.[62]

Industrial training for girls, like its male counterpart, was always justified on the basis of meeting the particular needs of the individual children. At times, however, the self-serving interests of proponents surfaced. The motive of the Pittsburgh Domestic Arts Association speaks for itself. The association was composed of a "little group" of Pittsburgh society women concerned over the lack of opportunity for less fortunate girls to learn the homemaking arts. To meet this need, they founded the Pittsburgh School of Domestic Arts in 1900. A sympathetic contemporary description of the institution observed that "graduates of the school found excellent positions awaiting them in the homes of members of the association." Within one year of its founding, the executive board of the association added a course for training "professional housekeepers" because "the numerous large and well-appointed homes of Pittsburgh offer an attractive field for the practice of this seldom considered profession." The description of the association's work concluded: "If the nearly one million employers of domestic service in these United States would unite in a determined and persistent effort to raise the standard of homemaking as an art 'the domestic service problem' would be solved by this generation."[63] The writer voiced a common sentiment among proponents of industrial training: the needs of the working-class child could best be met if she or he were trained for efficient service.

Industrial training for girls and for blacks was not an anomaly in the industrial training movement. It exemplified the movement's basic principle, that each child had a particular future, which the public school should discern and subsequently fit him or her to fulfill. Because the school prepared blacks for the bottom rungs of the labor force and girls for only those occupations suited to the role of mother and homemaker, these children were denied the opportunity for an equal education. In

---

62. See, for example, Mary Schenck Woolman, "Private Trade School for Girls," *Charities and the Commons*, October 5, 1907, pp. 839–48.

63. Mary Clark, "An Experiment in Domestic Service Reform," Chicago Association of Commerce, *Industrial and Commercial Education*, pp. 48, 49.

all cases, the occupational orientation of the educational experience worked to reduce the possibility of any but the school-projected future of the child.

INDUSTRIAL TRAINING AND ACADEMIC PREPARATIONS

Surprisingly, most proponents of vocational training agreed with George H. Mead's claim that such training would not detract from the academic thrust of the school program.[64] This claim, however, contradicted not only the basic rationale of the programs, but also common sense, simple arithmetic, and the evidence provided in vocational course descriptions. Vocational programs, justified as appropriate for students unable to appreciate or master bookish academic subjects, decreased the time devoted to academic courses by as much as one-third to one-half of the school day. In general, students fitted for higher positions in the industrial hierarchy received more academic or cultural work in order to develop their ability to make independent decisions, while those fitted for the rank-and-file positions were less exposed to traditional subject matter. Students in New York City's high school of commerce and girls' technical high school devoted slightly more than two-thirds of their class time to academic subjects and the remainder to technical subjects. The students' time in the manual training high schools was apportioned three-fifths to academic work and two-fifths to vocational training. These three institutions sought to train students for leadership roles above that of the actual mechanic. Conversely, students in the Manhattan Trade School for Girls and those enrolled in the industrial course at Stuyvesant High School, destined for lower types of occupations, spent two-thirds of their school career in vocational courses and only one-third in academic courses. Admission to the latter schools usually did not even require completion of elementary school work. Many working-class children thus did not have the advantage of academic training afforded by the elementary schools.[65] The New York division of time for

---

64. City Club of Chicago, *Report on Vocational Training*, pp. 9, 19.

65. *New York Annual Report*, 1903, pp. 57–60; *New York Annual Report*, 1904 , pp. 60–63; *New York Annual Report*, 1912, p. 343; *New York Annual Report*, 1907, pp. 251–52; *New York Annual Report*, 1910, p. 183; and "Report of Subcommittee on Industrial and Technical Education," pp. 78–79.

students fated for the industrial rank and file seems fairly consistent with the rest of the nation. In Chicago; Cleveland; Freeport, Illinois; Springfield, Massachusetts; Rochester, New York; and Columbus, Georgia children in schools like Manhattan or Stuyvesant would spend one-half or less of their class hours in academic courses.[66] It made sense that, in the interests of industrial efficiency, those destined for subservient roles should not be trained for autonomy.

The fact that children headed for the industrial proletariat would receive less than half as much work in academic subjects as upper-class children inhibited their social and intellectual development. Even more significant than restricted academic or cultural study, though, was the major disfigurement these restrictions caused. Children in vocational training curricula did not study the same kind of math or English, or science or history, or even literature as did students from upper-class families who, at least theoretically, were educated to make independent decisions and assume leadership positions in the industrial army. The NEA's influential report on industrial training outlined the work of some "exemplary" programs. In the Manhattan Trade School for Girls, "academic work is reduced to a minimum, but arithmetic, drawing, and some other studies are followed largely with reference to their bearing on the particular industries followed." "Academic work" in the New Bedford, Massachusetts industrial school was "based on the concrete or shop work." In the Rochester, New York factory school, "almost all of the academic work was based on industrial conditions or needs."[67] In the same vein, The New York City superintendent outlined the academic side of the curriculum in his vocational school for boys as follows:

    B. Non-vocational Subjects.
      a. Trade Mathematics.
        1. Arithmetic.
        2. Use of Symbols (Elementary Algebra).
        3. Plane Geometry as Used in Trade.
        4. Trigonmetry as Used in Trade.

---

66. For figures on Chicago, Cleveland, Freeport, and Springfield, see Chicago Association of Commerce, *Industrial and Commercial Education,* pp. 40–55; for Rochester and Columbus, see "Report of Subcommittee on Industrial and Technical Education," pp. 79–80.

67. "Report of Subcommittee on Industrial and Technical Education," p. 79. For a similar description of the academic aspect to industrial training in Springfield, Massachusetts and Cleveland, Ohio, see Chicago Association of Commerce, *Industrial and Commercial Education,* pp. 53–56, 98.

b. English.
 1. Business Letters.
 2. Reading, with Oral and Written Expression.
 3. Drawing of Contracts.
 4. Writing Specifications, etc.
c. Industrial History; Civic.
d. Industrial and Commercial Geography.
e. Applied Physics and Chemistry.
f. Simple Bookkeeping.
g. Elements of Commercial Law.[68]

An examination of some of the texts used in vocational curricula to organize the academic subjects around the needs of industry indicates that academic classes oriented the children toward industrial roles. The authors of the report for the City Club of Chicago, after they had questioned teachers in vocational schools, compiled the following list of "academic" texts used in vocational schools throughout the country:

Geography
 Adam's Commercial Geography
 Carpenter's Geographical Reader of North America
 Day's Commercial Geography of the World
 Olin's Commercial Geography
History
 American Inventors and Inventions
 Bogart's Economic History of the United States
 Coleman's Industrial History of the United States
 Dopp's Place of Industries in Elementary Education
 The Story of Iron and Steel
 Thurston's Economic and Industrial History for Secondary Schools
Mathematics
 Duncan's Applied Mechanics
 Elementary Algebra and Mensuration
 Handbook of Arithmetic and Geometry
 Kent's Formulas in Gearing
 Machine Shop Calculations
 Mechanical Engineer's Handbook
 Tables for Engineers and Businessmen
 Useful Information for Businessmen[69]

---

68. *New York Annual Report*, 1910, p. 184.
69. City Club of Chicago, *Report on Vocational Training*, pp. 230–31.

The Fitchburg, Massachusetts vocational program required collateral reading for students in its English classes. The list of titles the boys were to choose from was approvingly outlined in a U.S. Bureau of Education *Bulletin*. Any resemblance between the following list and readings designed for standard English classes was clearly unintentional. The list suggest how vocational training might help fit the boy into his intended slot in the industrial labor force:

> *Artist's Way of Working in the Various Handicrafts and Arts of Design*
> *Boys' Book of Inventions*
> *Boys' Second Book of Inventions*
> *Bulletins of Vocational Bureau of Boston*
> *Careers of Danger and Daring*
> *Hand Work in Wood*
> *Harper's Electricity Book for Boys*
> *Harper's How to Understand Electrical Work*
> *Harper's Machinery Book for Boys*
> *History of the Telephone*
> *Lives of Undistinguished Americans*
> *Romance of Industry and Invention*
> *Romance of Modern Electricity*
> *Romance of Modern Engineering*
> *Romance of Modern Invention*
> *Romance of Modern Manufacture*
> *Romance of Modern Mechanism*
> *Romance of Modern Steam Locomotion*
> *Story of the Railroad*
> *Triumphs of Science*
> *Vocations for Girls*
> *The Workers*
> *Young Folk's Library of Vocations*[70]

It is no secret that the intellectual stimulation provided in cultural or academic courses can open new vistas and new worlds. It takes little insight to discern the kind of stimulation a working-class child might get from reading the *Lives of Undistinguished Americans, Harper's Machinery Book for Boys,* or *The Romance of Modern Steam Locomo-*

---

70. Mathew R. McCann, "The Fitchburg Plan of Cooperative Industrial Education," *Bulletin of the U.S. Bureau of Education,* 1913, no. 50, p. 17.

tion. A mathematics course that used *Machine Shop Calculations* as its basic text, and a history course devoted to the rise of industry, would encourage the child to believe that reality was limited to the factory and the machine that he was destined to tend.

INDUSTRIAL EDUCATION AND THE "REAL WORLD"

Academic courses, however, were not the primary weapons in the arsenal of the industrial training programs. The most effective device for inhibiting intellectual growth was the atmosphere created in the vocational segment of the school program. This atmosphere, a replication of that of the factory, was created on the principle that the transferability of class learning would be proportional to the degree of similarity between school and work environments. If the child could be led to accept what many educators called the "shop atmosphere" as the basis of his reality, he might more easily accept the work discipline of corporate industrialism as the natural order of his existence. The psychological predisposition modeled in a "real shop" environment was the most important contribution of the vocational classes to inculcating conformity to the requirements of industry.

An early experiment in Boston's Agassiz School conditioned the boys to labor specialization and denigrated artisan methods by making courses "conform as closely as possible to actual industrial work in real life." In one class the boys were taught to make paper boxes. They were first shown how to make the boxes, and then each future factory recruit was set busy making one entire box. Subsequently, the boys were divided into teams, each member having his specialized function. Eventually an assembly line, complete with student foreman and efficiency calculations, was incorporated into the work procedure.[71] This helped the boys to accept the superiority of the "industrial method." Clearly, this lesson was more valuable for production schedules than any skills the program might have taught.

The Chicago public schools made the most explicit attempt to combat modern industry's perennial and most costly enemy—the inability of workers to withstand boredom. The new industrial work regimen re-

---

71. "Report of Subcommittee on Place of Industries in the Elementary School," *Report of the Committee on the Place of Industries in Public Education*, pp. 56–57.

quired most workers to spend their day at a single task that demanded little skill and less initiative. Under such conditions, the workers' attention often wandered from the task at hand, resulting in loss of production efficiency. The Chicago superintendent of schools recognized this as an "educational problem" and instituted an experiment designed to raise children's tolerance for boredom, thus fitting them better to meet the needs of industry. In her 1913 annual report, the superintendent observed that in modern industry, "the specialized work makes apparently so few demands on the equipment of the young apprentice or office assistant that the foreman, the head of the office, and the employer look with dismay at the inaccuracies of the product of the schools." It was useless, she said, to attempt to discover the conditions that caused the problem because "efficiency, not theory, is what the schools should furnish." According to Superintendent Young, inefficiency arose because the schools offered students too much variety; this diversity caused the "incompetency of the raw recruit" when he entered industrial employment. The Chicago superintendent argued that "long and frequent periods devoted to the same piece of work" would be more "stimulating" than the characteristic 30-minute class. The term "stimulating" must have had a peculiar meaning in the Chicago schools, for even at that time psychologists had examined the attention span of children in their early teens and explored the effect of enforced activity over an interval exceeding their relatively short attention span. Educators usually could find a psychological theory supporting their effort to assist the industrial system. In this instance, where their need contradicted most learning and behavior theories, psychology was simply denied. "Many of the tabulated experiments made by students of psychology to determine the limits of attention in children are misleading," declared the superintendent. She concluded that the curriculum should be less varied and the time spent on each of the remaining areas greatly increased. Within a year, elementary schools with vocational training programs had followed these recommendations. The length of classes for the children who were projected as the rank and file of the industrial army lasted from 70 minutes to three hours.[72] Schools have long contributed to modern industry's need by producing students who can tolerate boredom, and this Chicago experiment must rank high as an open and conscious attempt to do so.

---

72. *Chicago Annual Report*, 1913, p. 112–13; and *Chicago Annual Report*, 1914, p. 313.

If the Chicago experiment was the most explicit attempt to increase the student's insensitivity to boredom, then New York's Vocational School for Boys was the most successful replication of the factory atmosphere. The school, opened in 1909, was designed primarily for children who had not completed elementary school and who were to labor near the bottom of the industrial hierarchy. Superintendent Maxwell's 1910 report noted that the school's organization was "radically" different from that of ordinary schools "to avoid the school-room method of procedure, and to substitute that of the shop." He believed that "the success of such a school as this depends in great part on the 'atmosphere' that prevails." Students "must be made to feel that they are moving in an atmosphere much like that which obtains in the business world. . . ." Thus, the school was run on a factory schedule with children reporting to their "foremen" at eight in the morning and after a lunch hour returning to their work stations until five in the afternoon. Most of the program consisted of industrial work taught by actual mechanics "who have the knack of imparting instruction." This work was integrated with a series of "industrial visitations" to give the boys a better appreciation for the factory atmosphere.[73] It is difficult to imagine any scheme of school organization, short of actually placing the boys in the factory for part of their schooling, that could better fit them to meet the demands of the industrial workplace. The latter expedient was considered in New York but was not implemented because industrialists feared the possible inefficiency of intermittent child labor.[74]

The expedient of sending the children to the actual factory to receive part of their schooling was used in a number of cities, including Fitchburg, Beverly, and Worcester, Massachusetts; Chicago, Moline, and Freeport, Illinois; and Cincinnati, Ohio.[75] These programs were usually called part-time or cooperative industrial training courses. The most well-known and widely copied program originated in Fitchburg. Here, the boys were matched in pairs; each spent alternate two-week periods in school and in the factory, thus giving the employer a continuity of help. School time in Fitchburg was equally divided between shop work and what passed for academic work. Consequently, each boy spent only 20 weeks in "academic" work. The tenor of the program, with its heavy emphasis on fitting the boy to the demands of the work-

---

73. *New York Annual Report*, 1910, p. 185.
74. *New York Annual Report*, 1912, p. 166.
75. City Club of Chicago, *Report on Vocational Training*, p. 127ff.

place, was encapsulated in the information sheet presented to each co-op as he entered the program:

Co-op Information

Read this carefully. It will save you and us trouble.

Remember that the object of work is production. Your foreman measures you by the quantity and quality of your work. Social position does not enter. In the shop you are not a high-school boy; you are an apprentice. Wear clothes accordingly. If you get the mistaken idea that any work given you is beneath the dignity of a high-school boy, just remember you are an apprentice and get 100 percent busy.

It is your business to get along smoothly with the workmen and foreman; not theirs to get along with you.

Do not expect any personal attention from the superintendent. He will probably ignore you entirely, but he knows whether or not you are making good, and in most cases his idea of you depends upon your ability to please your foreman.

Don't be a kicker and don't continually bother your foreman for higher wages. If you are not receiving your raises as agreed upon, or if you have other grievances, let the director adjust matters through the firm's office.

An idle machine means a cash loss to the firm. Let yours never be idle without previous arrangement. To "lay off" without permission is a serious offense for a working-man and is just as serious for an apprentice, regardless of the relative importance of the work he does. The foreman always plans ahead for every man's work, yours included. Therefore, notify your foreman before you leave on any regular vacation. A little thoughtfulness may prevent serious misunderstanding. And always, if sick and unable to report in person, send a telephone message to your foreman. He can arrange then to have your work done for you; otherwise he will naturally cease to depend on you.

Never try to conceal defective work. Take your full measure of blame, and do not make the same mistake twice.

Watch, in a quiet way, what things are being done around you, and don't be afraid to ask sensible questions. A good rule is to think over a question twice before asking. A reputation for having "horse sense" means that you are making good.

Foreman and workmen will take pleasure in showing you, if you show yourself genuinely appreciative of little attentions. If they tell you something you already know, don't spoil their pleasure by telling them you already know it, but let it be impressed on your mind all the deeper; for the conversation may lead to something which is entirely new to you.

If your foreman refuses to grant any requests, and you value his good will, do not refer the matter to a higher official. Let the director, Mr. Hunter, help you.

The fool act of one co-op hurts every co-op. See that your actions in and out of the shop do not bring discredit on the co-op course.

Confer freely with Mr. Hunter about your work. He is here to help you do the right thing and be a success.[76]

Although the amount of the time spent on the job varied from one city to another, the cooperative idea found extensive expression in many American urban school systems—especially after a favorable description of the Fitchburg plan, written by Mathew McCann, a high school physics teacher from Worcester, Massachusetts, was distributed by the United States Bureau of Education in 1913. Adaptations of cooperative training still exist in all parts of the nation today. The following "student agreement" form currently in use in the cooperative work experience program at Atwood, Illinois, illustrates the amazing historical continuity of the Fitchburg plan when compared with its 1913 information sheet:

One Example of a Student Agreement Form
Student Agreement

The _____program in cooperative vocational education is planned to develop a student academically, economically, and socially. To meet the goal, there are responsibilities the student must realize and he must agree to cooperate in carrying them out to the fullest extent. As a participant in the program, are you willing to assume these responsibilities in the program?

1. To realize that I am under the jurisdiction of the school throughout the school day.
2. To know that the coordinator is the recognized authority for making adjustments or changes in the training on the job.
3. To know that it is my responsibility throughout the year to be well-dressed and groomed both in school and on the job.

---

76. Quoted in R. McCann, "The Fitchburg Plan of Cooperative Industrial Education," pp. 22–23.

4. To carry out my training on the job in such a manner that I will reflect credit upon myself and upon the cooperative vocational education program.
5. To perform all my duties in a commendable manner and perform related study assignments with earnestness and sincerity.
6. To work toward the group and individual achievement goals.
7. To be regular in attendance in school and on the job. (This includes days on the job when school is not in session such as teacher's meetings, Christmas vacations, etc.)
8. To be on time at school and on the job.
9. To notify my employer as soon as I know that I will be absent from work.
10. To notify the coordinator as early in the day as possible on days that I am absent from school.
11. If I am absent from school I must also be absent from work on that day.
12. To know that if I use a car as transportation to and from my work, I will observe all traffic regulations and school policies with extreme care. Any infraction of the traffic laws may be sufficient cause to terminate the use of my car in connection with cooperative vocational education program.
13. To conduct myself in a satisfactory manner, both on the job and in the classroom, or my training may be discontinued and I may be removed from the program.
14. To know that if I am removed from the program due to failure either in the class instruction or work experience that I will receive a failing grade for the program and will lose both credits.
15. To understand that if I am required to leave school because of any disciplinary reason, I understand that I cannot report to my training station as this is the same as any other classroom subject in which I am enrolled.

THE COST OF INDUSTRIAL TRAINING

It has been implied that public school officials, who were not particularly concerned with immigrant and working-class children, used the new industrial training programs as a way of getting them out of the school as quickly and with as little expense as possible.[77] The evidence

---

77. See for example, Colin Greer, *The Great School Legend* (New York: Basic Books, 1972).

does not support such an interpretation. In the first place, it was well recognized that industrial training would be considerably more expensive than the traditional education that upper-class children received. The NEA report admitted that its proposed intermediate industrial school would "be relatively expensive for each pupil."[78] In Grand Rapids, Michigan, it cost almost twice as much to train each pupil in the vocational classes of the intermediate school as it did to teach the student who received traditional education in the regular elementary grades. At the eighth-grade level, the comparative semester figures were $12 per student in the regular classes and $20 per student in the intermediate school. Costs were even more disproportionately high for students being trained for the lower levels of the industrial army at Brookline, Massachusetts. The district expended $181.03 per pupil for the 1915–1916 school year in its school of practical arts, and only $62.46 during the same period for each student in its regular elementary school. The same picture held true for high school costs. During 1906, Chicago spent $85.94 per student in its manual training high school and only $58.76 per student in its regular high schools. Figures published in 1915 by *School Review* regarding the mean cost in 25 cities of 1,000 pupil recitations for various subjects revealed that the Chicago figures were in line with those across the nation. The mean cost for shop and drawing was placed at $93, while English cost $51, and science, $60.[79]

Their willingness to undertake these higher costs indicates that school officials did not want working-class children to drop out of school or to be failures either in school or in life. Examination of the educational literature of the early decades of the twentieth century discloses profound concern for the success of working-class children. Too often these professionals are given too little credit for their penetrating understanding of the social order. Perhaps more than any educators before or since, these men and women fathomed the requirements of the contemporary power structure. They perceived that the success of corporate industry depended on the efforts of the industrial proletariat. The industrial workplace required laborers with particular abilities, personality structures, patterns of habitual responses, and an insensitivity to

78. "Report of the Subcommittee on Intermediate Industrial Schools," p. 76.

79. Harold O. Rugg, "The Cost of Public Education in Grand Rapids," *School Survey; Grand Rapids, Michigan,* p. 437; *Educational Survey of the Public Schools of Brookline, Massachusetts* (Cambridge, Mass.; Murray and Emery, 1917), p. 52; *Chicago Annual Report,* 1907, p. 90; and quoted in Rugg, "Cost of Education in Grand Rapids," p. 430.

dehumanizing conditions of work. The educators of the early 1900s saw their mission as fitting the children of the working class to these requirements. They believed theirs to be a formidable task, the success of which would have enormous repercussions on the industrial future of the nation. One might take issue with their conception of education or with the kind of success they projected for the working-class children under their charge, but it is a serious mistake to believe that they were indifferent to these children.

Rhetoric supporting the conception of education developed by these school superintendents and theorists has flowed from the pens of intellectuals, industrialists, and other educators. Most of the school officials discussed in this chapter seemed to accept the belief that corporate industrialism and its work structure was inevitable, and they also embraced the Platonic notion of innate differences among men. Since some workers would have to perform the tasks required by the new system, they believed that it was best for all concerned if those so destined to toil were trained to labor efficiently and reliably. Protests against this conception of education had little impact, as they ran counter to the perceived needs of the nation. Although received with amused antipathy and considered archaic, some of the protests were indeed powerful. One of the most insightful was Ernest Carroll Moore's 1902 article in *The Arena*.

Early in his article, Moore boldly proclaimed the basis of his rejection of the new conception of education and, at once, demonstrated the obsolescence of his argument. He said, "That education was good and is good which educates the whole man, not a part of him. The test of true education is in the man, not in society." It was monstrous to call an experience "education for any man which society countenances as fitting him to fill the place which society has allotted to him." Moore contended that "the question of education is not how to make a man fit the demands of the marketplace, nor yet how to make him shine in society, but how to make the best of the whole man. And this question attaches to every man." With uncanny anticipation of the arguments of educators like Ellwood Cubberley and James E. Russell, who would later contend that bookish, abstract cultural education could only harm the future industrial worker, Moore offered this rebuttal:

> Something must be radically wrong in a world in which the same process both fits and unfits men for their work. Why does education fit the professional man for his work and unfit the laborer for his? I can find no logical reason for this result. I am compelled to say that the statement is false,

although it seems to be true, and has become a common law through the approving votes of an overwhelming majority. Education cannot unfit him for his work—it may unfit the present conditions in which that work is performed for him. It may bring about better hours, better places, better estimation of labor; but unfit him for his work it cannot do, for the chief factor in determining his work is the pronoun, not the noun.

Moore, a humanist, looked first to the man, insisting that work should fit human criteria. The proponents of industrial education, however, when confronted with a mismatch between man and industrial labor requirements, determined that the state should train the man to fit the job. Moore believed that because those trained to fit the requirements of the marketplace rather than educated as men would be unlikely to make independent decisions, they would be ill equipped to determine their own destinies. Quoting the classics, he said, "Plato described a slave as 'one who in his actions does not express his own ideas.'" Unfortunately, this was precisely the condition which industrial training promoted in the working-class child. Moore argued that "measured by the best Greek standard, most men among us are not free."[80] Sadly, this statement still rings true.

---

80. Ernest Carroll Moore. "The Place of Education in Reform," *The Arena* 27 (May 1902): 499–512.

Chapter 8

Vocational Guidance

In his perceptive critique of modern industrial societies, Jacques Ellul maintained that vocational guidance played a crucial role in system stability by accommodating humans to industrial processes. Although vocational counseling claims to be able to categorize people according to their purported ability to adapt to various aspects of industrial work, Ellul argued that it simply "discovers" the kinds of abilities that industry needs at a particular time. Thus, counselors today can discover a large number of high school students with "aptitudes" in math and science to meet the demands of a space age technology. Should industrial requirements shift, counselors will be apt to find many fewer students so gifted. Changes in career patterns indicate not merely the flexibility of human potential but also the influence of guidance techniques. Ellul concludes that vocational guidance "deprives man of freedom and responsibility, makes him into a 'thing' and puts him where he is most desirable . . . where he is most efficient."[1]

If Ellul's analysis is substantially correct—and there is much evidence to suggest that it is—then the history of vocational guidance in the United States presents another example of the degeneration of an initially humanizing impulse into an instrument of repression. Vocational guidance began to assume its present form around the turn of the century, when its objectives, location, and essential techniques emerged.

---

1. Jacques Ellul, *The Technological Society* (New York: Vintage, 1964), pp. 358–62.

VOCATIONAL GUIDANCE AND SOCIAL SETTLEMENTS

Like playgrounds, penny lunches, competitive athletics, clubs, and many other programs incorporated into the urban public school during the first third of the twentieth century, vocational guidance began in the settlement houses. For the turn-of-the-century urban working class, and especially for the foreign-born laborer, procuring employment entailed difficult and dehumanizing problems and circumstances. It was common for foremen to auction jobs to the lowest bidder at the factory gate. Frequently, an unsuspecting immigrant would pay an employment agent for a nonexistent job and then travel many miles, only to discover his folly. Proprietors of saloons and poolrooms, precinct leaders of the local political machine, and parish priests were often the only reasonably reliable sources for "finding a place in American industry."[2]

The search for a job was even more precarious for the child laborer who ventured into the uncharted trails of job hunting without skills or experience. Increasingly, the youngsters turned to the residents of the settlement houses for assistance. From almost the very founding of the various settlements, the residents reported that they were called upon to answer the anguished cries of unemployed children seeking jobs. At first the help was unorganized and was offered on an individual basis. The head resident of Boston's South End House stated that "pioneer residents, almost before they were aware of what was happening, found themselves deeply involved in the hopes and trials of job getting. Trustees, board members, contributors, and volunteers were importuned in favor of proteges." According to this chronicler of the settlement movement, "Every settlement soon treasured a list of employers who were relied upon to take recommended boys and girls. Young people thus launched began their industrial careers a level or two higher than they might otherwise have achieved, and the settlement household rejoiced at the superior wage scale, more inspiring work, and ultimately better home conditions made possible."[3]

The enormous social problems facing the urban working class and immigrant neighborhoods, however, usually blighted the rejoicing

2. See William M. Leiserson, *Adjusting Immigrant and Industry* (New York: Harper and Brothers, 1924), pp. 28–49.

3. Robert A. Woods and Albert J. Kennedy, *The Settlement Horizon* (New York: Russell Sage Foundation, 1922), p. 138.

over individual victories and personal successes. The settlement residents' first glow of satisfaction with the effectiveness of their haphazard and incidental efforts to find jobs for their friends was soon dulled by reality. As Robert Woods said, "The question kept rising whether individual strokes in the way of securing positions did not represent a subtle form of favoritism and whether in the larger view of the problem any real gain was made."[4] The problem envisioned by settlement workers was twofold: first, most of the working children they dealt with needed additional training before they could be placed in the better jobs; second, a more effective job placement service had to be developed.

Since working-class children needed to be better trained to find better jobs, simple job placement could not solve their problems. Early in the vocational guidance movement, settlement residents, among the leaders of industrial education, voiced a concern that would become the major feature of the effort. They insisted that vocational guidance must become educational guidance before it could become truly effective. The more efficient job placement service encouraged by the residents developed as an institutionalization of their early, personal efforts in behalf of individual workers. Vocational bureaus designed to meet corporate industry on its own terms emerged. These agencies processed large numbers of job seekers in a bureaucratic fashion, charting the individual applicant's aptitudes and personality on standardized forms and matching the resulting profile with the specifications for particular positions required by corporate industry.

Numerous settlements set up vocational bureaus, often in cooperation with other agencies and sometimes in conjunction with the public schools. The Henry Street Settlement established such a bureau in New York's P.S. 147.[5] Jane Addams' Hull House was part of a consortium, including the Chicago Women's Clubs and the Chicago Association of Commerce, which employed vocational workers who were given space and access to the pupils' records in the Chicago public schools in 1913.[6] Both Henry Street House and Hull House conducted early experiments in industrial training, and their vocational bureaus, like those of others, concentrated on placing school

---

4. Woods and Kennedy, *Settlement Horizon*, p. 138.

5. Lilian Wald, *Windows on Henry Street* (Boston: Little, Brown, 1934), p. 144.

6. *Chicago Annual Report*, 1913, p. 204.

dropouts. The bureaus tried to place children in jobs that matched their ability and personality. One of the first tasks of the bureaus was to conduct an industrial survey of their city to determine what kinds of jobs were available and most appropriate for eligible children. Bureau workers tried to keep children out of what they considered "demoralizing" or "dead-end" occupations. Quickly, however, they discovered that very few jobs were appropriate for children under the age of 16. Many employers did not want to be bothered with the additional trouble associated with child laborers because industrial technology was making child labor obsolete. Hence, vocational bureaus soon lessened their efforts in job placement and concentrated instead on convincing the child to stay in school for further training that would render him more useful in the newer forms of industrial labor.

Probably the most successful and certainly the most visible of these job agencies was the Boston Vocational Bureau, established in 1901 by the Civic Service House and financed by Mrs. Quincy A. Shaw. The bureau was headed by Frank Parsons, often called "the father of vocational guidance." Under Parsons's leadership until his death in 1908, the bureau engaged in short-term but intensive counseling. A series of interviews and tests first established a candidate's aptitudes and attributes; then he was directed toward an occupation that fit his profile. An interesting example of the kind of profile developed by Parsons was "the case of the would-be doctor," described in his *Choosing a Vocation*.[7] Parsons persuaded the client that medicine was an undesirable goal because of his humble social and economic background and also because of his race. These criteria weighed heavily against working-class and immigrant clients because the Anglo-Saxon middle-class model defined Parsons's ideal for higher status and better-paying vocations. Working-class children were thus discouraged from aspiring to prestigious callings and made to believe that they had been "scientifically" selected for low-level occupations. As job placement centers, the early vocational bureaus assisted cor-

---

7. John M. Brewer, *The Vocational-Guidance Movement* (New York: Macmillan, 1918), p. 23. See also Eleanor Kemler Feinberg, "Frank Parsons and the Role of Vocational Counseling in Education" (Ph.D. diss., University of Illinois, 1973), p. 6; Howard V. Davis, *Frank Parsons: Prophet, Innovator, Counselor* (Carbondale, Ill.: Southern Illinois University Press, 1969); John Brewer, *History of Vocational Guidance* (New York: Hayer and Brothers, 1942); Arthur Mann, *Yankee Reformers in the Urban Age* (Cambridge, Mass.: The Belknap Press of Harvard University Press, 1954), pp. 126–44; and Frank Parsons, *Choosing a Vocation* (Boston: Houghton Mifflin, 1909), p. 117.

porate industry by supplying a steady stream of workers selected because their aptitude and personality profiles conformed to the requirements of a particular job. These workers were also potentially more content with that assigned slot because it had been systematically selected. Parsons assured prospective employers that his bureau aimed "to reduce the percentage of inefficiency and change you may experience in your working force, and the care it entails in employment expense, waste of training, and low-grade service—due to the haphazard way which young men and women drift into this or that employment, with little regard to adaptability, and without adequate preparation. . . ."[8]

Soon after Parsons's death, the Boston Vocational Bureau expanded its mission. Job placement became a less important function as the bureau became increasingly involved in the research and development of vocational guidance. After a series of industrial surveys, it published a number of vocational pamphlets, each detailing a special vocation and including the requirements a prospective employee should possess. These pamphlets were widely used in industrial training classes throughout the country. In 1910, under the sponsorship of the Boston Chamber of Commerce, the bureau organized the first national conference on vocational guidance, the forerunner of the National Vocational Guidance Association. Then, in 1911, the bureau diversified further by establishing the first university training course for vocational counselors at the Harvard summer school; by 1917, it had conducted such courses at Indiana University, Boston University, the University of California, and Columbia Teachers' College. The bureau also was busy helping school districts organize their vocational guidance departments as early as 1917.[9] The Boston Vocational Bureau, it is clear, initiated and exemplified the pattern of the vocational guidance movement. The agency began in association with settlement house attempts at job placement and then shifted to larger areas of endeavor. Throughout its history it led both by example and by proselytizing.

---

8. Quoted in W. Richard Stephens, *Social Reform and the Origins of Vocational Guidance* (Washington, D.C.: National Vocational Guidance Association, 1970), p. 21. Stephens' work represents the first systematic effort to interpret the development of vocational guidance.

9. Brewer, *Vocational-Guidance Movement*, pp. 24–32; see also, Paul H. Hanus, "Vocational Guidance and Public Education," in *Readings in Vocational Guidance*, ed. Meyer Bloomfield (Boston: Ginn and Company, 1915), p. 92.

THE CHILD STUDY MOVEMENT

Although job placement was a significant antecedent, it was not the only source of the vocational guidance movement. The child study movement also made an important contribution. Educators have been investigating differences among children at least since Rousseau, Pestalozzi, and Emerson make them aware that those differences existed. An impetus to the child study movement in American education was the enactment of compulsory attendance legislation. These laws gathered into the public schools masses of students theretofore ignored by school officials. Those with physical disabilities—the crippled, the deaf, and the blind—and those with perceived intellectual deficiencies presented professionals, already inundated with masses of "normal" pupils, with special problems that they believed could be solved only by isolating the "defective" in special schools or classes. Most large cities opened special schools soon after the passage of compulsory attendance laws. "The necessity for the establishment of these schools," observed Ben Blewett, the St. Louis superintendent of instruction, "was emphasized in St. Louis as it had been in other places through the conditions forced by the adoption of a law compelling attendance." The first special school began in 1906, and by 1908 six were in operation. Superintendent Blewett, emphasizing a view shared by many educators, acknowledged that these special schools were particularly important because they relieved normal classes of "deficient" or, as they soon came to be called, "exceptional" children.[10]

The problem of segregating "exceptional" pupils was double-edged. Educators believed that because these children could not learn in the normal classroom, they should, for their own welfare, quietly be placed in a special school. These special classes would not cover as much or even the same kind of work as the normal class; they would concentrate on manual training and handicrafts. Boston's superintendent of schools, Stratton D. Brooks, reflected a common outlook when he justified that city's special class curriculum by admitting that even if the students made little intellectual progress,

---

10. Ben Blewett, "Provision for Exceptional Children in the Public Schools of St. Louis," *NEA Addresses and Proceedings,* 1909, pp. 356–58; see also Leonard P. Ayres, *The Cleveland School Survey (Summary Volume 26)* (Philadelphia: Fell, 1917), pp. 203–4; and Stratton D. Brooks, "Provision for Exceptional Children in the Public Schools of Boston," *NEA Addresses and Proceedings,* 1909, p. 361.

the habits and motor abilities which they developed would render them "safe" for society.[11]

While it was deemed important to channel the exceptional child into the special class, it was equally urgent that the normal child not be placed into this class because he would then be deprived of an opportunity to develop his full potential. Earl Barnes aired some of the dimensions of the dilemma for the 1908 meeting of the Special Department of the NEA: "Granted that these children exist in every community, the problem of separating those who need special treatment from their fellows is most difficult. It is almost impossible to draw a line of definition between the normal and the special child." He noted that "the parent cannot be trusted to make this selection" because kinship created bias. Nor could the teachers make such judgments because they were not qualified in the field. The only solution was to train experts. Barnes concluded, "From time to time all the children of the state should pass through the hands of trained experts who, after advising with teachers and parents, should be empowered to separate children who need special care from the general group."[12] Of course, parents might still raise problems. Responding to Barnes's proposal for experts, Jane Addams suggested a policy that became a hallmark of twentieth-century liberalism. She cautioned against outright conflict between experts and parents. The parents' misguided resistance was, she believed, based on praiseworthy affection for the child. Correctly informed, this feeling could be put to good use: "To convince the parent," Addams said, "that by following a certain line of action [prescribed by experts] his child will be enormously benefited is simply to turn affection into a scientifically prepared channel."[13]

Katherine E. Dopp, of the University of Chicago, expressed the current wisdom in admiring the efficiency of Plato's educational proposals for sorting and subsequent training of children according to their special abilities. Unlike many of her contemporaries, however, she warned that "until the sciences which underlie this knowledge shall be developed to a far greater extent than they are at present, we shall do well to refrain from mortgaging the child's future on the

---

11. Brooks, "Provision for Exceptional Children," p. 362.

12. Earl Barnes, "The Public School and the Special Child," NEA Addresses and Proceedings, 1908, p. 1120.

13. Jane Addams, "The Home and the Special Child," NEA Addresses and Proceedings, 1908, p. 1127.

basis of our superficial judgment."[14] This cautionary advice should have dampened the ardor of the child sorters, especially when juxtaposed with an often-quoted comment of the much-admired William James: "However closely psychical changes may conform to law, it is safe to say that individual histories and biographies will never be written in advance no matter how 'evolved' psychology may become."[15] Nevertheless, educators, philosophers, intellectuals, and lesser psychologists than James continued to improvise cataloging schemes designed to categorize children and to "write their biographies in advance."

Varieties of this human taxonomy offered such classifications as physically disabled, which included the crippled, blind, deaf, adenoidal, and tubercular; mentally deficient, including subnormal, neglected, and retarded; gifted; and the morally defective.[16] Although the boundaries between these classifications of exceptional and normal children were imprecise, by 1910 there was general agreement among professionals that such divisions were essential for the well-being of both exceptional and normal pupils. At the time these categories were being devised, educators busily studied individual children. Identification of physically exceptional children was comparatively the easiest task, most often accomplished by referring children to some form of medical examination. The frequent confusion of morally defective, mentally subnormal, and simply behaviorally deviant indicated the difficulty inherent in the other categories and the lack of clear criteria distinguishing the exceptional from the normal child. Problems of definition were not, however, caused by a lack of investigation. School systems expended enormous efforts to study their students; the slogan proposed by G. S. Hall, "no exceptional child unstudied," was liberally applied in practice.[17]

---

14. Katherine E. Dopp, "Equality of Opportunity Can be Secured Only by a Systematic Recognition of Individual Differences in Native Capacity and in Prospective Career," *NEA Addresses and Proceedings*, 1908, pp. 743–46.

15. William James, quoted in Brewer, *Vocational-Guidance Movement*, p. 159.

16. See, for example, "Report of Committee on Books and Tests Pertaining to the Study of Exceptional and Mentally Deficient Children," *NEA Addresses and Proceedings*, 1909, pp. 901–14; Frank G. Bruner, "Abnormal Children: Their Classification and Instruction," *NEA Addresses and Proceedings*, 1909, pp. 350–55; Robert T. Aley, "Care of Exceptional Children in the Grades," *NEA Addresses and Proceedings*, 1910, pp. 881–93; and James H. Van Sickle, "Provisions for Gifted Children in Public Schools," *NEA Addresses and Proceedings*, 1910, pp. 155–60.

17. G. S. Hall, "The National Child Welfare Conference: Its Work and Its Relation to Child Study," *NEA Addresses and Proceedings*, 1910, p. 894.

Most investigators seemed to agree that the proportion of mentally subnormal children was relatively low. Estimates made by H. H. Goddard, Leonard Ayres, G. S. Hall, and Baltimore school superintendent James Van Sickle generally ranged from one-half of 1 percent to 3 percent of the total school population.[18] Children rated mentally subnormal were frequently put in special schools or in special classes, sometimes called nongraded classes. One problem with these provisions was that many children assigned to nongraded classes were actually behavior problems or truants. Thus, at times, special classes became dumping grounds for students not wanted in regular classes.

Emphasis on the exceptional or defective child and the child study movement developed simultaneously, and both interrelated with concern for job placement and vocational guidance. By 1910, most of those involved in placement procedures in the vocational bureaus concluded that if the counselor was to significantly influence the child's vocational biography, it was necessary to begin vocational guidance before entry into the job market. Guidance advocates were turning away from the idea of placement and toward the idea of educational counseling to prepare the child for his future role in the labor force. With the emergence of this new idea, the lessons of special education would have significant import. Work with exceptional children purported to show that there were special categories of children and that these groups needed differentiated training. Vocational guidance leaders accepted this hypothesis as an educational principle applicable to all children. When considered in conjunction with the industrial training movement, the hypothesis meant that all children needed special training based on their individual differences, aptitudes, and prospective vocations in order to render them efficient members of urban-industrial society.

FROM JOB TO EDUCATIONAL PLACEMENT

This shift in strategy was summarized by the director of the Child Labor Division of Cincinnati's public schools, Helen T. Woolley, at

---

18. See, for example, Henry H. Goddard, "What Can the Public School Do for Subnormal Children?" *NEA Addresses and Proceedings*, 1910, pp. 712–919; Leonard P. Ayres, "What Constitutes Retardation?" *NEA Addresses and Proceedings*, 1910, p. 153; Hall, "National Child Welfare Conference," p. 894; and Van Sickle, "Provisions for Gifted Children," p. 155.

the 1913 Grand Rapids meeting of the Vocational Guidance Association. Tracing the history of the movement from its early job placement orientation, Woolley noted that the shift to educational placement occurred when counselors discovered not only a shortage of "the right sort of niches," but also many prospective employees who had been "spoiled in the making" because they had received the wrong type of education. Thus, "the curative point of view" gave way to "the preventive point of view."[19]

In part, the shift away from job assignment was prompted by the recognition that more complete and intimate information about the individual was necessary to insure safe placement in an appropriate industrial function. For example, John Brewer, Parsons's successor as head of the Boston Vocational Bureau, suggested that employment managers in private and religious organizations such as the YMCA were unable to give adequate guidance to many clients because the counselors could not obtain adequate knowledge of the client in a few meetings.[20] It became apparent to leaders in the guidance movement that several interviews and the results from one or two standardized tests were insufficient to reveal the complex potentialities of the prospective worker. Longitudinal studies of each child were needed for efficient placements. This understanding contributed heavily to the propensity of American schools to collect extensive personal dossiers on each student. As early as 1909, the New York City schools began organizing cumulative uniform card records on each student primarily for the purpose of aiding in placement.[21] This practice soon spread to other city school systems. In 1913, the Cincinnati schools developed a system for eighth-grade students to "schedule and record on guidance record cards those general characteristics which influence the vocational success or failure of the individual."[22] The following is an approximation of the record card:

---

19. Helen T. Woolley, "The Present Trend of Vocational Guidance in the United States," in "Vocational Guidance," *Bulletin of the U.S. Bureau of Education*, 1914, no. 14, p. 43.

20. Brewer, *Vocational-Guidance Movement*, pp. 46–47.

21. *New York Annual Report*, 1909, p. 192.

22. Frank P. Goodwin, "Vocational Guidance in Cincinnati," in Bloomfield, *Readings in Vocational Guidance*, p. 131.

Vocational Record Card   Eighth Grade

Name _____   School _____

Date of birth · _____   Nationality _____

Parent's name _____   Residence _____

1. Health and physical characteristics (from the physician); height, weight; sense organs: eyes, ears.
2. Powers of observation: good, medium, poor.
3. Memory: good, medium, poor.
4. Attention: good, medium, poor.
5. Association: rapid mental coordination, medium rate of coordination, slow mental coordination.
6. Type of activity: deliberate, impulsive, neither.
7. Intellectual ability: good, medium, poor.
8. Manual ability (domestic-science or manual-training): good, medium, poor.
9. Social leadership: well developed, moderate, absent (a follower).
10. Perseverance: good, medium, poor.
11. Habits of promptness: good, medium, poor.
12. Studies: preferences, successes, dislikes, failures.
13. Vocation of parents.
14. Which high-school course?
15. What vocation has the child in mind? [23]

As business corporations became more concerned with the psychological makeup of their workers, it became more important for those in charge of the labor supply to expand their knowledge of the personal characteristics of potential workers. Thus the public schools began to collect and record a wider variety of information about their students.

Another factor in the expansion of vocational guidance from job placement to what was called educational placement was the rapidly diminishing number of industrial jobs for children under 16 years of age. By 1913, most vocational guidance experts understood this trend. The 1912 report of the New York City Vocational Guidance Survey, organized the previous year under the auspices of the Junior League and the Public Education Association, concluded that "a system of vocational guidance which would mean finding jobs for children under 16 would be not only futile but dangerously near exploitation, however well meant the intention might be. The facts showed, broadly speaking,

---

23. Goodwin, "Vocational Guidance in Cincinnati," p. 131; see also Ernest L. Talbert, "Opportunities in School and Industry for Children of the Stockyards District," in Bloomfield, *Readings in Vocational Guidance*, p. 451.

that there are no jobs for children under sixteen which they ought to take." The report asserted that children needed and wanted vocational training and that "vocational guidance should mean guidance for training, not guidance for jobs." As a result, the Vocational Guidance Survey symbolically changed its name to the Vocational Education Survey and took as its goal the collection of data "about actual industrial conditions for use of the schools in working out types of industrial training."[24]

The enlarged conception of vocational guidance did not eliminate the concern for finding jobs; it merely made placement the end of a process that guided the child through a series of educational experiences designed to fit him for his future role as a worker. George Herbert Mead was speaking of this continuum when he stated that "vocational training and vocational guidance are normally linked together."[25] The concern of the vocational guidance movement to fit each child for his place in the work force through schooling was underscored by the New York City Committee on High Schools and Training Schools. In its 1914 report, this body quoted Meyer Bloomfield's claim that "booklets on occupations. . .intended for guidance, are valuable only to the extent of their appeal to motives which prolong school life, which help send children into further training opportunities."[26] Vocational guidance had evolved from a movement primarily committed to fitting individuals into the correct niches to a movement concerned with processing individuals. The assumption underlying this shift of focus was that the public schools should process children in conformity with the manpower needs of corporate industry.

This change in outlook meant that the educational mission of the schools would have to expand along the lines of industrial training (as discussed in the preceding chapter). Describing the vocational guidance program in the Cincinnati schools, Frank P. Goodwin summarized the new and broadened commitment:

> In response to a demand caused by changed industrial conditions, vocational education has become an important part of our public-school system; our high-school courses are, in a great measure, organized in accordance with the vocational idea, and vocational or pre-vocational

---

24. *New York Annual Report*, 1912, pp. 395–97.

25. George Herbert Mead, "The Larger Educational Bearings of Vocational Guidance," in Bloomfield, *Readings in Vocational Guidance*, p. 47; see also: C. A. Prosser, "Practical Arts and Vocational Guidance," *NEA Addresses and Proceedings*, 1912, p. 647.

26. Bloomfield, quoted in "Vocational Guidance," in Bloomfield, *Readings in Vocational Guidance*, p. 315.

education for children who will not go to high school will soon become an essential part of the work of our educational system. This introduction of vocational courses, combined with the complexity of modern vocational life, has forced upon us the necessity of attempting some direction of students in their choice of a life-career and in their preparation for same.[27]

Many of the early attempts at formal educational guidance in the urban schools were simply efforts to channel prospective high school students into the expanded course offerings resulting from the development of industrial, commercial, and other vocational curricula. As early as 1908, for example, the New York City superintendent reported that elementary school graduates who desired high school training were offered a choice of over five different curricula ranging from college preparation courses to trade training in bookbinding. Superintendent Maxwell said that "it is of the utmost importance that children should select that high school course for which they are best adapted by natural talent." He believed, however, that many students were not making wise choices and that often their parents were giving them bad advice. "Misdirected effort at any age is always to be regretted. It involves loss of power, wealth, and happiness to the individual and to the community of which he is a part," said Maxwell. "Misdirected effort, however, at the time the child is entering high school is little short of calamity, at that stage it means that the energy of a life-time will probably be led into paths for which it is not best fitted." The gravity of such consequences led him to feel "that the principals and teachers of the elementary schools ought to assume responsibility for advising each graduate and the graduate's parents as to the high school course the student is naturally adapted to pursue." In order to bring home this responsibility to the elementary principals and teachers, the superintendent "prepared a blank form on which they should advise parents as to the kind of high school course for which the pupil is best fitted."[28] Maxwell included with the form a series of charts showing the number of students in the various boroughs who had been advised and the number who indicated that they were going to follow the advice. Three years later, over 22,000 of 31,000 students advised by elementary principals declared that they intended to follow their counsel.[29] This counseling device was, of course, a stopgap

---

27. Goodwin, "Vocational Guidance in Cincinnati," p. 129.
28. *New York Annual Report*, 1908, pp. 75, 76.
29. *New York Annual Report*, 1911, p. 97.

measure awaiting the institutionalization of a regular educational guidance bureaucracy in the New York system.

The year after New York's first experiment with formal educational guidance, Boston faced a problem caused by its schools' failure to channel students. The Boston High School of Commerce and the High School of Practical Arts were both overenrolled by almost twice their capacity for entering freshmen. When such conditions had arisen in the past, schools were forced to admit students by lottery or on the basis of scholarship, but the 1909 introduction of vocational counselors into the elementary schools permitted a new procedure. The principal of each elementary school was sent a list of the students from his school who applied for admittance to the crowded high schools. This list and an outline of the qualities thought essential for successful pursuit of studies at the high schools were then given to the vocational counselors in each elementary school. These advisors selected the students for entry. Stratton Brooks, then superintendent in Boston, expressed the hope that the new method of selection would prove superior to earlier practices.[30]

The expanded offerings of the high schools and the increased numbers of students in post-elementary schools presented problems of placement to other urban school systems. At about the time that New York and Boston experimented with placement schemes, the Cincinnati schools instituted a program for educational guidance. The superintendent argued, "The greatly increased attendance in high schools and the greater number of courses to choose from have made it necessary for children and parents to have some help in order that they may choose with due consideration of the future of the children." Cincinnati's program, which provided systematic guidance before and during the high school career, reflected the general trend of the guidance movement. The aims of the Cincinnati program were listed as:

1. To impress upon child and parent the need for thoughtful consideration of career.
2. To secure information whereby the pupil may be aided in arriving at a judgment, and to furnish parent and teacher with material to assist in guiding the pupil.
3. To secure or plan methods of guiding and to keep records of such data as will help in forming judgments.

---

30. Stratton D. Brooks, "Vocational Guidance in the Boston Schools," in Bloomfield, *Readings in Vocational Guidance*, pp. 87–88.

    4. To aid the pupil at the time of his leaving school: i.e. secure employ-
    ment, help in the selection of college, and keep in touch with
    him.[31]

This program, like its counterparts in New York and Boston, sought
more efficient placement of students in the existing educational channels. It represented one of the early attempts to expand the vocational
guidance movement from job placement.

    Charles A. Prosser expressed the need to broaden vocational guid-
ance when he said, "We are swinging around to the idea that it is to be
the mission of the schools in the future to select by testing and training—to adjust boys and girls for life by having them undergo varied
experiences in order to uncover their varied traits and aptitudes and to
direct and to train them in the avenues for which they display the most
capacity."[32] In a similar vein, the Committee on High Schools and
Training Schools of the New York City Board of Education suggested
that vocational guidance should not be an exclusive function of the high
school but "a fundamental motive of the entire educational system."
The committee later proposed that the school system should expose the
child to a variety of occupations and begin training in a specific vocation before the age of vocational choice.[33]

THE IMPACT OF GUIDANCE ON SCHOOL CURRICULA

Many leaders of the guidance movement were active in developing strategies for implementing the principle of vocational training at the programmatic level. F. E. Spaulding, superintendent of schools in
Minneapolis, argued that vocational guidance must understand both the
needs and capacities of the students and the needs of society, especially
the opportunities for service that society offers. This special knowledge,
he believed, placed the vocational department in a position to change
the schools. Spaulding cautioned the guidance department to influence
the "conscious and intentional efforts of the school to train the character
as well as the intellect." Vocational guidance, the superintendent said,
had to be especially concerned with "the continuous, unavoidable, yet

---

31. *Cincinnati Annual Report,* 1911, pp. 33–34.
32. Prosser, "Practical Arts and Vocational Guidance," p. 647.
33. "Vocational Guidance," pp. 297, 308.

rarely appreciated effect of the conditions imposed upon the pupil through the organization, administration, and conduct of the school and of the work of the school." Here Spaulding was referring to what later became known as the structural imperatives of any institutional system. Vocational guidance should encourage every student to develop traits necessary for success in corporate industry:

> The school must learn to adapt its work and requirements to the natural desire to succeed, so that the entire school life of every pupil may be a series of successes, to the end that—however meager the intellectual accomplishment—the habit of success may be formed. Without this fixed habit of success any young person is poorly prepared to face the discouraging conditions so prevalent in the world of industry. The young person entering industry with the habit of failure developed in school has already made several grades toward graduation into the class of unemployables.[34]

The Minneapolis superintendent proposed to subordinate the educational program of the public schools to the objectives of vocationalism. Students, teachers, and schools must accept the possibility of "meager intellectual accomplishments" if that was necessary to produce the kind of worker needed on the assembly line.

If Superintendent Spaulding suggested a general strategy for vocational guidance to transform the schools into institutions more compatible with the needs of vocationalism, other officials worked on the tactical aspects of this transformation. These tactics involved at least three areas of effort: reorganization of traditional curricula, development of new courses designed specifically to teach about vocations, and closer articulation of industrial training and prevocational classes with the actual conditions and requirements of corporate industry. The last area was, perhaps, the most predictable development. Vocational guidance officers were asked to conduct industrial surveys to ascertain firsthand and accurate information about the occupational opportunities and requirements in their city. Nearly every survey included suggestions on how the information should affect the training program in the schools. As a result of their acquaintance with industry, guidance personnel were expected to influence the content and methods in the industrial training and prevocational curricula.

---

34. F. E. Spaulding, "Problems of Vocational Guidance," in Bloomfield, *Readings in Vocational Guidance*, pp. 70–72.

Counselors also influenced the development of new curricular offerings, especially those concerned with teaching about vocations. The level at which these subjects should be introduced into the curriculum caused some disagreement. While some educators suggested the subjects be taught in kindergarten, Brewer, in his widely read *Vocational-Guidance Movement*, published in 1918, recommended that such courses start in the fourth grade.[35] Few questioned the value of vocational offerings, and most agreed that they should be a part of the public school curriculum at least by the junior high period. The so-called "life-career classes" were designed to teach children about the opportunities that different occupations afforded. In 1913, the Boston elementary schools taught boys about medicine, civil service, business, building trades, and printing, while girls were introduced to retail sales, nursing, dressmaking, and teaching. This kind of study was supposed to increase the share of children choosing the trades and business occupations.[36] By 1918, it was reported that over 150 high schools had begun vocational courses.[37] Apart from helping children to decide upon a calling, the purpose of life-career studies was to vitalize school work with "realistic" types of learning. Children would be motivated to academic studies if schooling became more relevant to their lives and futures.

The other courses in the curriculum did not escape the influence of the vocational guidance movement. Educators came to believe that every subject should in some way be modified to strengthen the schools' effort to find an appropriate vocational place for each child. The report of the New York City School Board's Committee of High Schools and Training Schools included an extensive section prepared by vocational guidance experts. In that section, they indicated how the traditional subjects like mathematics, geography, history, and civics could be modified in order to further the vocational guidance function of the school.[38] Some guidance advocates even suggested that any subject that did not directly contribute to the vocational purposes of schooling should be eliminated from the curriculum. John Brewer felt that "if the child is to be regarded by the teacher as a prospective worker, . . . each lesson having something to contribute to the vocational efficiency of the

---

35. Brewer, *Vocational-Guidance Movement* pp. 229–30; see also, "Vocational Guidance," pp. 296–99.

36. Ellen M. Greany, "A Study of the Vocational Guidance of Grammar School Pupils," in Bloomfield, *Readings in Vocational Guidance*, pp. 270–76.

37. Brewer, *Vocational-Guidance Movement*, p. 44.

38. "Vocational Guidance," pp. 301–10.

child should be taught with that fact in mind. The vocational uses will appear in almost all of the studies and will predominate in many of them."[39] The assumption that the child should be considered primarily as a prospective worker by the schools seemed to be accepted without critical examination. Hence, it was logical to consider public education as a series of roads to be traveled and bridges to be traversed toward the final objective of a permanent place in the economic structure of corporate industry.

The most often cited experiment modifying the traditional school subjects was initiated in Grand Rapids, Michigan in 1909. The program was analyzed three years later by Jesse B. Davis, principal of Grand Rapids' Central High School. Davis began with the standard assumption that "every pupil who enters the high school presents himself as a candidate for some successful career in life." Students and parents expected the school to transport these youth along the road to occupational success. That the schools had thus far failed could easily be ascertained by observing the "educated misfits — round pegs in square holes" who abounded everywhere. Attempting to remedy this situation, Central High developed a plan to give vocational emphasis in all areas of its curriculum. Significantly, the plan involved moral training. "We found that the plan not only tended to give vocational aim to the high-school course," observed Davis, "but, as the work progressed, it developed into a very practical course of moral instruction."[40] Many of the leaders in the vocational movement correctly viewed their campaign as having a significant moral dimension. Uplift was essential in the effort to create a contented labor force. As suggested in the preceding chapter, the development of skills was in many ways the lesser concern of educators dedicated to creating the kind of working class needed by industrial society; they thought it more important to convince prospective workers that their role in the economic structure was important, that it was in their best interest to accept that role, and that the role represented the natural order of things.

At Central High this more necessary component of industrial training found its locus in a restructuring of the traditional English classes. Beginning in the eighth grade and continuing through the next four years, approximately one-fourth of written and oral composition time

---

39. Brewer, *Vocational Guidance Movement,* p. 66.

40. Jesse B. Davis, "Vocational and Moral Guidance Through English Composition in High School," *NEA Addresses and Proceedings,* 1912, pp. 713–18.

was devoted to vocationalism. In the eighth grade, theme topics were based on the value of high school training and the importance of choosing the appropriate course of study. During the first semester of the ninth grade, the children devoted their efforts to investigating the lives of successful men and women "for the purpose of discovering the habits of life and work that have contributed to their success." The second semester of the ninth year concentrated on "self-analysis." The pupils were led to discover their own likes, strengths, and aptitudes and then shown how to apply these qualities to a vocational situation. In their compositions they were asked to discuss, among other topics, the business assets of personal appearance and good manners. Sophomore English composition offered a survey of occupations, with procedures for choosing among them. Students presented reports outlining the conditions of various callings and explaining how to align their own aptitudes with the requirements of the occupations under consideration. By the end of the sophomore year, it was expected that the student would have chosen his future career or at least narrowed the choice to a general vocational area. During the eleventh grade, the students organized the vocational quarter of their English course around topics dealing with the ethics and standards of the occupation for which they were now preparing themselves. The seniors examined the relationship of their special vocation to the larger social organization of society to get a concrete and personal knowledge of applied social ethics.[41] By devoting one quarter of the time of the English class during the last five years of public schooling to vocationalism, the Grand Rapids schools no doubt effectively presented the world of work to their students. Here vocations and the moral codes associated with corporate industrialism were presented as aspects of social reality by teachers of a subject with seemingly little vested professional interest in the economic structure that they tacitly supported. As vocationalism became more entrenched in the curriculum, propaganda aimed at encouraging future workers to accept their place within the industrial system became more pervasive. Such diffusion made the propaganda more difficult to discern as such; increasingly, it was accepted as an empirical description of reality. The effect of this massive transformation of the traditional school curriculum may well be one reason why, in the United States, unlike in European countries, alternative economic systems failed to gain popular credence as legitimate challenges to industrial capitalism.

---

41. Davis, "Guidance Through English Composition," pp. 713–18.

SELF-SELECTION

While massive changes were made in the school's curriculum, a subtle, but important, shift occurred within the vocational guidance movement. The belief that guidance experts should direct children into those occupations that the counselors had decided were best for them and for society was gradually replaced by the notion that the children themselves should make the actual career decision. This change can be seen as a dimension of twentieth-century liberalism. Its effect, like the effect of the curriculum changes, was to bind the future worker even more closely to his destined place in the labor force. By 1912, the idea of "self-selection" was widely accepted by leaders of the vocational guidance movement. "We do not prescribe or decide a particular occupation for anyone," wrote Meyer Bloomfield. "This is the business of the parents and the natural protectors of the child or home. Decision must come from within and not from without. We are not trying to divert anyone from any class of pursuits or to direct particular attention toward them." In this description of the Boston plan for guidance presented to the NEA's Department of Superintendence, Bloomfield clearly opted for so-called autonomous career choices. He continued:

> It is not the business of vocational advising to favor or disfavor occupations. It is primarily its function to know the facts, analyze, classify, simplify, and apply them, where they will do the most good. Let the facts speak for themselves, but drive them home. The responsibility rests on the shoulders of those who make the decision. But knowing the facts is no child's play, neither is their skillful dissemination.[42]

During the same meeting, George Knox, assistant superintendent of schools from St. Louis, after rejecting the job placement concept of vocational guidance, reinforced Bloomfield's characterization of the appropriate kind of guidance.[43] At the November 1912 Boston Masters' Association meeting, William T. Miller of the Agassiz District of that city also endorsed self-selection as opposed to reliance on counselor-determined choice. Similar endorsements were given by the 1914 teacher's committee that surveyed the Chicago public schools' vocational guid-

42. Meyer Bloomfield, "Vocational Guidance," *NEA Addresses and Proceedings*, 1912, p. 433.

43. George Platt Knox, "How Should the School System Contribute to an Intelligent Choice of Vocation on the Part of the Pupil?" *NEA Addresses and Proceedings*, 1912, p. 417.

ance program and by the 1918 Committee on the Reorganization of Secondary Education.[44]

The statements of Bloomfield, Knox, Miller, and the various committees appear to indicate that by 1912 the vocational guidance movement supported truly free choice of vocations by students; that no student would be guided into a vocational area because of his particular social, economic, or ethnic heritage; that aptitude and interest were really the major factors which advisors recommended as determinants in the students' vocational choice; and that if students decided not to enter a particular vocation, counselors would assume that the vocation should be either changed or eliminated. A more careful examination, however, reveals that vocational guidance continued to channel and slot students into those occupational areas most needed by corporate industry.

The vocational guidance movement reflected the general direction of liberal social philosophy in moving away from coercion to more subtle and effective kinds of social control. Rather than impose industry's will by command or exhortation, the new techniques relied upon the internalization of goals and ideals which had been previously selected by experts. At times, individuals were even allowed to choose their own goals—if these were acceptable to the professionals. Because compulsion was disdained as ineffective, long-term schooling became increasingly important in the vocational conditioning process. The difference between the new, subtle kind of social control and the older type can be seen by comparing the way the English yeoman farmer was driven off the land and into the factories with the American process of transforming immigrants and native laborers from preindustrial to factory workers. The English working class was created by force through the Enclosure Acts and the Poor Laws. The former took away the land that the farmers had traditionally worked, and the latter reduced parish charity. These laws presented the English farmer with the free choice of working in the factories or starving.[45] In the United States, although there was considerable violence in the relations between workers and the owners of

44. William T. Miller, "Vocational Guidance from the View Point of Its Application to Boys in Elementary Schools," in Bloomfield, Readings in Vocational Guidance, p. 121; Chicago Annual Report, 1914, p. 343; see also Brewer, Vocational-Guidance Movement, p. 12; and "Vocational Guidance in Secondary Education," Bulletin of the U.S. Bureau of Education, 1918, no. 19, p. 9.

45. For a more extended analysis of this process see E. P. Thompson, The Making of the English Working Class (New York: Vintage, 1963); and C. B. Macpherson, Democratic Theory (Great Britain: Oxford, 1973).

industry, schooling replaced coercion in socializing the industrial labor force. The Americans relied more heavily on the ability of the public school to present a version of social reality that future workers would internalize; the extensive use of physical compulsion to usher workers into the assembly lines was thus eliminated. The reality depicted by the public schools, and especially the vocational guidance movement, portrayed industrial vocations as normal expectations for working-class children. Within the prescribed boundaries of this reality, students could choose their future vocations.

Significantly, the statements supporting autonomous occupational selection indicated that vocational guidance should be "a continuous process," or that the aim of guidance "must be to bring the child to understand the real values in his environment and to detect the best opportunities," or that its responsibility was to present "the facts" and then "let the facts speak for themselves, but drive them home." The creation of reality constructs takes a long time and requires continuous care, and American educators realized that long-term schooling was necessary to create those constructs. However, when we consider a captive audience of children presented with a certain selection of "facts" for several years, and the alteration of the school curriculum to support industrial capitalism, we must question how much "free choice" children were permitted in determining their futures.

The report of the NEA's Commission on the Reorganization of Secondary Education discloses the limits of freedom under the controlled classroom conditions. "Vocational guidance must not only teach the child to adjust himself to his environment," it asserted, "but must also equip him to change that environment." A significant change in the industrial environment had occurred: "Employers are finding that recognition of social welfare in the conduct of their enterprises is not only good citizenship but is good business." The advent of welfare capitalism required that "faith in the effectiveness of plans that promote community helpfulness must be instilled into the pupils, who will be the adult citizens of the next generation." The report clearly conformed to the trend of twentieth-century corporate industrialism and predicted that "twenty years from now, undoubtedly the spirit of cooperation will permeate vocational life more than it does today." Accordingly, "school children must acquire the spirit of cooperation and be trained in cooperation through the social organization of classroom and community."[46]

---

46. Quoted in "Vocational Guidance in Secondary Education," p. 23.

Thus, vocational guidance had to produce future workers who believed in the modern economic system. Counseling helped create an allegiance to corporate industry. While the child could make limited judgments regarding his future and the destiny of his social order, clearly such volition was circumscribed by the demands of modern capitalism.

Many leaders in the vocational guidance movement favored student autonomy over counselor-dictated choice because they believed the former procedure more effective even if more time consuming. Charles W. Eliot claimed that "it is highly inexpedient, as well as unjust, to force any child or youth into a trade which does not attract him, for in it he will be both inefficient and unhappy."[47] The former president of Harvard University reflected the commonsense observation that individuals might react negatively to externally imposed determinations of their life chances. Leaders of the vocational guidance movement opted for a long-term process of schooling that would create an environment in which the "correct" career decision would appear to have come from within the child. Eliot had suggested that a child forced into a vocation may become dissatisfied and thus inefficient; moreover, someone coerced into an unsuitable job might blame his plight on the school, the state, or the economic order. If, however, a person could be led to believe that the "decision came from within," he would more likely accept responsibility for his condition, and any subsequent dissatisfaction would be deflected from the economic order into self-condemnation.[48] Indeed, the 1914 Chicago teachers' committee recognized that many children would be placed in undesirable positions in the industrial order: "Even the strongest advocates of vocational guidance do not dream that all pupils will become skilled workers. For many it will mean only the directing into the least harmful employment. . . ."[49]

A realistic and frank appraisal of the problems of self-selection and vocational dictation was made by the superintendent of schools of Ironwood, Michigan. Superintendent John V. Brennan confessed that "the demand for economic efficiency has made vocational guidance one of the leading educational questions of the hour." Educators viewed America's traditional ideals of personal independence and social equality as problematic for vocational placement. Because the right to

47. Charles W. Eliot, "The Value of Life-Career Motive," in Bloomfield, *Readings in Vocational Guidance*, p. 9.

48. *Chicago Annual Report*, 1914, p. 343.

49. *Chicago Annual Report* 1914, p. 343.

aspire and achieve was also important for national economic efficiency, the basic issue before the vocational guidance movement was "to preserve to the individual his right to aspire, to make of himself what he will, and at the same time [to help him] find himself early, accurately and with certainty. . . ." It was the schools' responsibility to determine "how to preserve individualism with a high standard of community efficiency; in other words how to keep alive in the breasts of the youth of this country the ambition to venture, to experiment, and to attain, while at the same time directing him along certain definite paths best suited to his aptitudes and talents."[50] Vocational guidance would resolve this dilemma by structuring the learning environment of the child so that he would internalize the aims of corporate industry and select the appropriate vocation from among the presented alternatives. This would insure a sense of independence, a desire for achievement, and—equally important—economic efficiency.

Industrialists and leaders of the industrial education movement had long complained that American youth disdained working-class jobs in favor of professional and "clean clothes" occupations. Some evidence supports their claim that substantial effort was needed to direct the youth into the factories. Irving King examined the vocational preferences of high school youth in several Iowa schools and compared his findings with a study done in New York City by J. K. Van Denburg. Both studies found a high proportion of students desiring to enter professional callings, while relatively few chose trades and industrial pursuits. Similarly, Bessie Davis discovered in Somerville (Massachusetts) High School that "of the 1,226 [students questioned] only 11 indicated desire to engage in the work of trades."[51] She concluded that vocational guidance was needed in the Somerville High School. J. B. Sears's study of Oakland, California seventh and eighth-grade students indicated the concern of many educators with vocational placement problems. Although Sears studied the subject of spelling in the Oakland schools, he managed to gather information regarding the occupations of the students' fathers and the vocational preferences of the students. Of the 1,039 boys queried, over 90 percent had definite ideas about their future careers. The Stanford educator, however, believed that "too large

---

50. John V. Brennan, "The Schools and Vocational Guidance," in Bloomfield, *Readings in Vocational Guidance*, pp. 76, 79.

51. Irving King, "The Vocational Interests, Study Habits, and Amusements of the Pupils in Certain High Schools in Iowa," in Bloomfield, *Readings in Vocational Guidance*, pp. 172–89; and Bessie D. Davis, "An Inquiry into Vocational Aims of High School Pupils," in Bloomfield, *Readings in Vocational Guidance*, p. 194.

a percentage of the boys wished to enter the professions." He found, too, that many of the children were not attracted to their fathers' occupations. In Sears's opinion, "The boys are to a large extent aiming at something they can never reach," a situation which "shows also that much need exists for intelligent vocational guidance, and it makes very clear the specific nature of such need, and the extent to which it exists and must be met by the schools if they are to solve their whole problem." He felt that "the function of the schools is first to rationalize those aspirations, and then to carry foward the present plans for occupational training suggested above which the writer has observed in successful operation in at least one large vocational school in the city."[52]

The studies by King, Van Denburg, Davis, and Sears showed that in at least seven cities—two in the East, four in the Midwest, and one on the West Coast—students recorded a strong preference for white collar vocations. In light of the rhetoric regarding self-selection, it is interesting that, on the basis of no other data except the failure of Somerville High School students to choose blue collar occupations, did Davis conclude that they needed vocational guidance. It is difficult to understand how Professor Sears could assert that "too large a percentage of the boys wished to enter the professions" when presumably the only evidence he had about their abilities were their fathers' occupations and their spelling scores. Perhaps the Stanford educator had developed a new method of predicting vocational destiny on the basis of junior high school spelling achievement. While such a method may have proved as successful as most of the other methods in vogue, since he never published any account of such a concept, it probably was not the basis of his judgment. As the notion of vocational placement based on the inheritance of occupations was not in vogue, it is equally unlikely that the information regarding paternal occupations accounted for his decision most likely— and the internal evidence of his article bears this out—Sears based his conclusion simply on the kinds of jobs available in corporate industry. Even a cursory examination of the industrial workplace demonstrated that modern capitalism could accommodate only a small percentage of its work force in the professions and that the vast majority would have to become laborers if the economic structure was to survive intact. Thus, in spite of the talk about self-selection, the vocational guidance movement did not lose sight of the broad manpower requirements of

---

52. J. B. Sears, "Occupations of Fathers and Occupational Choices of 1,039 Boys in Grades Seven and Eight in the Oakland Schools," *School and Society*, May 22, 1915, pp. 750–56.

corporate industry. The choices of students were to be guided by those requirements.

Nondirective vocational guidance may have increased the proportion of students chosing working-class occupations while decreasing the share of those students unclear about their future vocations. The results of Boston's experimental program of vocational guidance in eighth-grade classes provides some evidence for this contention, but not enough data is available to substantiate any definite conclusions on this aspect of vocational guidance influence. During March and April of 1913, students were divided into an experimental and a control group. Each group was given a brief vocational interest questionnaire both at the beginning and at the end of the experiment. Prior to the final questionnaire, the experimental group received nine lessons of the "informational" variety involving exposure to "the facts" about various occupations. The control group received no instruction. On the final questionnaire, over 70 percent of the experimental group chose occupations which had been subjects of lessons. Most significantly, the percentage of "undecided in the experimental group dropped by 22 percent, while the same category in the control group rose by 9 percent. Not surprisingly, the percentage of those in the experimental group choosing working-class occupations increased by 9 percent. Few other categories of occupations suffered significant loss; therefore, a reasonable conclusion is that most of the gain came from the undecided group. This shift suggests that the program had been successful in helping formerly undecided children to choose working-class vocations. The share of the uninstructed group opting for working-class occupations remained exactly the same during the two-month period.[53] This evidence suggests that vocational guidance might deliver the "uncommitted" youth to industry by a forceful presentation of "the facts." Apparently, children not yet decided upon their future life's work were most easily guided in their career decision.

The children who had decided that they would prefer to enter professions, however, presented a more difficult challenge for vocational guidance counselors committed to filling the manpower requirements of industry through the technique of student self-selection. In a section of his *Vocational-Guidance Movement* entitled "Methods of Inducing a Young Person to Change His Aim," Brewer asked, "How shall a boy or girl be induced to reconsider a determination to be a lawyer or a doctor

---

53. Greany, "Vocational Guidance of Grammar School Pupils," pp. 267–87.

or engineer when it appears that he has no conception of the battle ahead of him?" Rejecting "direct counsel of a negative sort," Brewer advocated allowing the student to make the decision himself. This "free" decision, however, would be made only after the counselor had helped the child to study the occupation in question with an emphasis on the difficulties of preparation, the stringent personal qualifications for the occupation, and the disadvantages of the occupation.[54] It is not difficult to understand how, once they had been brought to realize the long, arduous, and expensive educational trail which would have to be climbed, children of working-class background could be induced to make a decision "from within" to forsake a professional career for a more attainable occupation.

GUIDANCE AND INDUSTRIAL EFFICIENCY

Agreement between the orientation of vocational guidance and the manpower requirements of corporate industry was neither accidental nor incidental. This congruence had been built into the objectives of the guidance movement by its leaders and formed a major part of its *raison d'être*. In 1914, the New York City Committee on High Schools and Training Schools asserted that vocational guidance should promote employment and occupational efficiency by preparing future workers for the types of labor needed in the modern economic system.[55] Nor was the New York committee alone in its belief that the schools should supply the types of workers demanded by industry. Edward Elliott, writing in 1908, pointed out, "Until we possess reliable data upon which to base a rational scheme of reorganization, the public schools cannot hope to become instruments for 'industrial determination.' Neither will they cease to prevent the present positive misselection of individuals for their proper station of efficiency and happiness." According to Elliott, "Rightful selection must precede and underlie the maintenance of the educational equilibrium of democracy."[56] Leaders of the vocational guidance movement generally agreed that the guidance they advocated

---

54. Brewer, *Vocational-Guidance Movement*, pp. 23, 104, 123, 124.

55. "Vocational Guidance," p. 289.

56. Edward C. Elliott, "Equality of Opportunity," *NEA Addresses and Proceedings*, 1908, p. 161.

could enable the schools to effect "industrial determination" in order to provide the "educational equilibrium" necessary for democracy.

It was also recognized, though, that this "equilibrium" would require redefinition of the traditional meaning of democracy. At the first national conference on vocational guidance, held in Boston in 1910, the president of the Massachusetts Institute of Technology, Richard D. MacLaurin, observed that "the old watchwords, which were so useful in their days, the watchwords of our fathers and grandfathers, such as 'Breath,' 'Freedom,' 'Liberty,' are less frequently heard in these days." These slogans were now less useful, MacLaurin said, because they proclaimed unattainable ideals and thus failed to inspire youth. Bread and butter goals, on the other hand, would motivate youth.

The MIT president probably heard little dissent from the assembled vocational guidance personnel when he stated: "We have to face everywhere in the field of education the problem of fitting men for the actual conditions of the world today and tomorrow; we must have an educational device that will make our youth see that to succeed they will have to work seriously; we must have an educational system that will fit them for particular professions."[57] Within the vocational guidance movement the "actual conditions of the world" meant industrial conditions, and fitting children for these conditions meant preparing them for the industrial workplace. The prefatory statement to the collected papers read at the organizational meeting of the Vocational Guidance Association in 1913 in Grand Rapids, Michigan left no doubt about the universality of the practical point of view. The statement noted that one of the three sources of vocational guidance was "an economic demand, made in recognition of the fact that our industrial system needs a better and more efficiently chosen body of employees."[58] The following year, John V. Brennan asserted, "For the present, at least, vocational guidance is to be especially concerned with industry."[59]

In an article appropriately titled "Sorting Students," Frank N. Freeman, a professor at the University of Chicago, argued that the public school should extend its practice of grouping students homogeneously in order to direct them into occupational slots where they could receive

---

57. Richard C. MacLaurin, "Vocational Guidance," in Bloomfield, *Readings in Vocational Guidance*, pp. 13, 14.

58. "Vocational Guidance," *Bulletin of the U.S. Bureau of Education*, 1914, no. 14, p. 6.

59. Brennan, "Schools and Vocational Guidance," p. 75; see also Goodwin, "Vocational Guidance in Cincinnati," p. 129.

the type of training that would make them more efficient and docile future workers. Like others in the guidance movement, Professor Freeman believed that "it is the business of the school to help the child to acquire such an attitude toward the inequalities of life, whether in accomplishment or in reward, that he may adjust himself to its conditions with the least possible friction." Perhaps anticipating the criticism that the unfair system of rewards in corporate industry should be opposed, Freeman dismissed the possibility with the usual detached air of the university scholar: "The school is not responsible for the world's system of rewards." One might wonder how the school could ethically prepare children to fit industry's labor requirements without being "responsible" for the reward system of industry. Surely, this issue would bother those who assumed that the public school, as an agency of the state, had some responsibility for assuring equality among its students, or at least for assuring that the state supplied educational opportunities to individual children on an equal basis. This assumption was explicitly rejected by the Chicago educator: "The real difficulty with this whole line of reasoning is that it assumes that education is a gift by the state to the individual for the benefit of the individual. The only valid conception of public education is that it is for the purpose of fitting the individual to take his place in the life of the community."[60] This reasoning echoed the justifications for compulsory attendance laws. In Freeman's case, the protection of the state and the interests of corporate industry became synonymous.

Leaders of the vocational guidance movement as they attempted to use the public school to classify and train the general population to fit the manpower needs of corporate industry, perceived the complexities of those needs. The preceding chapter showed that educators designed the vocational training programs of the differentiated curriculum to accommodate the modern hierarchical and rationalized structure of the labor force. Another example further demonstrates the sensitivity of public school officials to the needs of corporate industry. Only recently have social historians rediscovered the extensive geographic mobility of the industrial labor force.[61] In 1913, however, Leonard Ayres, working for the Russell Sage Foundation, examined conditions affecting industrial education in American cities with populations of 25,000 to

---

60. Frank N. Freeman, "Sorting Students," *Educational Review 68* (November 1924): 169–74. I am indebted to Clarence Karier for bringing this source to my attention.

61. See Stephen Thurnstrom, *Poverty and Progress* (New York: Athenum, 1972), pp. 84–90.

200,000. He discovered that "only about one father in six is now living in the city of his birth and that among the boys only a few more than one-half are now living where they were born." Ayres quickly drew from this data conclusions about the structure of industrial training. "These facts are significant," he said, "because if it is often urged that the schools should develop courses of industrial education that will directly prepare the children to enter the local industries, but if present conditions maintain in the future, the majority of adults are not going to work in the same communities in which they received their schooling."[62] The significance of these facts did not escape the purview of the vocational guidance leaders. Brewer cited the Ayres study when he urged that children be prepared for a national as well as a local labor market.[63] In this instance, as in many others, the vocational guidance movement demonstrated a sophisticated and sensitive understanding of the manpower needs of corporate industry.

Though the vocational guidance movement's primary objective was to fit children for the needs of industry in order that the economy might operate on the most efficient labor basis, this goal did not render all the leaders of the movement insensitive to the health, prosperity, or happiness of the future industrial worker. Herman Schneider, dean of the University of Cincinnati's College of Engineering, declared that "a man is most efficient when his work gives him the greatest satisfaction, when he is doing the thing his Creator intended he should do." Schneider felt that "every working man, from the hewer of wood and drawer of water to the research scientist, should get three things out of his work: first, mental and physical development and discipline; second, joy in doing it (or at least satisfaction); and third, a decent living." Displaying a more human side of the movement, Schneider went on to assert that "the man who has found the job his soul is blindly craving, the job for which he has inborn talents, gets these [three necessities]. But the man whose whole being revolts at his task becomes a captious citizen, an inefficient worker, a meager earner."[64] Schneider felt that an analysis of the industrial workplace would show some jobs requiring creative effort while others demanded routine repetitions. Interestingly, however, he con-

---

62. Leonard P. Ayres, "Some Conditions Affecting Problems of Industrial Education in Seventy-Eight American School Systems," in Bloomfield, *Readings in Vocational Guidance*, pp. 150–71.

63. Brewer, *Vocational-Guidance Movement*, p. 140.

64. Herman Schneider, "Selecting Young Men for Particular Jobs," in Bloomfield, *Readings in Vocational Guidance*, p. 370.

tended that the task of guidance was to discover which children were innately endowed with the characteristics required by the different kinds of jobs. Apparently, the Cincinnati administrator believed that the Creator had engineered men to fit the manpower needs of corporate industry.

Others in the vocational guidance movement were less sanguine about the possibility of fitting students to fill all of the occupational slots in industry. Some were convinced that not all callings deserved support of the public school. At the 1912 NEA meeting of the Department of Superintendence, Meyer Bloomfield appealed to educators to recognize that the school should not recruit children as future workers for occupations detrimental to their well-being. "We go to great pain and sacrifice to fit our boys and girls for the job," he said, and "we want the job to be fit for the boy and girl. We want to give the world of work the best trained, best advised, and best prepared corps of workers we can turn out; we ask that this investment and this equipment shall be not ruined even if not enhanced."[65] Despite crass metaphors referring to students as equipment and investment, a sympathetic reading of both Bloomfield's and Brewer's works on vocational guidance reveals genuine interest in the students' welfare. Unfortunately, this concern was probably not predominant in the movement. Statements like Bloomfield's, which condemned some jobs or occupations as unfit for workers, occasionally surfaced, but little evidence exists to suggest that vocational guidance personnel actively campaigned to eliminate particular occupations or that schools attempted to influence students to shun particular jobs that reasonable observers might designate detrimental to employee well-being. When faced with the immense economic and political power of corporate industry, public schools have rarely offered active or even passive resistance.

Failure to object to adverse working conditions discloses a basic flaw in the assumptions of the vocational guidance movement. Experts in this field claimed that, because schools advocated students' interests against the selfishness of industry, children would be best protected if the public schools actively entered the occupational selection process. Even if the school acted in this manner, though, the awesome power of corporate industry makes the belief that schools could stand as bastions

---

65. Bloomfield, "Vocational Guidance," p. 436.

against it an exercise in pure folly. Rarely in twentieth-century America have the objectives of corporate industry been frustrated.

In fact, the schools did not protect students from industrial interests. Research shows overwhelmingly that schools cooperated with the business system. The values, beliefs, prejudices, and sympathies that formed the outlook of the leaders of corporate industry were identical to the views of the public educators. The public school was transformed during the early years of the twentieth century into an instrument for achieving the objectives and meeting the needs of corporate industry not because school officials were forced against their will to accede to policies they might freely have rejected, nor because they were disingenuous, nor because they had entered some secret conspiracy with the scions of big business. The transformation in schools occurred because educators, like most other middle-class Americans, held the same world view as corporate industrialists and thus, truly believed that their policies were the best public policy.

The vocational guidance movement always tried to fit individuals to the manpower needs of modern capitalism. From its early role of job placement to its development as an agency of educational placement, it attempted to change the public schools into a realization of the Platonic educational ideal. The ancient Greek philosopher proposed that education should be a state-controlled device to select and train citizens for leadership and subordinate roles in society, and many advocates of the vocational guidance movement recognized the intellectual heritage of their objectives. However, the Austrian philosopher, Karl R. Popper, offered a penetrating critique of the use of education to channel individuals into roles. Popper maintained that it was probably impossible to construct any institution that could select outstanding individuals for leadership, and he said that schools should never undertake such a task:

> This tendency transforms our educational system into a racecourse, and turns a course of studies into a hurdle-race. Instead of encouraging the student to devote himself to his studies for the sake of studying, instead of encouraging in him a real love for his subject and for inquiry, he is encouraged to study for the sake of his personal career; he is led to acquire only such knowledge as is serviceable in getting him over the hurdles which he must clear for the sake of his advancement. In other words, even in the field of science, our methods of selection are based upon an appeal to personal ambition of a somewhat crude form. (It is a natural reaction to this appeal if the eager student is looked upon with suspicion by his colleagues.) The impossible demand for an institutional

selection of intellectual leaders endangers the very life not only of science, but of intelligence.[66]

There is little question that Popper's critique applies to the conditions that the vocational guidance movement helped create in American public education.

---

66. Karl R. Popper, *The Open Society and Its Enemies,* 2 vols. (Princeton, N.J.: Princeton University Press, 1971), 1:135–36.

Chapter 9

Conclusion

The massive transformation that American public education experienced between 1890 and 1930 altered its basic structure and character and produced an institution fundamentally different from the one that Americans had grown accustomed to during the preceding two centuries. By the Great Depression, public schooling was national in scope and compulsory until mid-adolescence. The curriculum of traditional literary and classical studies had been expanded to include courses of study designed to prepare the student to function as a wage earner and consumer in the new urban-industrial setting. Schools employed professional personnel whose purpose was to help each student find an appropriate place within this expanded curriculum and ultimately within the industrial economy. Extracurricular activities were systematically organized and directed by the schools and allied agencies so that the nonacademic aspects of the child's life would promote desired psychological traits, personal habits, and character types.

Several themes recur in each of these developments. State authority increased prodigiously, and in no other governmental agency was its expanded power more apparent than in the twentieth-century public school. The school's impingement into the private lives and personal beliefs of individuals derived from a relatively new political principle that separated the new liberals of the twentieth century from the classical liberals of the nineteenth century. This idea held that the state was justified in taking any action deemed necessary to insure its well-being. Throughout the twentieth century, the new liberals, who dominated the positions of power in urban education, translated this idea into educational theory and practice. They insisted that sound citizenship was essential for the survival of the state; they then justified any extension of the school's control over the lives of students by claiming that the new program contributed to good citizenship. The campaign to compel school attendance until mid-adolescence, for example, emanated from the belief that the safety of the state would be threatened unless future citizens were socialized in the schools. The movement to fit children into places in the modern work force was accompanied by the argument that the ability and desire to earn a livelihood was necessary for good citizenship and thus the health of the state. Americanization programs and supervised extracurricular and play activities were also thought to enhance good citizenship. The practice of protecting the state through programs designed to assure acceptable citizenship resulted in amplification of public school authority and a concomitant diminution of the power of the individual.

A second theme resonating through urban schooling in twentieth-century America is the impact of industrial capitalism. Educators found the requirements for good citizenship to be identical to those for efficient service in the modern economic system. This symbiotic relationship fostered not only vocational training and guidance programs, but the play movement, extracurricular activities, and Americanization campaigns as well. Examination of the explicit objectives and activities of these programs shows that all sought to produce adults who met the requirements for an industrial work force. Modern capitalism needed employees who were punctual, accurate, and willing to act as a production team within the boundaries set by superiors. There was no room for the loner, who might design his own plan and carry it out at his own pace and according to his idiosyncrasies. Individuality was banned from the playground and from extracurricular activities, emphasis being placed instead on team games, group goals, subordination of self to the group, and adherence to externally imposed norms. These urban school programs were an effort to instill an industrial consciousness into a preindustrial or premodern people, whether immigrants or rural migrants.

It should not be inferred that school officials were simply lackeys for corporate industry or that they knowingly sold out the future of their students to the interests of big business. Such an interpretation ignores a far more complex reality. These educators felt the estrangement of the "strangers in the land"; they heard the "bitter cry of the children" in the slums; many observed firsthand the suffering of "the other half"; and still others were personally affected by the "shame of the cities." When they saw mammoth corporations clawing their way to the commanding heights of American society by the first decade of the twentieth century, educators accepted the modern social order as reality for the foreseeable future. They were impressed by economic and technological advances, which they thought would alleviate many social ills. Most educators believed that the best future for their students lay in industrial society. Since they felt it was in the student's best interests to share this industrial consciousness, the resultant programs emerged from an honest commitment.

The methods employed in these programs to nurture a modern industrial consciousness constitute a third dominant theme in American urban education. A long and hallowed tradition in American education held that the purpose of schooling was to produce men able to make independent decisions, an objective best accomplished by immersing the student in the cultural traditions of Western civilization. Contemporary educational psychology suggested that the trials and triumphs of past heroes would provide models for the student to emulate in his own life.

The old notion of cultural and intellectual training was rendered obsolete for the majority of students when, at the end of the nineteenth century, several new factors entered the educational equation. Once American public education committed itself to compulsory universal schooling, the idea of education for leadership and independent decision making became dysfunctional. A number of respected professionals warned that any state attempting to provide the same education for leaders and followers would surely experience labor unrest. Leadership and the exercise of independent judgment, even if they could be promoted by the public schools, were not desirable qualities for production line workers. Most educators believed that these qualities could not be fostered in the twentieth-century public school because immigrant, working-class, and minority—increasing in number with compulsory attendance—were allegedly quite different from those of the past. These new pupils were supposedly incapable of comprehending the intellectual and cultural heritage of the West. Because attempts to train these children through intellectual appeals were considered futile and hence frustrating, educators devised different methodology for training the initiates.

The new techniques involved an overt attempt to train and control the nonintellectual sources of behavior. Faculty psychology was displaced by newer theories which emphasized the role of emotional conditioning for behavioral control. Freud demonstrated the importance of impulse in human behavior; social psychology stressed the ability of primary groups to mold the attitudes of their members; and Edward L. Thorndike suggested that future behavior could be determined by selective schedules of positive and negative reinforcement. From these and other sources, educators learned that other methods of influencing human behavior were more effective than appeals to the intellect. It is against such a background that one must examine progressive education's slogan, "learn by doing," and the various training programs that arose from it in settlement houses, playgrounds, and public schools. Educators, social workers, and other experts probably were correct in thinking that nonintellectual impulses were the most influential forces in the human personality. Attempts to control behavior through appeals to the intellect are, at best, inefficient, for concepts and arguments, by their very nature, invite rebuttal. The new methodology for reality structuring and consciousness formation was considerably more efficient. Children were taught specific reactions to stimuli that educators believed were typical in the adult world of work. Thus did the experts hope to build specific constellations of personality structures, and appropriate emotional responses. Alternative outlooks or modes of behavior were treated not simply as different interpretations of a social situation, or peculiar personal responses, but as signs of unreality or even of insanity. Rejection of behavioral patterns embedded in the personality structure through nonintellectual appeals proved far more difficult than reaction against concepts and arguments presented intellectually.

This new methodology permeated nearly every phase of public schooling. In assembly and music programs, on the playgrounds, and during athletic contests, an overt and continuous effort was made to shape the emotional responses of students into a pattern of acceptable behavior. During school athletic contests, for example, cheerleaders channeled the emotional responses of the student spectators. In such programs, efforts to condition emotional reflexes that would determine proper adult behavior were not always obvious because they were aimed at the development of a general outlook. Curricular efforts to develop an industrial consciousness, being more specific, were also more obvious. Industrial-training classrooms took on the actual physical characteristics of the factory workshop. Desultory criticism that school shops failed to teach the right skills because of obsolete equipment misses the point by a wide margin. These programs were not primarily concerned with producing actual skills for factory use, for such skills could be learned on most jobs in a very short time. The schools actually sought to develop what was called "industrial intelligence"—a sense of reality or a consciousness that led children to envision themselves as industrial workers. The schools wanted to equip these children with personality structures and emotional habits suitable to the industrial workplace. Other areas of the curriculum were similarly revised to so condition children slotted for factory service. These children, for example, spent little time pondering the dilemma of Hamlet, or the character flaws of Oedipus, or the creative accomplishments of Michaelangelo. They read about *Romance of Modern Electricity* or *Lives of Undistinguished Americans* in their English classes, where they also learned how to fill out job applications and read job specification instructions.

The institutional structures, the educational goals, and the themes that underlay the transformation of American urban schools during the first third of the twentieth century remained dominant during the succeeding four decades. Educational developments through the sixties illustrate the continuity in American education from the early decades of this century until the present.

A noteworthy innovation in education during the thirties was the massive entry of the federal government into the schooling process through educational programs in the Civilian Conservation Corps. On the surface, the CCC might appear to be simply an humanitarian effort to provide work relief for unemployed youths; a closer examination, however, shows it to be a complex educational enterprise utilizing many of the techniques developed during the previous three decades and analyzed in the preceding chapters. The camps had organized recreational and leisure-time activities much like those extracurricular and playground activities developed earlier in the urban schools. They also had a rather extensive vocational-training component. The chief aim of the CCC was to hold young people out of an already flooded job market until the depression ended. In the interim, the youth were taught to accept the economic slump as a temporary aberration in the structure of industrial capitalism and were prepared to fit into that system when they would be needed. The attitudes, habits, and perspectives fostered at the CCC camps were much like those encouraged in urban public schools during the preceding three decades.[1]

1. See Howard Oxley, "Introducing CCC Enrollees into Citizenship," *School Lives*, April 1938, p. 236; Samuel F. Harby, *A Study of Education in the CCC Camps of the Second Corps Area* (Ann Arbor, Mich.: Edwards Bros., 1938); Ray Hayt, *We Can Take It: A Short Story of the CCC* (New York: American Book Co., 1935); Frank Ernest Hill, *The School in the Camps: The Educational Program of the CCC* (New York: American Association for Adult Education, 1935); *The Phi Delta Kappa* 19 (May 1937); and Hinson L. Triter, "Development of the Educational Program of the CCC" (Master's Thesis, Iowa State College, 1940).

There is little doubt that life-adjustment education was the major concern during the years immediately following the Second World War, nor is it mere coincidence that a leading figure in this movement, Charles Prosser, had also been a guiding light in the earlier industrial-training crusade. The new life-adjustment curriculum was obviously aimed at the majority of public school students destined neither for college nor for skilled labor positions. It was established to help them adjust to the conditions of contemporary life, both on and off the job.[2] In many ways it simply repackaged older techniques and objectives to suit the changed material conditions in postwar American society.

The Bestor-Rickover reaction to life-adjustment education, culminating in James B. Conant's revisions for the American high schools during the fifties, might seem a significant departure from this philosophy. In reality, though, this reaction stemmed from a similar outlook. Conant did not suggest that all students should enter his revised curriculum, which featured innovations in the hard sciences and mathematics; on the contrary, he advised schools to become even more selective. Following his recommendations, the federal government financed the training of an enlarged corps of guidance counselors who would ensure that gifted students entered the technical areas in sufficient numbers to meet national manpower demands. In fact, nowhere in Conant's writings is there any hint that the student should be given training expressly for his personal benefit. As in the past, the safety and supremacy of the state determined what the children were taught in the public schools. In the era of Sputnik, that training happened to be in the sciences and mathematics.[3]

If Sputnik dominated education during the fifties, the "invisible man" did during the sixties. In the wake of the civil rights movement, the black child, heretofore unnoticed, became a visible entity in the public schools. School integration plans, Head Start and Upward Bound programs, project talent, and Afro-American history and black

---

2. See Arthur Bestor, *Educational Wastelands* (Urbana, Ill.: University of Illinois Press, 1953); and C. A. Bowers, *The Progressive Educator and the Depression* (New York: Random House, 1963), ch. 6.

3. See, for example, the following works by James Bryant Conant: *The American High School Today* (New York: McGraw-Hill, 1959); *The Child, the Parent, and the State* (Cambridge, Mass: Harvard University Press, 1959); *Education in a Divided World* (Cambridge, Mass.: Harvard University Press, 1948); and "Public Education and the Structure of American Society," *Teacher's College Record* 47 (December 1945): 145–94.

awareness courses were but a few of the responses to the educational needs of the new and often militant black student. As diverse as these projects appeared, they nonetheless shared a common element: the belated realization that industrial capitalism could not endure peacefully unless black Americans participated in the system on a basis of reasonable equality. Not only might cities burn, but businesses might suffer economic penalties if they ignored the labor and the consumer potential of 30 million Americans. Once these truths about the importance of blacks for social stability and commercial profit were recognized, as they had been recognized decades earlier regarding immigrants, the public school system began to respond with vigorous programs to bring blacks into the mainstream of American life. In many ways, these endeavors resembled the Americanization programs begun for immigrant children 50 years before.[4]

Ultimately, the historian who challenges the hallowed past is forced to answer the somewhat unhistorical question of alternatives, both for the past and for the present. Defenders of historical interpretations that support contemporary social arrangements ask, "What alternatives could these historical actors possibly have chosen?" This question implies that men are captives rather than creators of their history. The critical historian sees at least two other ominous questions embedded in it: Were no alternatives available other than the routes chosen? Is a critical evaluation of the past really fair play? While the range of possibilities available at any time is admittedly, restricted by the social, intellectual, and economic conditions of the historical era, the most severe limits on man's alternatives are usually his own lack of imagination and will. Regardless of external restrictions, no man can escape responsibility for his own choices. The critical historian, then, is obliged to evaluate the actions of historical figures. It is sometimes suggested that if other real alternatives were available the historian should detail what actions might have been taken. Such inquiry would take him out of the field of history and into the realm of speculation. His task, however, is not to write historical utopias, but to examine as clearly and as accurately as his evidence allows the alternatives that were in fact adopted.

---

4. See James Bryant Conant, *Slums and Suburbs* (New York: McGraw-Hill, 1961); and *Report of the National Advisory Commission on Civil Disorders* (New York: Bantam, 1968), esp. chs. 9 and 17.

Contemporary practitioners, too, often express concern regarding alternatives. Historical criticism can have serious implications for present educational programs and practices. A recreation director, after reading a draft of the play movement chapter, began to raise ethical questions about his own involvement in this field. Similar problems have been confronted by professionals in vocational education and vocational guidance. Their concerns rested upon the premise that if historical investigation is reasonably accurate then perhaps the present structure of their calling has been contaminated to the degree that they do not wish to be a part of it. These concerned practitioners should be aware that while few institutions or professional fields are completely free from their histories, the past rarely marches unaltered into the present to exercise a controlling influence over its progeny. This means that a program developed for purposes that a contemporary critic might have considered objectionable may now function in different and more acceptable ways. Professionals should examine the objectives of their chosen fields in light of the questions that have evolved from their historical analysis. They will then be in a reasonable position to decide whether to accept the present in an unqualified manner, to work for reforms, or if they believe that the present condition of the field is beyond redemption, to leave it. Historical studies should not be accepted as the final answer about the present. They should, ideally, only raise questions about it. Hopefully, this study has.

Index